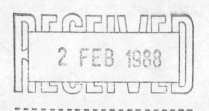

Property Before People

Property Before People

The Management of Twentieth-Century Council Housing

ANNE POWER

London School of Economics

London
ALLEN & UNWIN
Boston   Sydney   Wellington

Allen & Unwin, the academic imprint of
Unwin Hyman Ltd
PO Box 18, Park Lane, Hemel Hempstead, Herts HP2 4TE, UK
40 Museum Street, London WC1A 1LU, UK
37/39 Queen Elizabeth Street, London SE1 2QB

Allen & Unwin Inc.,
8 Winchester Place, Winchester, Mass. 01890, USA

Allen & Unwin (Australia) Ltd,
8 Napier Street, North Sydney, NSW 2060, Australia

Allen & Unwin (New Zealand) Ltd in association with the
Port Nicholson Press Ltd,
60 Cambridge Terrace, Wellington, New Zealand

British Library Cataloguing in Publication Data

Power, Anne.
    Property before people : the management of twentieth-century
    council housing.
1. Public housing—Great Britain—
Management—History
I. Title
352.7'5'0941   HD7288.78.G7
ISBN 0–04–350069–2
ISBN 0–04–350070–6 Pbk

Library of Congress Cataloging-in-Publication Data

Power, Anne.
    Property before people.
Bibliography: p.
Includes index.
1. Public Housing—Great Britain—Management.
I. Title
HD7288.78.G7P69 1987   363.5'8   86–28751
ISBN 0–04–350069–2 (alk. paper)
ISNB 0–04–350070–6 (pbk.: alk. paper)

Set in 10 on 11 point Sabon by Latimer Trend
and printed in Great Britain by Billing and Sons Limited,
London and Worcester

Contents

	page
List of Plates	ix
Acknowledgements	xi
Introduction	xiii

Part One   *The Origins of the Housing Service*

1	Nineteenth-Century Origins of the Landlord Tradition	3
2	The Interwar Years	22
3	Postwar Mass Housing	40
4	Postwar Housing Departments	66
5	Housing for All or Housing of Last Resort?	91

Part Two   *A Survey of New Housing Problems*

6	The Worst Estates	119
7	The Design of Unpopular Estates	137
8	The Management of Unpopular Estates: Allocations and Empty Property	151
9	Repairs, Rents, Cleansing and Caretaking	165

Part Three   *Changing the Landlord Tradition: Findings of the Survey*

10	Local Offices on Unpopular Estates	185
11	Social Change	217
12	Summary of Main Themes and Conclusions: A Way Forward	232

| Bibliography | 249 |
| Index | 261 |

Plates

1   Inner city slum: Upper Ground Place, Southwark, 1923 (*London County Council*).

2   Local estate office: London County Council estate office, Pleasance Road, Roehampton, 1926 (*London County Council*).

3   Slum clearance (*Shelter*).

4   Slum clearance site: St Ann's Estate, Stepney, London, 1961 (*London County Council*).

5   Industrialized building in progress: GLC Savona Estate, London, early 1970s (*Greater London Council*).

6   Honor Oak Estate, Lewisham, built in the 1930s.

7   St Cuthbert's Village Estate, Gateshead, built 1969–71.

8   Penrhys Estate, Rhondda – vandalism, litter and dogs, 1984.

9   Stockwell Park Estate, Lambeth – entrance corridor, 1982.

10 Wenlock Barn Estate, Hackney – before improvement, 1979.

11 Goscote Estate, Walsall – before improvement, 1982.

12 Goscote Estate, Walsall – after improvement, 1982.

13 Honor Oak Estate, Lewisham – environmental improvements, 1982.

14 Maisonette block in Knowsley before improvement.

15 Maisonette block in Knowsley after 'lopping off' improvements.

16 Broadwater Farm Estate, Haringey – neighbourhood housing office, 1985.

17 Cloverhall Tenant Cooperative, Rochdale – Tenant Selection Committee, 1985 (*Paul Herrmann*).

18 Cottage estate in the North West in the 1970s (*Richard Olivier, Save the Children Fund*).

19 Tulse Hill Estate, Lambeth – playgroup 1980 (*Jane Bown*).

20 Penrhys Estate, Rhondda – mothers and children (*Photo Valley Workshop*).

Acknowledgements

Without the help of Professor Brian Abel-Smith of the Department of Social Administration at the London School of Economics, I would not have attempted to trace the origins of unpopular council estates. A grant from the Joseph Rowntree Memorial Trust enabled me to leave my work for the Department of the Environment and the Priority Estates Project for one day a week over two years to write up what I had seen and heard.

Margaret Pitt, now course assistant for the Housing Diploma at LSE, unearthed old documents, collected materials from local authorities and estate offices throughout the country and checked information many times over. Hilda Gage typed and retyped scripts, often against unreasonable deadlines, and kept meticulous track of materials and corrections from the many housing bodies who helped compile this version of events. Lesley Owen located missing references, uncovered recent statistics, and combed through the final corrections.

A number of specialists shed new light on what I was trying to say: Michael Burbidge of the DOE, who was responsible for the original investigation of difficult-to-let council estates; Professor David Donnison of the University of Glasgow, who made penetrating observations on an issue he had long studied; David Piachaud of the Department of Social Administration (LSE) who highlighted the contradictions of policy; Duncan Bowie of Newham Housing Department who corrected the biases in my version of events.

The following people read all or part of the book and offered important suggestions: Alan Holmans of the DOE; Peter Williams of the Institute of Housing; John Macey of the Samuel Lewis Housing Trust, formerly Controller of Housing at the Greater London Council; Patrick Allen, Keith Kirby, Sue Duncan, Robin Sharp and Alison Curtis of the DOE; John Hills of the Welfare State Programme (LSE); Patrick Dunleavy of the Department of Government (LSE); Tricia Zipfel, Sally Phillips, Richard Ellis, Maggie Hindley, Lesley Andrews and other workers within the Priority Estates Project.

The Greater London Council, the London Boroughs of Lambeth, Tower Hamlets and Islington, Rhondda Borough Council, the Metropolitan Borough of Rochdale, and the City of Glasgow taught me much about council housing; and the nineteen local authorities that participated in the Priority Estates Project Survey of 1982 provided much of the material which is drawn on here. Their help was indispensable.

Many individuals have worked tirelessly over years to change housing conditions for people who suffer great stress and hardship, and the following residents in some of the areas where I have worked played a major role in the process, providing much of the background material for the book: Jeannette Caruana of Westbourne Road, Edna Perry of Charteris Road, John Williams, Shirley Pennant and Madeleine Prince of the Holloway Tenant Co-operative, Cynthia Walker, Mary Herbret, Mrs Kitrilakis, Gladys, Sheila, and Hazel Turay of the Tulse Hill Estate, Jim and June Haggerty of Cloverhall Co-operative, Denise and Chris Yeates, Cy Jones and Peter Bolger of Penrhys Estate; Maureen Leigh of Hornsey Lane Estate; Stafford Scott and Clasford Stirling of the Broadwater Farm Youth Association. I must also thank my original teachers, Kit and Sheridan Russell, Chris Holmes of the Campaign for the Homeless and Rootless, Mrs Abbott for the hospitality of her café at Woodbridge, and Margaret Lonnergan for babysitting. My family helped me greatly while I was writing *Property Before People* and played their part in many of the housing developments I have described, not sparing their own suggestions where they thought I was wrong. There are many, many others. I must accept full responsibility for the mistakes and shortcomings of the book. The inherent contradictions remain.

The information from the Priority Estates Project Survey of twenty estates, in Parts Two and Three, was commissioned by the Department of the Environment and collected by the author. It is Crown copyright and is reproduced with the permission of the Controller of Her Majesty's Stationery Office.

The writer alone is responsible for the opinions expressed in this book. Nothing in the book should be taken as reflecting the view of the Government or any local authority.

Introduction

It's not the way it ought to be.
People before property.
(From a song by Leon Rosselson)

Property Before People is an examination of the attempt by successive governments to combat slum conditions and homelessness, to reform landlord–tenant relations and to provide sound modern dwellings with full amenities for all who need them. After 5.5 million council dwellings had been built, some central questions remained unanswered: why were some estates of flats in inner cities and some peripheral estates of houses and gardens rejected by desperate housing applicants? Why were landlord services firmly located within town halls instead of on the estates where the tenants lived? Why were the women who played such an innovative and humanizing role in the early days of housing reform neutralized as public housing gained momentum? Why did housing policy discussion focus so relentlessly on building to the detriment of management of rented housing? Why did local politicians become direct landlords instead of delegating the provision to housing organizations as happened in other European countries? There are no ready answers to these questions, though this book, with the benefit of hindsight, tries to unravel the chain of decisions and events that led to the current 'crisis in council housing' (Audit Commission, 1986, p. 1). Central to the history of housing development is the almost total absence of attention to housing management.

Local authorities did not originally set out to be landlords, only builders or enablers (Cooper, 1985, p. 15). They did not forge coherent relations with their tenants in their dealings over rents, repairs, lettings, communal maintenance or welfare. At the same time, from 1930 onwards, they increasingly housed low-income households whose own resources to make good the shortfall in landlord services were strictly limited. As a result, the quality of housing in all its aspects on some primarily low-income housing estates gradually deteriorated to a point where the original problems of slum housing began to re-emerge.

A major contributor to this circular process was the almost

obsessive emphasis on property rather than people. The conditions of the private rented sector, the role of markets and subsidies, the imperatives of slum clearance, the respective roles of central and local government in the building process, the numbers, styles, locations and sizes of estates dominated housing thinking. The strong belief that housing had to be produced on a massive scale to combat poor conditions and house a growing population led to this one-sided focus. The almost exclusive reliance on councils as direct landlords caused the scale of council housing to be out of all proportion to the management skills or community needs of local areas.

As council housing threw up new problems – estates that were difficult to let, slack demand for rented housing in parts of the country, structural defects in some modern estates, racial discrimination in the allocation of council housing – so attention gradually shifted away from 'the numbers game' to the problems of managing the stock. It is now all too apparent that running public rented housing is no less problem-prone than running private rented housing. Above all, it has become clear in the course of this study that the vast scale of council house development and the remote style of council house management have through quirks of history created new and unforeseen problems (Burbidge, 1981).

On the other hand, there is scope for change. Socially owned, rented housing is expected to remain at over 4 million dwellings far into the future. A majority of council tenants do not expect to become owner-occupiers in the near future (General Household Survey, 1983), and four out of five do not want to buy their existing council house. Two-thirds of council tenants are dependent on Housing Benefit and could not afford to buy and repair a dwelling without substantial help. About 1.5 million flats and maisonettes, many system-built on large, dense developments of over 500 units, are unlikely to be attractive to would-be purchasers. Demolition and rebuilding are not considered to be realistic options for more than a small proportion of the stock. Therefore the issues of housing management of a large rented sector will be of paramount importance over the next generation if we are to escape the scourge of new slums.

This book examines the issues of housing management in three parts. Part One outlines the history of housing management from the intensive, personal, reforming role of Octavia Hill and the women housing workers to the birth of local authority housing departments and the growth of slum-clearance programmes. Three central strands emerged in the postwar era: the 'mass housing' boom leading to unpopular styles and scales of building; the growth of town hall based, functionally divided housing empires; and the allocation of council housing, first to the most deserving and then to the most needy, but with selective concentrations of the most vulnerable on the least desirable estates. Part Two discusses the emergence in the 1970s of estates which were difficult to let while council house-building was still endorsed virtually uncritically. Material collected from twenty unpopular, run-down estates throughout the country is examined to show major problems of design, management and the development of social 'ghettos'. Part Three looks at the same twenty estates under the impact of housing management initiatives, set up by the local authority landlords. Could a new style of localized housing service reverse the often shocking conditions on the worst estates?

The discussion of run-down council housing does not attempt to cover in detail the politics of housing development nor the role of housing finance in development. The political swings and roundabouts are not central to the management story, because no political party or government until recently paid serious attention to management issues. Management went largely by default.

Being a landlord was not politically attractive, whereas building new homes was. Policies towards housing finance have been similarly focused around the provision of housing, not its management. Hence the current impassioned debates about *cuts* in the housing programme, with almost no recognition of the continuing rise in spending on housing management and maintenance in real terms between 1979 and 1983 (Atkinson, Hills and Le Grand, 1986).

Because of these large gaps in the policy debate, *Property Before People* attempts to show what was happening to the running of council housing and leaves the issues of development largely to one side. The book relies heavily on government and local authority reports to trace the developments in housing management. The standard works on housing policy of the last ten years make only brief incursions into *landlord* issues. The central questions for policy – why different tenures, why different subsidies, why different types of housing – have ignored other housing areas: why were rents handled by one department, repairs by another and allocations by another? Why were tenants graded for their suitability for different quality dwellings? Why did publicly owned estates almost invariably look dirtier and uglier than their private counterparts?

What of design? If much council housing has been built in intrinsically unpopular styles, leading to rapid deterioration and breakdown in standards of behaviour, as Alice Coleman aimed to show in her book *Utopia on Trial* (1985), surely management cannot solve the problem? Certainly management is only one part of the business of housing people. The buildings are of paramount importance and how they are put up profoundly influences their popularity and their maintenance. Design can be improved. But rented housing requires good landlords, regardless of design, as the old privately owned slum terraces showed. So whatever is done to enhance design, or remedy past mistakes, there must be a full housing management service if rented housing is to work.

In addition to the impact of design, the interrelationship of many complex factors, including the allocation of housing, the provision of a repairs service, the economic well-being of residents and the needs of children and young people, affect an estate's development. Solutions are rarely one-dimensional, and there are no longer any certainties about housing futures. We cannot condemn the last generation of publicly owned housing until we have at least tried to run it properly. That is the theme of *Property Before People*.

Statistics cover England and Wales unless otherwise stated. The Difficult to Let investigation, the Priority Estates Project Survey and Housing Investment Programme information cover England only. Specific examples from Scotland and Wales are also mentioned. The studies by David Donnison, Claire Ungerson and Patrick Dunleavy, which provide further general statistics, cover Great Britain as a whole. All housing Acts have now been consolidated into the 1985 Housing Act. Historic titles and dates of Acts have been left as it is easier to show the sequence in which they were introduced. The London County Council minutes are referenced by date of recording as are Council reports.

PART ONE

The Origins of the Housing Service

Chapter One

Nineteenth-Century Origins of the Landlord Tradition

Transplant them tomorrow to healthy and commodious houses and they would pollute and destroy them.   (Hill, 1883, p. 10)

The Industrial Revolution in the late eighteenth and early nineteenth centuries caused a huge movement of people from countryside to town. Large new cities sprang up around the factories, and humble shoddy dwellings were packed into the urban landscape in a way that had never happened before. People had to live near their work, for they had no transport; factory and mining hours were long – sixteen hours a day was quite common. 'Back-to-backs' and 'two-up-two-down' became the classic housing style of the masses.

The social and health problems caused by nineteenth-century urban conditions were overwhelming. With no sanitation, no piped water, a damp climate, and families with an average of five children, epidemics of cholera, smallpox, typhoid and tuberculosis were common. The death rate rose in the crowded streets of industrial cities. By the end of the nineteenth century, a pattern of utilitarian squalor embraced the majority of the population (Trevelyan, 1944). Its marks have endured until now; in the major centres of population they have only been displaced by a more modern and possibly as ugly utilitarianism.

Throughout the nineteenth century, private landlords provided the vast majority of housing for rich and poor alike. By 1914, it is estimated that only 800,000 dwellings were owner-occupied, while over 7 million were rented from private landlords. Councils, which had started building to replace insanitary dwellings in the 1880s, owned a mere 20,000 dwellings in 1914 (DOE, 1977, Part 1, p. 38). In the city areas where land was scarce and jobs plentiful, housing had long been expensive, crowded, and in bad condition for the mass of the poor. The housing needs of the bursting city populations were often in conflict with the land hunger of the factory owners and, increasingly as the nineteenth century advanced, with the needs of the railway companies, road builders, model dwelling companies, housing trusts, and even school boards, which from 1871 were required to provide schools in districts where none had yet been built. Even the initial attempts by local authorities to provide decent housing often displaced the poorest and most vulnerable households, making their problems worse. Most landlords did not want to cater for the very poor, who were seen at worst as feckless, disorderly or diseased, and at best as unprofitable.

The 1885 Royal Commission

The clearest insight into conditions of overcrowding, ill health and exploitation in the homes of the very poor is given by the 1885 Royal Commission on the Housing of the Working Classes. In spite of a substantial increase in the total number of dwellings, a general rise in living standards, and improved sanitary and public health conditions, Lord Shaftesbury, the great social reformer, asserted to the Commission that 'the evils of overcrowding . . . were still a public scandal and were becoming in certain localities more serious than they ever were' (Royal Commission, 1885, p. 7). Demolition, whether for sanitary reasons by local authorities or for developments such as railways, model dwellings and schools, was seen as the major cause of worsening conditions for the poorest, and of large-scale displacement.

> The overcrowded state of Spitalfields is attributed in great measure to such clearances, and the rise in rent which has doubled . . . is largely owing to demolitions . . . When the new model dwellings are completed the very poor displaced do not generally find accommodation in them, and therefore the overcrowding continues notwithstanding the new erections. (Royal Commission, 1885, p. 20)

The continued influx of immigrants from the countryside, Ireland, Scotland and Europe added to the overcrowding. These workers, according to the Royal Commission (ibid., p. 19), often enjoyed better health and were therefore more popular with employers. But their arrival intensified the problems of overcrowding in the poorest, most transient districts. The Commission concluded that 'the pulling down of buildings inhabited by the very poor, whether undertaken for philanthropic, sanitary or commercial purposes, does cause overcrowding into the neighbouring slums with the further consequence of keeping up the high rents' (ibid., p. 21).

The Commission examined evidence of wage levels in relation to rents and found that dockers and costermongers earned between eight shillings and ten shillings a week, depending on employment and markets. Artisans earned about £1 5s and the average for all labourers in Clerkenwell was about 16s. The average rent for one room across several London districts was about 3s 6d; for two rooms 6s. In the provinces, the average was 2s 6d. Thus the average rent for one room in London was around a quarter of the average wage (ibid., p. 17). But for the poorest families, rent would amount to nearly half their wages. Poverty was thus the dominant cause of overcrowding. People without work or drifting in and out of the multitude of casual jobs would be constantly on the move, evicted from room after room.

Looking at conditions of overcrowding and rent levels among the poor, the Royal Commission found that:

> It was common practice in London for each family to have only a single room for the rent of which nearly half of them paid between 25 per cent and 50 per cent of their wages ... A contributory cause was the existence of the disreputable middle man. (ibid., p. 17)

The middleman was in effect the housing manager, fixing and collecting rents, letting rooms and evicting tenants, doing repairs to a minimal standard or not at all. His basic job appeared to be packing in as many people as possible to maximize rents. The same rents were often charged by middlemen to the very poor for part of a room as were charged by housing reformer Octavia Hill and other more conscientious landlords for a simple flat.

It is worth quoting one or two actual examples of the conditions of rented property:

> *St Pancras* – an underground back kitchen 12 feet by 9 feet and 8 feet high inhabited by seven persons.
> *Bermondsey* – the washhouse at the back, 10 feet by 5, a father and mother, two children and two older sons.
> *Newcastle-upon-Tyne* – 140 families in 34 houses, which each consist of four rooms and two cellars ... 50 houses with 230 families ... 62 houses with 310 families. (Royal Commission, 1885, pp. 7–8)

Usually in each house there was only one water supply and one closet for all the families. In some cases the closet was shared by several houses. In Clerkenwell a case was found of sixteen houses using one closet. The state of the houses let under these conditions was often a cause of scandal. The street doors were not secured, so stairways and entrances were commonly 'crowded by persons who, presumably having no other place of shelter, come there to sleep' (ibid., p. 9).

Although the Commission cites parish vestries and district boards as being responsible for hiring scavengers to remove 'dirt, ashes, rubbish and filth', it is clear that this duty was rarely performed adequately. 'There is much room for improvement in the matter of ashpits and dustbins ... Vegetable substance ... is frequently thrown into open dustholes ... lying for weeks decomposing and poisoning the atmosphere of the close courts [courtyards]' (ibid., p. 9).

The question of repairs was most complex. According to the Commission the owner was responsible, but he would usually lease the house to a middleman with responsibility for repairs in exchange for a share of the profit from rent collection. This system was considered a major cause of the break-up of single family houses into one-room tenements. A case was cited to the Commission of the landlord, Lord Northampton, renting a house to a middleman for £20 a year, who in turn rented it out room by room for a total of £100 a year. The middleman expected to make between 50 and 150 per cent profit on the rent he paid over to the landlord (ibid., pp. 21–2). Repairs were minimal and gross overcrowding was the crude method of expanding the rent income. Lord Northampton claimed that he did not like to enforce repairs in case it led to even higher rents.

Absurdly, because of the low wages and high rents, rent arrears were often a serious problem. Octavia Hill gave evidence to the Commission of large rent debts accumulated in properties she acquired. This was inevitable, given the wage and rent levels quoted, and led to constant moves by poor families. The Commission claimed that 'it is likely that more than one half the population of certain poor districts are constantly shifting' (ibid., p. 19). These conditions had a devastating impact on family life. Lord Shaftesbury described the human cost:

> An intelligent active young man ... comes up to London: he must have lodgings near his work; he is obliged to take, he and his wife, the first house that he can find, perhaps even in an alley ... his health is broken down; he himself succumbs, and he either dies or becomes perfectly useless. The wife falls into despair; in vain she tries to keep her house clean; her children increase upon her and at last they become reckless ... Their hearts are broken. They do not know how soon they shall go; they are merely wanderers on the face of the earth. (ibid., p. 15)

Many other witnesses to the Commission described the impoverished classes in less sympathetic terms, attributing their atrocious conditions to their own fecklessness and addiction to drink. The Commissioners did not resolve the cause and effect:

To return however to the question whether drink and evil habits are the cause or consequence of the condition in which the poor live, the answer is probably the unsatisfactory one that drink and poverty act and react upon one another ... the poor who live under the conditions described have the greatest difficulty in leading decent lives and of maintaining decent habitations. (ibid., p. 16)

The Royal Commission sought evidence from Octavia Hill about her work among the 'rejects' of society, asking if her role was 'to reform the tenants that nobody else will touch' (ibid., 1885, p. 304, para 9119). Her answer underlined the close interdependence of cause and effect: 'The tenants *and* the houses' (Hill, 1872–1907, p. 306). Her indignation at slum conditions and exploitative landlords was coupled with horror at the social abuses that she believed slum conditions bred. Her overriding commitment to helping only the very poor was coloured by her Christian socialist background, lending a reforming zeal to her intimate and personal involvement in the details of housing management. She, like all reformers, was convinced that there was a way out. 'The principle on which the whole work rests is that the inhabitants and their surroundings must be improved together. It has never yet failed to succeed' (Hill, 1883, p. 51).

Octavia Hill, the First Advocate of Housing Management

Octavia Hill, oldest of five daughters in an impoverished, fatherless family, had begun to acquire slum property a generation before the Commission sat, when she was only in her early 20s. She prevailed upon rich benefactors, such as John Ruskin, to invest their own money in poor, tenanted property adjacent to where she lived in Marylebone, and allow her to restore it by sound management. Sometimes houses were actually given to her which she could begin to manage efficiently. The condition of the properties she acquired was often appalling: 'out of 192 [window] panes, only eight were unbroken. Such was the court in 1869; a truly wild, lawless and desolate little kingdom' (Hill, 1883, pp. 27, 41).

In *Homes of the London Poor*, she summed up the conditions she set out to combat and the simple management techniques she used:

In Marylebone, where I began work, nearly every family rented but one room ... There were no cooking ranges in the rooms; water was hardly ever carried up higher than the parlours ... Wages were very decidedly lower, hours of work were longer ...

7

From these and many other causes a London court in 1864 was a far more degraded and desolate place than it can be now ... Moreover in the rough courts [the tenants] were little meddled with and could pursue in ignorance their insanitary habits. (Hill, 1883, pp. 25–6)

The very first court that she took over with money from John Ruskin was a decayed slum: 'The place swarmed with vermin; the papers black with dirt, hung in long strips from the walls; the drains were stopped, the water supply out of order' (Hill, 1901, p. 22). She was shocked by what she found: 'It was truly appalling to think that there were human beings who lived habitually in such an atmosphere with such surroundings' (Hill, 1871, p. 32).

Octavia Hill blamed negligent private landlords in the most vividly scathing terms for the extortions of the system of management among the poor. She came across a private landlord who was an undertaker by profession and who told her of the large number of bad debts which he compensated for by the ready trade from his tenants in funerals: 'It's not the rents I look to but the deaths I get out of the houses' (Hill, 1883, p. 20). She found middlemen, acting on behalf of the landlords, often responsible for serious mismanagement. In an area of ill-repute which she took over in Nottingdale, she reported:

Our first duty was to remove the middle-men and to enter into direct relations with the tenants ... The dirty furniture was removed, and the people were encouraged to provide their own. In this way, the rent being lower for unfurnished rooms, families could take two rooms for the same rent as one, thus mitigating the crowding. The closets, washhouses and yards were supervised; the drunken and rowdy inmates were in a measure both influenced and restrained and the quiet poor were protected, encouraged and gradually raised to better conditions ... No large expenditure in building has been incurred. (Hill, 1904, p. 2)

She often found the management of such houses almost non-existent:

The dustbins were utterly unapproachable, and cabbage leaves, stale fish and every sort of dirt were lying in the passages and on the stairs; in some the back kitchen had been used as a dustbin but had not been emptied for years ... in some the kitchen stairs were many inches thick with dirt which was so hardened that a shovel had to be used to get it off. In some there was hardly any water to be had... (Hill, 1883, p. 40)

However, there was nothing inevitable in this mismanagement and exploitation, and Octavia Hill was committed to making the landlord–tenant relationship work with the existing impoverished tenants. 'Steady improvement of the people and the houses without selection of the former or sudden reconstruction of the latter was our first duty' (Hill, *Letters*, 1898–9, p. 2). To achieve this, she became a thoughtful business manager. She defined management as 'just governing rather than helping'. She was far from being a philanthropist or a lady-bountiful, convinced that all must pay their way: 'prompt payment of rent strikes a blow at the credit system that is the curse of the poor' (Hill, 1883, p. 52).

She thought that unless housing for the poor was made economically viable, landlords would never fulfil their duties properly nor would tenants ever get a reasonable deal. She also believed that workers should be paid a living wage by their employers so they could afford decent housing, knowing that without rents she could not repair the houses. Consequently, she was emphatic that 'I have never allowed a second week's rent to become due' (ibid., p. 52). She offered work to those temporarily unemployed and she made special arrangements when families were in particular distress. But she rejected the notion that arrears should be tolerated as a general rule. Therefore 'those who would not pay ... were ejected'. For 'where a man persistently refuses to exert himself, external help is worse than useless' (ibid., p. 33).

She claimed that eviction was almost never necessary. Her weekly visits broke through the barrier of mistrust and she ended up by devising a battery of supports for the many tenants who regularly hit hard times. She organized savings clubs, and she reduced overcrowding by giving families more rooms for nearly the same rent as they previously paid for only one room. She went to great lengths to persuade tenants to take an extra room whenever one became available or to move to another house to obtain a better home for their family. Full rent collection enabled her to charge less per room than other landlords. When she inherited severe arrears from previous landlords, she spent weeks or months building a new relationship with the tenants, only gradually re-establishing payment and offering tenants a deduction of threepence from their rent if they kept up their payments (Royal Commission, 1885, para. 8970). She reserved maintenance work for residents who lost their jobs, believing that 'It is far better to give work than money or goods' (Hill, 1883, p. 37). One dictum was: 'Perfect strictness in our business relations; perfect respectfulness in our personal relations' (ibid., p. 42). She did not enter tenants' dwellings without invitation, accepting their paramount right to private enjoyment of their homes. She rejected strongly the notion of patronage: 'refuse resolutely to give any help but such as rouses self-help' (Hill, 1901, p. 29). Her irritation with 'fashionable ladies' who tried to help (Royal Commission, 1885) came from her strong identification with poor people: 'I should instinctively feel the same respect for their privacy and their independence and should treat them with the same courtesy that I show towards any other personal friends' (Hill, 1883, p. 42).

Hill's priorities were: 'repairs promptly and efficiently attended to, references taken up, cleaning sedulously supervised, overcrowding put an end to, the blessing of ready money payments enforced, accounts strictly kept, and above all, tenants so sorted as to be helpful to one another' (Hill, *Letters*, 1898–9, pp. 2–3). She claimed not to reject any needy tenants unless their behaviour to fellow-tenants was threatening or unless they actually refused to pay their rent. 'I do not say that I will not have drunkards, I have quantities of drunkards' (Royal Commission, 1885, para. 8967). But she did move noisy tenants away from quiet ones, and tried to protect frail or ill tenants from any kind of disturbance. Her aim in 'sorting tenants' was to help curb the impact of disruptive tenants on neighbours and to protect those seeking a peaceful life. Residents with problems were not concentrated together in the courts she managed, but housed with more resilient neighbours so that help and support were on hand and so that informal networks could act as a brake on social disarray. She did not believe in rule books, preferring to evoke informal responses and what she regarded as innate human generosity. Therefore 'we have no rigid rules, except that no lodgers are allowed' (Royal Commission, 1885, p. 297, para. 8970). The ban on lodgers was to prevent renewed overcrowding.

She advocated strong action against anti-social behaviour: 'It is a most merciful thing to protect the poor from the pain of living next door to drunken, disorderly people' (Hill, 1883, p. 46); and she evicted tenants who, after warnings resulting from the complaints of neighbours, still made life miserable for other residents. 'Those who ... lead clearly immoral lives were ejected' (Hill, 1883, p. 27). Noise, alcohol and violence were the abuses that she cited. Respectability and Victorian morality were important in so far as they affected the communal life of a house or relations between tenants. She only cited continuous disturbance to neighbours or an absolute refusal to pay rent without any discernible cause as reasons for eviction. She believed that a landlord had to ensure communal peace within a rented tenement or subdivided house.

Octavia Hill talked passionately of one solitary old lady who begged to be moved so that she could die in peace without being able to hear her drunken, disorderly neighbour. But she did not evict the offending tenant without first giving him the choice of a truce with the neighbours, since she believed that disorder was often bred of poor standards of management. She found that reform was very often possible, and cites no case where she actually gave up. She usually resolved disputes by moving people rather than evicting.

She applied herself diligently to every trivial detail of management and maintenance, believing that 'it is on such infinitesimally small actions that the success of the whole work rests' (Hill, 1883, p. 31). While decay and neglect bred their own disarray, she felt that 'people are ashamed to abuse a place they find cared for . . . They will add dirt to dirt . . . but the more they find done for [the property] the more they will respect it till at last order and cleanliness prevail' (Hill, 1883, p. 45).

Octavia Hill and her growing band of trained helpers were a constant presence in the houses they ran, enforcing their own standards on people previously trapped in enslaving, communal squalor. 'The surest way to have any place kept clean is to go through it constantly yourself' (Hill, 1883, p. 36). She was able to make ends meet on modest rents but to respectable standards by organizing improvements incrementally on the basis of trade-offs with the tenants: 'reconstructing the estate can be successfully accomplished only if they [the landlords] can ensure the goodwill and co-operation of the present tenants' (Hill, 1901, p. 75). This was a prerequisite for improving the houses, 'a sort of co-operative system among the tenants' (Royal Commission, 1885, para. 9042).

Better amenities were introduced slowly and only to the extent that they could be paid for out of rents collected, and to the extent that existing improvements were respected. She invited tenants to choose their favoured improvements themselves, thus ensuring a high investment in protecting them. Where rebuilding or extensive renovation was taking place, she always aimed to retain the existing community and rehouse tenants back into the area. She held tenants' meetings regularly in her own home and later added common rooms to the courts which she managed in order to encourage tenants' associations. She believed firmly in resident supervisors, resident repairmen and so on. She used to employ girls from the tenants' families in cleaning the houses and yards and in supervising play areas, and she strongly advocated that open space be attached to all dwellings, no matter how small. She or her assistants personally visited all their tenants at least weekly, collecting rents, organizing repairs, sorting out disputes, enforcing standards and finally establishing personal friendship. This was her unique management tool.

Octavia Hill took a strong stand against flat-building, which by the 1880s was being advanced as the new answer to the slums. Her two main arguments against flats were 'the small scope they give to individual freedom', and the fact that 'people become brutal in large numbers' (Hill, 1901, p. 48). She objected to the segregation of rich and poor caused by large blocks of flats, believing that small areas of mixed families worked better. She disliked the public nature of flats, the many communal areas inviting disorder and abuse, and the complications for tenants of controlling family and social life in an anonymous block that generated so little intimacy. She did not accept that improved amenities and better layout compensated for the loss of outdoor space by each dwelling, since she believed that outdoor space was an essential ingredient of healthy family life. The 1885 Royal Commission on the Housing of the Working Classes asked her whether her experience bore out the common working-class objection to 'very large blocks'. In her evidence she replied: 'They feel the objection to them on the ground of the monotony and ugliness of them and that feeling seems to grow . . . The people always greatly preferred cottages, or houses accommodating a small number of families' (Royal Commission, 1885, p. 300). In addition the high cost of constructing blocks of modern flats meant that only the more affluent working classes could gain access to them, thereby extending over-crowding, high rents and poverty in the remaining slums. For example, she found that rents in Drury Lane rose by sixpence to one shilling a week in consequence of the Peabody development there (Royal Commission, 1885, p. 19).

Most of all she believed that blocks of flats could only work with authoritarian rule because of their density and communal arrangement. She preferred smaller-scale, more personal management in lower buildings (Hill, 1901, p. 47). She believed in exercising tight management control, not through policing and the threat of eviction, but through a familiar and trusting relationship, with clear responsibilities on both sides.

Octavia Hill not only opposed flat-building on design and financial grounds. She also opposed municipal housing in principle, believing that elected representatives should not control something as basic as the supply of homes to their electors. She abhorred the large-scale approach so readily adopted by public bodies. However, she increasingly recognized that the scale of the problem was beyond her scope and indeed praised the efforts made by Glasgow City Council to tackle their slums, taking fifty dwellings at a time (Hill, 1883, pp. 80–5), attempting to rehouse people within their own communities.

Her rejection of large, stark blocks of flats was coloured by her love of the countryside and her desire to beautify the environment of crowded city courts, on however small a scale: 'The sweet luxuriance of spring flowers is more enjoyed in that court than would readily be believed' (Hill, 1883, p. 29). As a crusading founder of the National Trust and a fighter for London's few open spaces, including Parliament Hill Fields, she felt that the poor should have access to sunlight and to growing green things. Therefore she always tried to provide open areas in spite of working under the most desperate conditions. She and her fellow workers arranged many trips to the countryside with tenants and their children, on one occasion returning with ninety bunches of wild flowers, one for each family. She also acquired country property to which children of the tenants and sometimes whole families could go to recover from illness and to enjoy the countryside.

By the end of her life in 1912, private landlords operating her system were finding it increasingly hard to make ends meet. She felt herself overwhelmed by the scale of the housing problems of the very poor, and appalled by the spectacle of unlet, publicly owned tenements, too expensive for the most needy. She left behind her a system of management and a body of trained workers, but at a critical stage failed to make any significant impact on the public bodies that were to become the major providers of housing for the poor. She did not expect councils to expand their housing activities very far, but in this she could not have been more wrong. Her strong belief in private philanthropy also exaggerated the potential of her movement and undercut the role that women might have played in the development of local authority landlords, at a time when public intervention was becoming more pressing and more common.

Throughout her career she recruited like-minded women who could act as visitors/rent-collectors/managers for the ever-expanding stock of property she controlled. She believed strongly that women rather than men should provide the personal, home-based service of housing management she had evolved, because women were much more in command of the home and family while men were often absent. Women were also more sympathetic in distress and more knowledgeable in questions of budgeting, diet, hygiene, and child development. She was clearly unhappy about the growing number of male estate superintendents in the blocks of flats then being built; they played the tough role of authoritarian guards and could not establish the personal trust on which her methods relied.

She did not establish formal training for her managers other than in book-keeping, about which she was rigorous. Instead she relied heavily on their individual initiative and responsibility and on direct experience. She felt she could train a capable person in six weeks. She devolved all responsibility for personal door-to-door management to each worker, who was given responsibility for about 300 properties. She wrote to them often; held meetings with them and reprimanded them for shortfalls in rent or any other lapse in standards. She wanted the job of housing management recognized in the way that nursing and teaching were coming to be recognized.

13

If there existed a body of ladies trained to more thorough work, qualified to supervise more minutely, likely to enter into such details as bear on the comfort of home life, they might be entrusted by owners with their houses. We all can remember how the training of nurses and of teachers has raised the standard of work required in both professions. The same change might be hoped for in the character of the management of dwellings let to the poor. (Hill, 1872–1907, p. 7)

When the Royal Commission asked her about training for housing management, she explained:

I think people with tact can do it . . . capable, sensible, ordinary people. What we want is a combination of interest in the people with a certain amount of business training . . . if people rush into managing or building without training, they will make a great mess of it. (Royal Commission, 1885, p. 297)

It is hard to deduce how many tenants Octavia Hill had. By the time she died about fifty trained women managers worked with her directly or with landlords who adopted her method of management. This means that she must have controlled or directly influenced the management of about 15,000 properties. In her evidence to the Royal Commission she was asked how much property she owned or managed and she responded that because she constantly disaggregated her operations and encouraged each new development to be autonomous, she had no idea at all of the numbers of properties or tenants involved. Eight years before the Commission sat, she had valued her own property at the equivalent of about 1,000 one-room tenements. 'I know I balanced off the accounts of £70,000 and that was then decentralised; I have never touched it again. All I have now has grown up since.' When asked how much, she replied 'I'm not sure' (Brion and Tinker, 1980, Ch. 7). Her work had spread across London and to other cities, but by the end of her life, public landlords were moving to the fore. In the years before she died, she failed to respond to the new challenge of public housing.

Octavia Hill sought to change the built environment of her time, with all its horrors, by running it properly rather than trusting to a new round of building enterprise to replace the old. Ahead of her time in thinking, she saw redevelopment as a terrible scourge on the poorest families, appalling as she found the existing conditions:

The high cost of building, the rise of rates, the sometimes absurd requirements of local bodies, make it impossible to reaccommodate families at the same rents as in the old houses. This makes it to my mind a very great duty on the part of owners and local

14

authorities to preserve so far as possible all old houses occupied by the poor, always supposing the drains and roofs are sound, and the rooms dry and light. The fashion of clearing away, which makes a grand show, has in my estimation, gone quite far enough ... so pause before you destroy an old house which is, or can be made healthy. (Hill, *Letters*, 1902, pp. 4–5)

She was almost the only housing reformer who neither argued for the replacement of slums with new and better homes, nor advocated political intervention, but relied almost entirely on how she ran or managed the existing houses. The few houses she built are still standing in Walworth, the property of the Church Commissioners and managed in accordance with her principles. She rehoused back into them all the tenants who had been displaced by the demolition of the crumbling old cottages on the site, she encouraged the formation of a tenants' association and she won the co-operation of her tenants by the quality of service her managers offered (Hill, *Letters*, 1902, 1906).

Octavia Hill cannot be readily classified as either a social reformer or as a successful businesswoman. Her main contribution was to develop a management technique which brought slum property up to minimal standards for the day at a cost that the mass of slum dwellers could afford. She spoke out against displacement of poor people, against impersonal blocks, and against political control of landlord services. She advocated meticulous management, continuous repairs, tenants' priorities for improvements, resident jobs, women's employment, and tenants' control over their own lives. But she did not understand that with over one million sharing households in 1911 (DOE, 1977b, Part 1, p. 16), the relatively small scale of her own efforts would be overtaken and to a large extent devalued.

The Philanthropic Trusts

The Peabody Trust was founded in 1862, and the Guinness, Sutton and Samuel Lewis Trusts later in the Victorian era. Appalled by the urban squalor that increasing wealth had spawned, several rich Victorians bequeathed fortunes for the purposes of building model dwellings to house the deserving poor. In dense city conditions, the trustees wrestled with their bequest, packing as many homes as possible on to the scarce land. These early trusts built thousands of model dwellings, usually in large blocks of tenement flats, on land cleared by local authorities under new public health powers. They housed the poor, but not the very poorest.

Octavia Hill's methods of intensive, unified, on-the-ground

management were widely adopted by the philanthropic trusts, although she disapproved of their dense, large-scale developments. The deeds of the Sutton Dwellings Trust (later to become the Sutton Housing Trust) specified that they would house the 'respectable poor' with 'proof of good character', and regulations like these certainly made the trusts' social tasks easier. They developed a system of resident estate management, with a resident superintendent in charge of each estate, controlling lettings, rents, repairs, communal cleaning, laundries and bath-houses, and ruling the blocks, sometimes with a rod of iron. One resident worker, caretaker, porter, repairman, manager or superintendent was employed for every fifty dwellings. The tradition has survived to this day. Throughout their 120 years' history the trusts have been the envy of many local authorities, although they have often also been accused of paternalism, selective lettings, and harsh management. While they might not have succeeded with the 'unrespectable' or disaffected, their intensive, coherent, local and resident management system has made physically unattractive blocks viable for low-income families for generations, which contrasts sharply with the experience of local authorities. In fact, the closely packed, multi-storey, spartan blocks of the early trusts have always been in high demand and popular with residents in spite of their oppressive style. The key factor which made them work over the years was the careful, if rather authoritarian, method of management. The trusts operated a style of local resident management and maintenance which led to close and interdependent relations between tenant and landlord, and inspired new thinking much later in the story of unpopular council estates.

Up to the First World War the philanthropic trusts had built more than three times the number of dwellings built by local authorities. But the trusts paid no heed to Octavia Hill's appeal to renovate the old terraced dwellings rather than build anew. The very poorest people were often displaced by the redevelopment. In any case they could not afford the new rents (Royal Commission, 1885, p. 20).

In the 1880s local authorities were given powers to construct model dwellings. The Royal Commission did not endorse the development of large tenement blocks of flats, both because they displaced the poorest families, making their housing conditions worse and their rents higher, and because they were intrinsically unpopular and hard to manage. The early history of the London County Council bore out their fears.

The Beginning of Local Authority Housing

The first Acts that gave local authorities the power to demolish unhealthy dwellings and replace them with sound working-class homes came between 1868 and 1879 and were known as the Torrens and the Cross Acts. Local authorities were propelled into a pathfinding role in housing provision which they only saw curtailed over 100 years later. Chronic overcrowding and the inability of poor people to pay economic rents were the major factors in public intervention.

Councils believed that public landlords could provide better conditions, standards and services than private landlords, although initially they did not attempt to solve the problems of the poorest (Daunton, 1984). Especially in cities, renting was becoming less attractive to private landlords as standards and costs rose, the stock of housing aged and land became scarce.

Average rents for council accommodation before the First World War were higher as a proportion of average income than they were in 1975 (DOE, 1977b, Part 1, p. 42). Overall rents dropped from an estimated 12.5 per cent of income in 1912 to 7.2 per cent in 1975 (ibid., p. 43). According to the 1977 Housing Policy Green Paper: 'average local authority rents in the late 1930s were lower in relation to average earnings than typical rents before 1914. But they were still high relative to income in comparison with the post-war years' (ibid., p. 43). Many households could not afford to rent a single dwelling and overcrowding was so intense as to defy effective public health action (Wohl, 1977).

From the start council housing was aimed at employed working families, and commanded higher rents than the average household was used to paying. The Housing Policy Green Paper of 1977 estimated that rent and rates for a new working-class dwelling in 1906 represented 23 per cent of *average* earnings (ibid., p. 5). It follows therefore that anyone earning *below* average wages or in unstable employment would not be able to afford a new council dwelling for which rents and rates were *not* subsidized at this stage. Nor were there rebates. Therefore 'local authorities for their part had perforce to secure a class of tenant which would be an asset and not a liability from a rent-paying standpoint' (CHAC, 1939, p. 6).

From its earliest days council housing had three flaws. First, it was not geared to what people wanted, cushioned as it was from consumer criticism by financing from the rates and by special powers under the various Acts. The demand for council housing and the rents it could command were disguised by subsidy. Secondly, some flats were difficult to let from the very earliest days. Thirdly, rents were too high for ordinary working people (Merrett, 1979, p. 30). London County

Council flats were being advertised for letting at the turn of the century with two to four weeks rent free as an inducement: 'The difficulty was not to find tenements, but to find tenants' (Moberly Bell, 1942, pp. 260–1).

Some London County Council estates had numbers of empty dwellings until the First World War created a shortage acute enough to generate demand for the unpopular blocks (LCC, Minutes of the Housing Committee, 7 Feb. 1928). 'In some of the less favourably situated block dwellings, there was for many years a high proportion of empties, and it was not until the pressure on housing due to the war was felt that some block dwellings were fully let' (ibid.).

The London County Council opted for the 'modern' idea of building flats rather than houses, considering amenities more important than design, and wanting to house as many families as possible on the scarce land. There was fierce argument in the Royal Commission over the advantages and drawbacks of flat-building. Octavia Hill reasoned forcibly that blocks of flats were not a response to housing demand but an imposed solution that would never be popular:

> The day has quite gone by for the erection of block buildings. They were never satisfactory, and nothing but the great pressure on the people ever made them resort to them. Now that the facilities of transit enable so many to get to the suburbs, and thus the great pressure on the central houses is removed, blocks would not let well, at least so I believe. (Hill, *Letters*, 1907, p. 4)

Her arguments did not prevail and flats became the norm for council building in inner-city areas, providing many more amenities than before and greater internal space to each family, but depriving it of privacy and outdoor space, however restricted: 'Even a third-rate house with a backyard of its own is better than the modern flats which the London County Council is now building because when the tenant can command his own front door and staircase, he can preserve the unity of his family' (Hill, *Letters*, 1906, p. 6). There was a radical change in the housing scene over the final twenty years of the last century, with a rapid expansion of public intervention in the built environment, with major redevelopment in cities for roads, railways, schools and other public buildings, the spread of flat-building, the suburban explosion, and the gradual impact of health and labour laws.

Local authorities were only just finding their feet on the housing front, and some started building without any careful evaluation of who needed help or how that help could best be provided. The result in the big cities where early council initiatives were most common, such as Birmingham, Glasgow and London, was the provision of

Table 1.1 Ownership of Housing in England and Wales, 1914

Tenure	No. of dwellings	% of dwellings
Owner-occupier	800,000	10.00
Local authorities	(20,000 total)*	0.25
Private and miscellaneous rented	7,100,000	90.00
Total	7,900,000	100.00

*Estimate.
   Source: DOE, 1977b, Part 1, p. 38.

relatively expensive, high-standard accommodation for the working classes. Shortages of very cheap accommodation were still acute but access to good housing was not possible for the poorest and the supply of land was strictly limited. Private renting still dominated at the outbreak of war in 1914.

The Birth of Housing Departments

Initially the management of council housing was not regarded as a major issue because of the class of tenants housed, although there are early references to social abuses creeping into the public tenement blocks, due to the dense design, lack of privacy and lack of careful management supervision. There are few accounts of the birth and early growth of local authority housing departments (Daunton, 1984), but a revealing insight into the rapid development of municipal housing management can be gleaned from the minutes of the London County Council, whose Housing of the Working Classes Committee was set up in 1889.[1] In 1893, it was linked with the new Public Health Committee, and while rents were collected under the direction of the Controller of Finance at headquarters, resident male superintendents for the large new estates were appointed by the Valuers' Department, which was responsible for day-to-day management.

From the beginning, estate-based staff were answerable to managers at County Hall. The estates housed securely employed working families and the council was reputed to be highly selective (Barclay, 1976, p. 18). Tenants took great pride in being selected for council accommodation and the council regarded its dwellings as standard-setters for the large private rented sector that still housed most of the working people in the country. Applicants were chosen for their

19

reliability of character, their standard of cleanliness and their ability to pay the council rent exactly on time. Irene Barclay (ibid., p. 18), in her history of the St Pancras Housing Association, describes somewhat bitterly the way the London County Council selected respectable tenants for their dwellings early in the century, leaving the poorest and most needy households to fend for themselves, even where the council was demolishing their homes:

> My serious criticism of the LCC pre-war [1914] housing was that only a proportion of the population displaced from slums was rehoused – the families where the wage earner was in regular employment: postmen, policemen, foremen in established firms, a few white-collar workers; the rest went where they could to escalate slum conditions by overcrowding the neighbourhood. (ibid., p. 18)

Even so, densities on early council estates were extremely high, often nearly 400 persons per acre (LCC, 1937, p. 4). There was an average of five persons per dwelling on the large Boundary Street estate built in 1907, which is still standing north of Stepney, its dense blocks largely filled now with Bengali families. The estate has over 700 flats.

By the turn of the century, the LCC had one housing employee for every sixty dwellings, including repairmen. Because of the scale of the operation, in 1912 a Housing Manager was appointed under a Housing Committee, with nearly 300 employees administering 10,000 dwellings, one employee for every thirty dwellings. Many of these employees were still based at County Hall. The Housing Manager was responsible for the first housing department in the country, with three distinct sections, each responsible for separate aspects of housing management:

(1) repairs, with its own maintenance staff;
(2) lettings, rent collection and empty property;
(3) investigations and inquiries, general housing matters, lodging houses.

Management was co-ordinated at headquarters and most flatted estates did not have a resident superintendent because they were not thought to be big enough. Even Boundary Street with 700 dwellings was not considered large enough to justify a resident superintendent. The very largest estates had resident managers, but all important decisions were passed up to separate departments in a remote County Hall.

Segmented, non-resident and functionally divided housing management had quickly grown up and taken root, while the dense, flatted estates of the LCC posed problems from the very outset. With 10,000 dwellings by the outbreak of the First World War, the LCC was the biggest and most developed municipal landlord in the country (Merrett, 1979, pp. 24, 26). The problems which were emerging included a large, remote landlord; dense estates of several hundred dwellings; a number of council departments directly involved in housing, leading to the creation of a sectionally divided housing department; a high ratio of staff to properties but a poor presence on the ground; unlet flats; and incipient problems of social abuse and vandalism.

In local authorities outside the LCC, housing management was either farmed out to estate agents (Butcher, 1942, p. 14), private companies or trusts (Macey and Baker, 1982, p. 14), or was handled piecemeal by a series of departments within the local authority, such as surveyors, valuers, treasurers, public health, or engineers (LCC, Minutes of the Housing Committee, 1899). Local authorities had set out to build decent homes and clear slums; housing management was an undeveloped area of public administration which they had not originally intended to embark upon (Cullingworth, 1966, p. 73).

Note to Chapter 1

1 The LCC minutes are used to trace housing management developments because the LCC was the earliest centrally organized housing department; it built large numbers of flats very early on and it became a large housing authority, before the First World War, comparable with the average-sized local authority in 1974. It established a comprehensive housing service long before other authorities. In addition London acts as the metropolitan barometer of wider developments in the country (Wohl, 1977).

Chapter Two

The Interwar Years

> It is suggested that there are many matters relating to the proper management of the home and the conduct of families as tenants of the Council in which a woman is specially fitted.
>
> (LCC, Minutes of the Housing Committee, May 1930)

The First World War created a housing crisis. Very little construction took place during the war, due to concentration on the war effort. Strict rent controls provoked in part by the major rent strike on Clydeside in 1915 (Daunton, 1984, p. 8) meant that private landlords could not make a profit, nor maintain their property in reasonable repair. The absence of large numbers of able-bodied men only served to make building and repairs problems worse. Even the benign landlords of the philanthropic housing movement, of which Octavia Hill had been such an important member, found it increasingly difficult to expand their work among the mass of poor urban dwellers. Housing for the poorest families was intensely overcrowded. Only subsidized public intervention on a large scale was likely to provide enough dwellings to meet the needs of returning soldiers and to bring city conditions up to acceptable standards. The fear of social unrest and even revolution was another major inducement to a committed house-building programme for poor people. Lloyd George proclaimed a target of half a million dwellings in three years under the catching pledge to build 'homes fit for heroes' (Merrett, 1979, p. 34).

Subsidies for Building

Soon after the war in 1919, Parliament passed the Addison Act which for the first time provided central government subsidies for house-building for working-class people, limiting the contribution that councils were required to make and guaranteeing a government subsidy above that level (Macey and Baker, 1982, p. 17). Lloyd

George's pledge was honoured for a short but impressive period, following recommendations from the Tudor Walters Committee to provide high quality homes for securely paid workers so that the mass of people could 'filter up' from the slums (Swenarton, 1981). Cottage estates were favoured against city flats, wherever this was possible.

The generous subsidies and higher building standards were quickly curtailed as the postwar economy flagged, but by 1924 the volume of public and private house-building, the more modest standards and the general fall in prices led to cheaper building and cheaper rents, and councils moved away from high quality building and began to build to modest standards to help low-income families. The result was a building boom, with local authorities building one-third of all new houses in the following five years. Councils became firmly established as major landlords. But even with central government and rate-fund subsidies, rents were still not 'within the means of the lowest-paid workers ... local authorities could still pick and choose' (CHAC, 1939, p. 6).

Although blocks of flats continued to be built in big city areas in dense, pokey tenements, most of the early postwar council housing was actually built outside the cities because city land was already intensively used. Problems of displacement were very great. Many estates were built on green field sites on the edge of the cities, often to generous standards for the day. 'Garden City' ideas had taken root whereby worker families were to be given space and individual homes in planned surroundings away from the city squalor. But the location of several of the early council cottage estates away from the main areas of employment on the edges of big cities made some of them unpopular over the years and they became difficult to let. However, on the whole, the council housing of the early postwar years, especially the 'cottage estates', stood the test of time and was built to higher standards of space and craftsmanship than the council homes built during the slum-clearance programmes of the 1930s or immediately after the Second World War up until the Parker Morris report of 1961. In the 1920s, there were no special cash incentives to clear slums or to help the most needy, and on the whole the emphasis was on the overriding priority of providing large numbers of homes for general needs, with a strong belief that well-built artisan housing would enable better-off workers to vacate the slums, allowing densely overcrowded families to spread out. Almost all LCC building from 1919 to 1927 was on cottage estates (16,178 out of 17,203 dwellings), but in 1924 the LCC began to build some 'lower standard' dwellings so that it could help poorer families. It afterwards found this policy to be a major cause of 'sink estates', as low rents attracted poor people, who in turn attracted a 'poor' reputation for the estate and thereby damaged its popularity. In later years the council also had to carry out extensive remedial works such as building back extensions to move baths out of kitchens (White, 1946). The LCC was often a step ahead in policy changes and its shift in emphasis in the mid-1920s towards helping more needy families was soon to be adopted by the government.

Subsidies for Slum Clearance and for Flats

With well over 1 million more households than dwellings, it was hoped that the postwar house-building drive would help eradicate slums. As the years passed and general standards rose, more and more of the old terraced houses were designated as only fit for clearance. Severe shortages continued in slum areas, with high unemployment and poverty through much of the postwar period culminating in the great depression of 1929–35. Parliament passed the Greenwood Act in 1930, for the first time giving direct subsidies to councils for the demolition of slums, followed by the ending of subsidies for general needs housing in 1933. The government gave councils £2 5s per person per year for each person they rehoused from a condemned slum. This gave councils a double incentive to demolish slums and to rehouse people living in bad conditions. The role of local authorities as landlords began to change. In addition to the existing subsidy for building costs, a special subsidy for expensive sites was introduced which was given *only* for buildings over three storeys high on sites above a certain price. Councils interpreted the additional subsidy for flats as a direct encouragement to build upwards. It was in fact the logical policy to adopt, following the decision to clear slums in city centres on a large scale while attempting to rebuild the homes being torn down to a higher standard.

The rationale for this subsidy was that flats, although more expensive to build, were necessary if housing conditions in crowded cities were to improve. There was a growing need to rehouse people back into expensive city sites. Flats were seen as the only way of fitting more people in, while at the same time building modern homes and giving overcrowded families more space and amenities. The problems of communal supervision and housing management were underestimated or ignored, and the virtues of terraced housing were unrecognized. No attempt was made to continue the familiar street patterns of the cities. Nor was the idea of renovation and installation of amenities considered as a way of tackling the widespread slum conditions.

Demolition had become the first prong of attack on bad housing conditions, and flats seemed the obvious answer to the continuing inner-city problems. By 1937, nearly 200,000 homes had been demolished and a further 200,000 were in demolition programmes. London,

Birmingham, Manchester and Liverpool had the biggest housing problems but other urban areas were caught up in the same process. The critical effect of the ambitious slum-clearance programme was that tenants had no choice. 'Families are being removed, whether willing or not' (CHAC, 1939, p. 73).

The new combination of subsidies, aimed at demolishing slums and encouraging local authorities to rehouse ex-slum-dwellers and over-crowded families in new council accommodation within the cities, actually changed the emphasis of council housing policy from an ambitious, high quality programme for a wide cross-section of the general population to a special provision for the poor and the needy. Some slum-clearance estates gradually built up a new life for the inhabitants, but some inherited the reputation and problems of the old areas. Some of today's most unpopular estates date from the 1930s when they were built to house slum populations. The government's 1939 report described the tenants' resettlement process:

> A number will adapt themselves quickly to their new surround-ings; some will not react to the change in their condition quite so readily and will need initial guidance. Others without contin-uous supervision will produce a slum atmosphere wherever they are sent; and a few, a very few, will be beyond reclamation altogether. (ibid., p. 7)

Several other important legislative changes in the 1930s had a direct impact on the future of council housing. In 1935, the Overcrowding Act increased subsidies to flats on expensive sites, following the abolition in 1933 of general subsidies for any housing that was not specifically designed to relieve overcrowding and slum conditions. A special new subsidy was provided by the government to Councils for each person rehoused to relieve overcrowding. This tied the public provision of housing very tightly to the most needy, low-income households, and marked the onset of welfare housing. It was regarded as unnecessary to provide direct government subsidies except for the most badly housed people, and the previous general subsidies were held to have caused sharp increases in house and building prices in the 1920s (CHAC, 1939, p. 7). The new subsidies were carefully targeted at the worst housing conditions.

A further Housing Act in 1938 clarified the type of household to be housed – either displaced by demolition of unfit areas or rehoused to abate overcrowding – and it set the minimum subsidy for flat-building at double the level for other dwellings, and payable for forty years. It also laid down that local authorities had to pay an amount equal to one half of the government subsidy (Macey, 1982, p. 25). The major changes in housing policy in the 1930s towards slum clearance, flat-

Table 2.1 Distribution of Housing Stock by Tenure

Year	Owner-occupied	Local authorities and new towns	Private landlord and others	Total
1914	800,000	20,000	7,100,000	7,920,000
1938	3,700,000	1,100,000	6,600,000	11,400,000

Source: DOE, 1977b, Part 1, p.38.

building within the city, and direct subsidies targeted at households in greatest need of rehousing coloured the development of council housing as a provision for low-income households. The LCC, encouraged by the subsidies for flat-building and following the withdrawal of general subsidies, reduced its commitment to peripheral estates of houses and gardens and concentrated on large-scale flat-building inside London. By the late 1930s the LCC was building nearly four flats for every house, in spite of evidence that some of the inner flatted estates were already unpopular (LCC, Minutes of the Housing Committee, 1928). They were constrained by the need to relieve overcrowding, to rebuild within the cleared areas, and to help the people who had lived in those areas. They were encouraged by the targeted subsidies. The LCC stock quadrupled between 1929 and 1939 to 100,000 dwellings. Other local authorities built nearly 1 million dwellings in the interwar period.

Overall, the housing stock expanded in the interwar years by 44 per cent while the proportion of council dwellings rose from 0.2 per cent at the onset of the First World War to nearly 10 per cent by 1938. Table 2.1 shows a major expansion in the stock across the board, but with owner-occupation expanding faster than any other tenure. Council housing was fairly close behind. Private landlords still dominated the total stock but their share had dropped from 90 per cent to 58 per cent.

From 1938 onwards, private renting was to enter an inexorable decline and owner-occupation was to become the central strand of housing provision, which council housing, because of the very large subsidies it required, was only rarely to match. Nonetheless, councils were moving rapidly towards becoming major landlords.

The Development of Allocation Policies

Specific central government intervention in the question of allocations did not arise until the 1935 Housing Act instructed local authorities to take account of need in allocating council housing. The Act was couched in somewhat ambiguous terms: 'Local authorities are obliged to give reasonable preference to persons who are occupying insanitary or overcrowded houses, have large families, or are living under unsatisfactory housing conditions' (CHAC, 1939, p. 8). The phrase 'reasonable preference' hardly made the local authorities' obligations crystal clear. But because of the generous subsidies paid to councils by central government for each tenant rehoused from a slum or from overcrowded conditions, councils switched their rehousing policies to favour needy households, away from applicants who could convince housing officers of their worthiness.

It was almost exclusively slum-clearance families who were rehoused in the 1930s. The shift in allocations from stable, affluent workers to poor, insecure slum dwellers was almost total. Such was the level of poverty that local authorities had on occasions to burn the tenants' belongings, as well as demolish their homes, because of infestations of vermin, lice and so on, when they were rehoused: 'We noticed dire poverty . . . They may begin [in a council house] with less than they had in their original homes because some of their effects have been destroyed to kill the vermin' (CHAC, 1939, p. 21). According to John Macey in his seminal work on housing management (Macey and Baker, 1982, p. 274), in the period before the Second World War up to 70 per cent of rehoused tenants had infested belongings. The medical officer of health for Stockton on Tees found that the death rate rose on new council estates in the 1930s because of poverty coupled with new high rents (Daunton, 1984, p. 24).

Early Slum Clearance and First Problem Estates

Tenants were moved *en bloc* from crowded old neighbourhoods with very few amenities to new estates built to high standards for the day. The old slum neighbourhoods would be demolished but the former residents carried the slum stigma with them and the new estates would sometimes acquire notoriety from the outset. Surprisingly, most of these estates were cottage estates of houses and gardens. In some cases the emergence of unpopular estates was a long process of attrition whereby over the years an accumulation of problems and pressures pushed the estate into a downward spiral. In others, notorious streets from the old Victorian inner cities (White, 1986, Introduction) became notorious enclaves of council housing. Dispersal would have been seen as spreading bad apples around. Local authorities had readily taken on board the new housing responsibilities towards needy families, without considering the best ways of eradicating some of the social problems they aimed to resolve. It is possible that many authorities believed a physical solution to housing was sufficient, or were simply unaware that housing management was vital to the creation of a viable rented sector. With displaced, forcibly uprooted, and often totally dispossessed families from crowded slum streets, the need for social support on a new estate was paramount, but frequently completely lacking.

'Dispersing Bad Tenants'

In a situation of severe housing stress, no one questioned the justice of allocating new publicly owned and heavily subsidized housing to deprived households. Nor did many question the assumptions behind the demolition of old slum areas or the wisdom of transplanting communities *en bloc* to brand new estates. However, in 1939 the government's Housing Advisory Sub-Committee on Housing Management became concerned over the allocation of housing to severely disadvantaged tenants and recommended the advisability of dispersing 'bad tenants' among good, even if it meant breaking up old social networks. They were not convinced that semi-penal measures, such as the Dutch adopted towards difficult tenants, involving segregation and strict supervision and rehabilitation, were either 'desirable or necessary in this country' (CHAC, 1939, p. 19). They felt that putting vulnerable households together would exacerbate the problems and make estates unmanageable: 'We favour the principle of separating unsatisfactory families from one another, so far as this is possible, and interspersing them among families of a good type' (ibid., p. 20). The Committee recognized the danger of ghettoization and the need to allocate sensitively to avoid concentrations of disturbed families, but their recommendation seems to have been ignored. Dispersal did not take place.

Housing Management

Following Octavia Hill's death in 1912, the managers who had been trained by her and had worked with her formed the Association of Women Housing Workers[1] in 1916 with fifty members (later to become the Society of Housing Managers), in order to advance the work of unified, intensive local housing management to a high standard (Brion and Tinker, 1980). Early members like Irene Barclay qualified as chartered surveyors, at the time a most unusual departure for women: 'A good deal of foolish fuss was made of us as the first

28

women surveyors' (Brion and Tinker, 1980, p. 70). Later the Association organized special training for its prospective members, asking the Royal Institute for Chartered Surveyors to set examinations for admission to their association. Trainees were carefully selected and it was considered quite a challenge to be allowed to embark on the professional career of housing management. The women involved had a very strong sense of responsibility towards their work and were rigorous in the selection of suitable trainees. In addition, members did a three-year apprenticeship in door-to-door housing management. Members gained the RICS qualification on passing the series of professional examinations.

The hallmarks of the Society were a high standard of professional competence, the total control under one manager of all aspects of landlord responsibility, from the organization and supervision of repairs to the enforcement of tenancy conditions, lettings and rents, as well as all aspects of welfare. The Society hotly defended Octavia Hill's insistence that Society managers should be female. There were numerous serious debates on the question of male members in the housing world (CHAC, 1939, p. 13), and the women only gave way on this point in 1948 – a move which some women housing managers today still think was a mistake. The women managers, however, strongly rejected, and resented, the exclusively do-gooding, welfare role traditionally considered appropriate to females. They were determined that the business areas – rent collection, maintenance and repair – should be their responsibility too. They worked almost exclusively in the private sector, with the philanthropic trusts, the Church Commissioners and the Crown Estate Commissioners.

Some of their work left its mark. During the First World War, in the absence of men, women managers ran big housing estates for the Ministry of Munitions, but they resigned in favour of the returning male managers at the end of the war. They also built up and ran large estates for the Crown Estate Commissioners, under the control of the notable follower of Octavia Hill, Miss M. Jeffrey. The management system survived and helped produce leading women members of the Institute of Housing, an organization which first appeared in 1932.

A most important development in the 1920s was the appointment of women housing managers in nine local authorities, almost entirely to run difficult or unpopular estates. Chesterfield, under the inspiration of their town clerk, Sir Parker Morris (of Parker Morris standards fame),[2] went to the Crown Estate Commissioners and, inspired by their intensive system of management, selected a woman housing manager, Janet Upcott, for the most difficult estate.

Janet Upcott, who had been trained by Octavia Hill (Smith, 1986), later organized the Conference of Women Municipal Managers in

1928 to represent what was seen as a growing area of work. The Ministry of Health had clearly stated as early as 1920 that

> The success of working class property depends very largely on its management ... Proper management will require a person specially skilled and trained for the work. The manager must be given ample authority ... Little is done except by the Association of Women House Property Managers, who have rendered such admirable service in redeeming unfit property. There will have to be more facilities for training if needs are to be met. (*Housing*, 1920, p. 11)

However, these early gains were not consolidated. Liverpool Corporation appointed a woman manager in 1936, only to rescind the appointment because she would have been in charge of men, an unacceptable departure.

Only forty-six women were employed by local authorities by the mid-1930s, with about 130 qualified Society members altogether. The hallmark of the Society continued to be that

> The women managers work in administrative control of the estate and at the same time in direct touch with the tenants ... including rent collection, court work, maintenance of properties including ordering and checking the work and accounts of direct labour staff, applications and tenancies, rehousing, social and educational work, committee work and relations with other departments. (Brion and Tinker, 1980, p. 75)

This was light years away from the early housing management style of the LCC or other city authorities such as Birmingham.

The Society itself had an increasingly chequered history, fighting a rearguard action against the admission of men throughout the inter-war period, when there were only 130–150 members. Some members began to accept with gratitude a welfare role on the large new slum-clearance estates of the 1930s, hoping that it would lead to a new departure in local authority housing management, but flying in the face of their dearly cherished management traditions. They were rarely given overall, co-ordinated responsibility for management; rather they were recruited to help impoverished new council tenants cope with the problems of a brand new, high quality dwelling in a totally alien community.

These women hoped that welfare had finally fused with housing management and that they would play a critical role in solving the new social problems of council housing:

By virtue of slum clearance and overcrowding, it [a local authority] has no option but to take all families whatever their income and character and trust that they will become satisfactory tenants. For this reason constant supervision and skill is always required . . . The permanent social service which housing has now become can be far more economically and efficiently administered by one [housing] department. (Besley, 1938)

But while the Society was hopeful that its ideas would take root in local authority housing management, by the late 1930s only seventy-five of its members were actually employed on council estates. Between them they were covering 35,000 properties, just under 500 properties each, and less than 5 per cent of the total council stock.

By the Second World War, only a small minority of councils had a housing department at all (Cullingworth, 1966, p. 73), or any concept of housing management as conceived by the Society. A much more typical pattern was the Birmingham model, propounded at the National Housing Conference in 1938: 'The collection of rents is divorced from the welfare work and a section of women home visitors is wholly employed in investigating and assisting cases of the unenlightened type' (Smith, 1938). The division of rents and repairs from allocations and welfare was fiercely if ineffectually opposed by the Society of Women Housing Estate Officers. But the women were on the defensive and their views were largely discarded.

In 1938 Mary Besley, a Housing Manager in Lincoln, criticized this fragmented approach:

They are employing several different officials to do separate parts of the work when they might employ people trained in the same work as a whole . . . Continuity of contact is invariably sacrificed if several different people conduct business with the tenant. It is obviously easier too for even the most amenable tenant to co-operate with one well-known official rather than with several. (Besley, 1938)

She argued forcibly that the method of unitary management of the Society of Women Housing Estate Officers was the only answer: 'Records are available to show they are a financial success' (ibid.).

With 1.1 million publicly owned homes by 1938 well over 3,000 trained managers would have been required in order to apply the methods of the Society. Their numbers were less than 200, and their influence was insignificant in relation to the problem they were attempting to address. Their voice went almost unheard and was certainly unheeded.

The Birth of the Institute of Housing

Meanwhile, the typical council structure comprised a variety of specialized technical departments delivering different parts of housing management, with repairs, rents, lettings and welfare handled respectively by engineers or surveyors, treasurers or town clerks, valuers, and public health, sanitation or housing officers.

The Municipal Yearbook of 1935 shows that only 13 per cent of the 450 local authorities in Britain had appointed a housing manager. The Central Housing Advisory Committee explained:

> In many districts, town clerks, treasurers, medical officers of health, engineers and surveyors are either separately or in combination, in control of the management of municipal houses ... and excellent though each official may be in his own sphere, skilled management is not only outside his province but housing management as such must always be to him a secondary consideration ... Little has been done by way of social service ... Management is incorporated in the ordinary machinery of local government, different officers being responsible for such part of the work as falls within their specialised duties. (CHAC, 1939, pp. 14, 15)

Construction was often the dominant interest of the 'professionals' and there was a well-rooted belief that men making a career of public administration could more competently handle the technical problems of rents, repairs, and lettings than well-intentioned women housing visitors, whose main role was seen as improving the lot of the poor.

In 1932, the Institute of Housing was formed with a male-dominated membership drawn almost exclusively from local authority employees, and propounding a very different approach to housing management than the existing women managers' organization, separating a social and welfare role completely from the more technical and professional questions of repairs and rents. The Institute of Housing dominated the local authority housing world with 'ex-town clerks trying to cope' (as one leading woman Housing Manager in the Institute of Housing described it in November 1983). It was born of different imperatives and propounded an opposite housing management tradition – the two bodies' 'contentions are largely conflicting' (CHAC, 1939, p. 26). The Institute had its own examinations, set to a lower standard than the Society, arguing that there was neither time nor money to replicate Octavia Hill's approach nor the Society's training: 'The cost would not be justified by results' (Macey, 1982, p. 337). The Institute held firmly to the belief that housing welfare should not be confused with the business and technical administration of housing which they regarded as 'men's work'.

The Society in turn refused to recognize the Institute, which in its early days provided no training, and would not allow joint membership after some initial attempts at co-operation. But by 1938, the Institute of Housing had a membership of 261, including seventy-eight members who were chief housing officers within their local authorities. This fact helps to explain why the Institute defended hotly the existing technical orientation of public housing management, and opposed the integrated, intensive and local approach by the women.

> The Institute of Housing are of the opinion that social service should be kept entirely apart from the other functions of housing, e.g. rent collecting and repairs, on the grounds that only a few tenants require supervision and that the majority can therefore be left entirely alone, thus avoiding unnecessary expenditure on management. (CHAC, 1939, p. 26)

They rejected out of hand the Society of Women Housing Estate Officers' advocacy of one manager for 300 properties, with additional resident caretakers, cleaners and repairs staff giving a ratio of one employee for every fifty dwellings, on the grounds of costs. Under the sectional/technical system that they advocated, local authorities usually employed (and still do) about one worker to every forty to sixty-five dwellings (LCC, Housing of the Working Class Committee minutes, 1912), but with each manager often covering 700 properties or more (Power, 1984, p. 60).

The Central Housing Advisory Committee's First Report

A landmark in the history of municipal housing was the publication in 1939 of the first report of the Central Housing Advisory Committee, appointed by the government to consider the problems of municipal council estates. It took evidence from both the Institute of Housing and the Society of Women Housing Estate Officers, as well as many local authorities. It also visited estates throughout the country.

The report brought into the open the central conflict between the two professional housing bodies, and on the whole favoured the Society's approach over that of the Institute. However, it failed to make clear-cut recommendations on many key issues: 'We are unable to recommend for general adoption in its entirety any of the systems which have been described to us' (CHAC, 1939, p. 28). It therefore failed to galvanize either support or opposition at a critical time in the evolution of housing management, when the overriding concern was how to cope with impoverished families and how to establish viable communities on the new estates.

The report posed a series of critical management questions, revealing the members' own sense of fear and anxiety over the 'slum problem' now transposed to municipal estates:

How shall the undesirables be dealt with?
What steps can be taken to prevent the bed bug?
How can he be supplied with the bare necessities
of comfort?
Who shall teach him to cultivate his garden?
(ibid., p. 28)

The Committee estimated that 80 per cent of tenants were 'of a good standard' and only about 5 per cent required 'continuous supervision'. The report recommended strongly the dispersal of this minority of problem-prone tenants in the hope that good neighbours would 'upgrade' them. They felt that this approach stood some chance on a spacious cottage estate with a resident manager.

But in the dense, flatted blocks the opposite was happening:

The impact of one antagonistic person on another, the quarrels of children, the behaviour of a noisy tenant, may be magnified out of proportion to the importance of the actual event and cause a general feeling of unrest and dissatisfaction. Local authorities recognize the value of exercising a somewhat closer supervisory control over families living in flats than over tenants on cottage estates. (ibid., p. 7)

In the event, local authorities only partially adopted a supervisory role, and problems built up rapidly. At no stage was it suggested that the 'antagonistic' tenants should not be rehoused in flats. This would have been the only possible solution, unless widespread and intensive policing was to be the management stance. However, flats were recognized as a permanent management responsibility because of their density, the proximity of neighbours and their unguarded common areas.

The report made a number of other useful points. It defended the door-to-door system of rent collection for all families, providing a vital point of contact. It stressed the need for good public transport to the outer estates and for social centres on all estates to rebuild a cohesive life for residents, especially since so many new residents from old slums were used to the vitality of city centres. The report also stressed that the landlord should retain responsibility for all functions including minor repairs and redecorations, otherwise poorer, more vulnerable families would always be falling behind in their standards. An interesting but largely overlooked piece of advice was that the manager of a large estate should hold a university degree, which in prewar times was an exceptional demand. Two universities, London and Cambridge, at that stage offered degrees in estate management.

On the question of women housing managers, the Committee was unequivocal in its approval, endorsing the personal approach and the combination of business with social matters, disagreeing with the Institute's view that social service should be kept separate from housing management:

> The housewife is usually willing to talk more freely to another woman and to entrust her with a fuller degree of confidence. It is easier for a woman than for a man to be admitted to a house ... These are in our view strong arguments for employing women ... (ibid., p. 28)

But the members of the Committee felt that they could not endorse unequivocally the central tenet of the Society of Women Housing Estate Officers that one manager should handle 'rent collection, ordering and supervision of repairs and costing, selection and allocation of tenants, keeping records and accounts, Court work in connection with notices to quit, and social service' (ibid., p. 26).

The report provided insight into the typical local authority response in the face of landlord responsibilities:

> In the main, management is incorporated in the ordinary machinery of local government, different officers being responsible for such parts of the work as fall within their specialised duties. The surveyor looks after the fabric of the houses, the treasurer sees to rent collecting and finance whilst the clerk exercises general supervisory functions. (ibid., p. 12)

It lamented somewhat timidly the fact that only 17 per cent of local authorities had appointed housing managers at all. But it maintained that no one system was best and that it had visited very well-run, popular estates under various systems of management.

One of the impressions to come over from the 1939 report is that people were uprooted and then rehoused in strange conditions that they did not readily take to and that they had to be helped to cope with. There was the blanket recommendation that all tenants should be assumed to be verminous and lice-infested: 'The cleansing process should be applied to all tenants as a routine' (ibid., p. 15). Then there was the admonition that 'Houses must be guarded against misuse and the interests of neighbours must be protected ... Firm handling introducing an element of compulsion, is occasionally necessary, for a family must not be allowed to break the conditions of tenancy' (ibid., p. 20). There was the added worry over flats 'where life is devoid of the spacious freedom of the cottage estate' (ibid., p. 23).

The Local Authority Management Problem

Developments in the LCC between the wars illustrate the lack of a clear sense of direction in local authority housing management. With the great burst of housing activity, the LCC in 1919 appointed a Director of Housing on the very high salary of £2,000 per annum. Housing development became a major part of the job and the Housing Manager of prewar times became the Housing Estates Manager under the Director. In the 1920s the LCC was building peripheral estates on a large scale, having reduced its inner-city flat-building to a very small share.

The early postwar houses were subsidized and built to a high standard and were therefore very attractive. All of these much more privileged suburban developments had resident superintendents, a system that seemed to work well, but for some inexplicable reason focused an integrated management service where it was least needed.[2]

At that time 5 per cent of the Council's stock was let to LCC employees, and several of the outer postwar estates in such places as Bromley and Roehampton were considered very desirable residences for administrative staff. John Macey, a long-serving LCC housing officer, later to become Controller of Housing at the GLC with nearly a quarter of a million properties under his direct responsibility, was an early LCC tenant under this scheme. The rest of the stock was to let at this stage on a system of date orders, though the volume of building and rent levels combined to make demand sometimes fall below supply. The waiting list for the Becontree estate in 1928 contained 700 fewer households than there were dwellings to let (Macey, private letter to author, 1984).

The resident superintendents were each responsible for 2,000 dwellings. The LCC by its management system tied itself to the logic of large estates, arguing that one resident superintendent *should* manage 2,000 dwellings. Within London, the estates were usually of several hundred dwellings and often did not warrant their own superintendent according to the LCC's standards. Although there was always resident caretaking staff, caretakers were considered lowly employees and the records show that they were employed on roughly the same level as lavatory attendants. They had little responsibility except for small repairs and cleaning. Women were also occasionally employed as caretakers. There was no estate-based manager in charge of most of the dense inner-city blocks, in sharp contrast with the trusts' housing.

By 1925, the LCC had 20,000 dwellings and it decided to allocate a quarter of new lettings to 'meet cases of hardship'. At that stage some of the better-paid LCC officers were asked to leave the outer estates by the council to make room for more needy tenants. With hindsight, it might have been preferable to retain a mixed community.

By the late 1920s, a number of factors coincided which led to a radical redirection of housing policy within the LCC and later at a national level. First was the decision in 1925 to give some priority to needy families. Secondly, a series of decisions between 1926 and 1928 led to a renewed emphasis on flat-building within the central areas, abandoning the early postwar policy of building cottage estates on the outskirts of London. Thirdly, building standards and conditions of tenancy were lowered to allow cheaper rents and to encourage poorer families to move in. Otherwise flat-building in inner areas would have failed to achieve the desired objective of attracting poor families, thereby improving slum conditions. A prime motivation in all this was the growing pressure in remaining slum areas, as the poorest families were constantly displaced by redevelopment and pushed into receding and rapidly deteriorating old areas.

The central management problem for the LCC was that for most of the inner-city blocks there was no coherent management system to cover rents, repairs, lettings and welfare problems. As a result, management problems grew while the populations rehoused became more needy. In 1930, the LCC recorded that

> The present system of management is an intelligent one which secures cleanly living on the part of the great majority of tenants ... Notwithstanding this there are undoubtedly some tenants who appear to be unable to appreciate to the full the accommodation afforded. (LCC, 13 May 1930)

No sooner had the council begun to rehouse genuinely needy tenants than this lack of coherent management became all too apparent. While the council blamed inadequate tenants for failing to make proper use of their new accommodation, it did also make a radical shift in its management organization. The LCC made the bold decision in 1930, ten years after the Ministry of Health had first recommended it, to employ women housing managers with responsibility for door-to-door rent collection, repairs, cleaning, tenancy matters and court action: 'Although it has not hitherto been the practice to employ women for the purpose ... a woman is specially fitted to be the helper and adviser of tenants' (ibid.). This decision was ahead of most other local authorities, which continued to defend the prevailing system of assorted departments handling fragments of the housing service. However, the LCC only sustained the intensive system for a few years and on a few estates, with the appointment of one woman manager and two female assistants in 1930. It reacted defensively and narrowly to the Government's report. It is worth quoting at some length from the council's response.

The question of adopting the Octavia Hill system ... has been considered on more than one occasion and many of those who advocated the system apparently took the view that the Council's system merely consisted of rent collection ... The Council's system, however, extends far beyond this and recognises the desirability of making contact with families from slum clearance areas as early as possible and the need for after-care measures ... The chief differences between the Council's system and the Octavia Hill system are:

1 The Council mainly employs trained men of practical ex-perience, while in the latter system trained women managers are responsible for the management.
2 The pivot of the Octavia Hill system is the combination of all functions of management and the door to door collection of rents in one person, whereas in the Council's system all questions of principle or matters of a difficult technical nature are dealt with at the central office, and the bulk of the rents is collected at local offices.

The Octavia Hill system is undoubtedly very successful when applied to working class dwellings previously subject to bad management and neglect, but it is doubtful whether it possesses any advantage over the Council's system.

We cannot subscribe to the view that it is essential in every case for one officer to maintain contact with a tenant for all purposes.

We do not accept the theory that women are, by reason of their sex, more suitable than men for this [housing management] work.

We see no adequate reason, therefore, in the interests either of the Council or its tenants, to suggest a radical change in the existing system. (LCC, *Report of the Housing and Public Health Committee on Housing Management*, March 1939)

In defence of its own centrally organized system, the LCC argued that door-to-door collection was more expensive than office collection; that social welfare combined with rent collection would slow down the rent collectors and involve a large increase in staff; and that in any case tenants were often visited by superintendents or surveyors from the centre and therefore local managers were unnecessary.

The LCC had a very intensive staff ratio, higher than even the resident, estate-based housing trusts, and could certainly have organ-ized integrated local management if it wanted. However, it would have had to break up its vast central empire, employing over 2,500 workers in 1939.

Notes to Chapter 2

1 The Association changed names a number of times before it finally merged with its rival, the Institute of Housing, in 1965:

1916 Association of Women Housing Workers, renamed Association of Women House Property Managers a few years later.

1928 Conference of Women Municipal Managers formed.

1928 Octavia Hill Club founded by Miss Jeffrey, one of her followers.

1932 The three bodies united as the Society of Women Housing Estate Officers.

1948 Admitted men and changed its name to the Society of Housing Managers.

1965 Merged with the Institute of Housing, to become the Institute of Housing Managers.

2 In 1961 a sub-committee of CNAC, under the chairmanship of Sir Parker Morris, published a report on housing standards entitled *Homes for Today and Tomorrow*.

3 As an interesting sidelight on management problems, in 1921 the LCC Housing Committee decided to prohibit the keeping of cockerels on its estates, though hens were allowed, and it also decided in 1923 to purchase four bicycles for staff to use on the largest estates. (At that time a bicycle cost about six times the average weekly wage, whereas today it costs half the weekly wage!) These two items, recorded in council proceedings, give some notion both of the involvement of politicians in detailed management decisions and the lack of devolution to a local scale.

Chapter Three

Postwar Mass Housing

The orientation of public housing in the 1960s towards unpopular and high cost forms of accommodation seems to have slowly but quite decisively reduced the levels of public support for Council Housing and to have strengthened support for private house ownership.   (Dunleavy, 1981, p. 355)

Postwar housing developments have been examined in great detail by political scientists (Dunleavy, 1981), economists (Merrett, 1979) and social policy experts (Donnison and Ungerson, 1982). Here we attempt to highlight a coincidence of factors culminating, within a generation, in the collapse of public confidence in 'mass housing' as a solution to overcrowding and slum conditions. The discussion in this chapter focuses on those trends and problems which led to the emergence of difficult-to-let estates, without covering in detail the full history of postwar housing policy.

The Second World War brought all building to a virtual halt and created another major housing shortage, this time partly through bomb damage, as well as a virtual stoppage in all house-building for six years. Three-quarters of a million homes out of a total 11.5 million were either demolished by bombing or seriously damaged. Rent controls continued on virtually all private rented dwellings, accelerating the decay of the old stock of city housing. Strict rent controls remained till the late 1950s, thereby depriving landlords of funds for repairs.

About two-thirds of homes at the end of the war dated from before the First World War and were in constant need of renovation. Conditions in private rented housing deteriorated while landlords found it less and less profitable to continue letting. Many private landlords gave up the rented market in the decades of tight rent control following the Second World War. In the 1950s about 1.5 million houses were transferred from renting to owning.

Because of scarcity and lack of repairs, the war gave a huge impetus to council housing programmes. The crude postwar shortage of homes forced the government to act, and the war itself generated an ethos of state intervention that made it easy for the postwar Labour government to take on the housing problem as a major plank of its social strategy, while the general decay of older city housing fed into the massive slum-clearance programmes that were to develop in the late 1950s and 1960s.

Labour's Housing for All

In 1945, the Labour government was determined to make council housing a general service like health and education, available to anyone, rather than a welfare provision for the poorest and the worst housed, as it had become in the 1930s. The government saw its role as inspiring and subsidizing housing development, with local authorities as the principal builders and landlords. New Towns were launched as a pathfinder to better social conditions, especially housing conditions, spearheaded by the state. The belief in town planning was never stronger. New Towns enjoyed the unique feature of being built by public authorities both for renting and owner-occupation, but they largely excluded the very poorest and most disadvantaged families by tying access to accommodation to jobs within New Town industries. Nonetheless, New Towns made a special contribution to the public sector housing stock by taking in a broader spectrum of social groups than had previously been provided for or than was usually contemplated in city council housing developments.

The groups with lowest incomes and least stable employment on the whole remained locked within the cities in private rented dwellings. The Labour government was conscious of the problems of acquiring and building on expensive city sites, and introduced a special additional subsidy in 1949 to encourage a mixture of houses and flats on such sites to diversify new city building away from flats alone. Improvement grants for older property were also introduced. Unfortunately, these imaginative new subsidies were not much taken up at up at that point.

The new Labour policy of providing for general needs was difficult to sustain. Unlike health and education, housing could not readily be provided universally by the state. There was such scarcity that demand was too great to be met by public effort only; in any case, private landlords still owned nearly 90 per cent of homes after the war and there were strong political differences over the desirability of mass council housing. Nonetheless, in the six years after the war, the bulk of new housing was built by councils – about 80 per cent of the total. By 1951, Labour had built over three-quarters of a million council homes, nearly as many in six years as were built in the whole interwar period, about one-fifth of them flats. But shortages continued with a further million homes still needed urgently. There was virtually no slum clearance until the mid-1950s since the housing shortage was acute, and councils either built on bombed sites or went outside the cities. The urban land shortage reinforced the trend towards flat-building which seemed the only answer to city problems. In the cities with the biggest housing problems, very few houses were built in spite of the 1949 additional subsidy for mixed developments of flats and houses.

The Conservatives' Massive Building Programme

Under the Conservative Minister of Housing, Harold Macmillan, a target of 300,000 homes a years was pledged, and this was met for most of the next eleven years. It was nearly double Labour's average rate. Three and a half million new houses were built, over half by local authorities in spite of the Conservative preference for private housing. Given the crude shortage of dwellings, the government wanted anybody who could get houses built to do so, councils included. By 1960, the stock of council dwellings had more than tripled from prewar levels, although by the end of the 1950s private building was beginning to overtake the rate of council building.

Table 3.1 illustrates the much faster rate of expansion in the council sector than in any other. While private renting shrank significantly and owner-occupation almost doubled, council renting more than tripled.

The Swing to Flatted Estates

In order to speed the production of homes, the Conservatives in 1952 drastically reduced space standards (DOE, 1977, Part 1, p. 31). Densities were increased to enable more homes on scarce and expensive land (Macey, 1982, p. 29). Housing, especially public housing, became meaner. Subsidies were increased for expensive sites, mostly in inner-city areas. In 1956 the government introduced a 'storey height' subsidy which went up with increasing storey height for flat-building. These subsidies became an albatross. Designed to overcome the barriers to council building where it was believed to be most needed, it actually encouraged councils to build in locations, in a style, at a density and on a scale that later proved highly unpopular and undesirable. In a sense it was killing the goose that laid the golden egg, 'site cramming' as it came to be called (Dunleavy, 1981, p. 162).

The scale of council housing under the impact of the continuous

Table 3.1 Public Sector and Private Sector New Building 1945–84

Year	Local authority completions	Private completions
1945	1,936	31,297
1946	25,013	
1947	97,340	40,980
1948	190,368	32,751
1949	165,946	25,790
1950	163,670	27,358
1951	162,584	22,551
1952	186,920	34,320
1953	229,305	62,921
1954	223,731	90,636
1955	181,331	113,457
1956	154,971	124,161
1957	154,137	126,455
1958	131,614	128,148
1959	114,324	150,708
1960	116,358	168,629
1961	105,529	177,513
1962	116,424	174,800
1963	112,780	174,864
1964	141,132	218,094
1965	151,305	213,799
1966	161,435	205,372
1967	181,467	200,438
1968	170,214	221,993
1969	162,910	181,703
1970	157,067	170,304
1971	134,000	191,612
1972	104,553	196,457
1973	88,148	186,628
1974	103,279	140,865
1975	129,883	150,752
1976	129,202	152,181
1977	119,644	140,820
1978	96,196	149,021
1979	75,573	140,481
1980	76,991	127,522
1981	54,956	114,216
1982	33,163	123,859
1983	32,742	144,309
1984	31,505	153,810

Sources: Holmans (1987), p. 114.
DOE, *Housing and Construction Statistics 1974–84*, pp. 68, 72.

Table 3.2 Ownership of Housing, 1938 and 1960 (millions)

Tenure	1938	1960	% of total in 1960
Owner-occupier	3.7	6.4	43.8
New Towns and Local authorities	1.1	3.6	24.7
Private rented and miscellaneous	6.6	4.6	31.5
Total	11.4	14.6	100.0

Source: DOE, 1977b, Part 1, p. 38.

upsurge in building was changing and becoming gigantesque. At the beginning of Conservative rule in 1951, over 85 per cent of council building was still in the form of houses, although the rate of council flat-building was already much higher than in the private sector. Government subsidies for flat-building inevitably led to a rise over a long period in the proportion of council dwellings in that form, as Table 3.3 illustrates. Flats were on the ascendancy throughout the 1950s, and by the mid-1960s comprised over half of the council dwellings being built. Among owner-occupiers the proportion of flats and maisonettes remained at a fairly steady low figure of 7 per cent.

The cost of building high-rise flats was 50 per cent greater than building houses. Yet the subsidy for a high-rise flat in the years 1956–61 was three times greater than for a house. This gave councils an incentive to build high. By 1965, the subsidy reduced to double (Table 3.4). Once the extra subsidy for high-rise flats was abolished in 1968, councils stopped building in that style. The subsidies had been justified by the government's firm belief that the postwar baby boom indicated longer-term population growth. Flat-building was the only foreseeable way in our crowded island to house the expanding population to reasonable standards, as spare land within cities was almost exhausted and green belts had been applied to all major towns (MHLG, 1955).

The Housing Subsidies Act of 1967 laid down the following sliding scale of subsidies, illustrating how they favoured high building (Macey and Baker, 1982, p. 32):

(1) Dwellings in a 4-storey block £8 a year per dwelling
(2) Dwellings in a 5-storey block £14 a year per dwelling
(3) Dwellings in blocks of over 5 storeys £26 a year per dwelling

There were strong regional variations in the proportion of flats,

Table 3.3 Number of Local Authority Dwellings Built as Houses, Flats and Maisonettes (thousands)

Year	Houses	Flats and Maisonettes	Total
1946–50	495*	55	550
1951–55	680	190	870
1956–60	385	205	590
1961–65	285	260	545
1966–70	360	370	730
1971–75	260	250	510
1976–80	275	222	497
1981–84†	79	75	154
Total	2,819	1,627	4,446

*Plus 116,000 prefabs.
†Covers four-year period only.
 Sources: DOE, *Housing and Construction Statistics* (1974–84), p. 54.
Merrett (1979), pp. 239, 247, 256, 261.

relating directly to land costs and therefore eligibility for extra subsidy. In 1967, 91 per cent of the homes built by the GLC were in flats, 65 per cent of which were in high-rise blocks. By 1971, two-thirds of the council stock in the London area was in the form of flats compared with 10 per cent for rural areas (DOE, 1977b, Part 1, p. 55). In the inner areas of Birmingham, Liverpool and Manchester, proportions were approaching the London figures. Flats became a hallmark of council housing in the large centres of population.

Figure 3.1 illustrates the change in style of construction and the strong swing to flat-building from the early 1950s onwards. The sharp increase in high-rise flats over a short period is very noticeable. The part played by government advocacy of system-building methods is discussed later.

Table 3.4 Proportional Cost of Building Flats Compared with Houses, 1964, and Subsidy Levels (1956–65)

Style	Cost (base 100)	Subsidy (actual 1956–61)	Subsidy 1965
House	100	£22	£64
4-storey flats	114	£32	£89
10-storey flats	145	£57	£109
15-storey flats	150	£66	£107

Source: Dunleavy, 1981, pp. 89, 162.

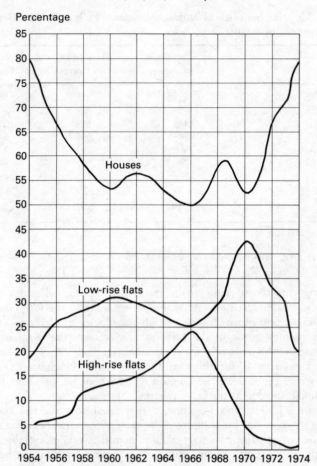

Percentage

Figure 3.1   Types of local authority dwellings 1954–74

Source: Dunleavy, 1981, p. 40.

Size of Estates

It is difficult to know the numbers of dwellings being built per estate in the council sector compared with the private sector during the period, as no record can be traced of such information. The most informative examinations of housing policy, history and development have overlooked this important element. However, the mass building of council estates on a large scale by one landlord was bound to lead to attempts at land consolidation in the hope that economies of scale would come into play. Council landlords favoured single large contracts rather

Table 3.5 Proportions of New Construction, Showing Size of Contracts, Contract Value Ranges, 1969

Value of contracts	Public sector housing (–)	Private sector housing (%)
Under £100,000	15	80
£100,001–250,000	12	12
£250,001–500,000	19	5
£500,001–1,000,000	20	2
£1,000,001–2,000,000	14	2
Over £2,000,000	19	0

Source: Dunleavy, 1981, p. 27.

than multiple small contracts, also encouraging large-scale estates. Large contractors played a major part in council building programmes, and because of their scale favoured estate building on large sites. The LCC records show that postwar estates tended to be larger than prewar (CHAC, 1959, p. 9). The Priority Estates Project reports (DOE, 1981a; Power, 1982; Power, 1984, p. 9) show that the more modern estates of the 1960s and 1970s were bigger than the 1930s to 1950s estates.

The most direct evidence we have is collected by Patrick Dunleavy in his lengthy study of flat-building and the high-rise movement. He showed the contrast in size between the private and public house-building contracts. Table 3.5 illustrates the heavy bias in the private sector towards small contracts, four-fifths producing twenty houses or less in a single contract, compared with one-third of public sector contracts covering at least 200 dwellings.

Thus under the aggressive housing policies first of the euphoric postwar Labour government and then of the housing-conscious Conservative administration of 1951–64, the large, inhuman style of many modern flatted council estates gradually emerged.

Redevelopment

Councils and governments, while encouraging industry, offices and homes to move out of cities, had not recognized the steady decline of city areas and continued to build homes at a rate density set by outdated expectations of city requirements. While city populations dropped by three million, the national population rose by seven

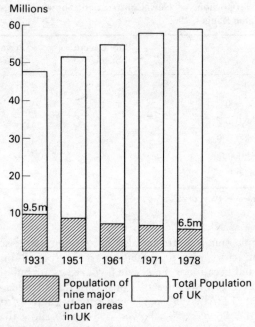

Figure 3.2 Decline in city population and increase in national population.

Source: Census data, 1931–81.

million. Figure 3.2 shows population trends in nine major urban areas in the UK (Inner London, Birmingham, Kingston-upon-Hull, Leeds, Liverpool, Manchester, Newcastle-upon-Tyne, Nottingham, Sheffield) in 1931–81, compared to national population trends. Outer boroughs and county councils restricted council building, partly to preserve the green belt, partly to reserve land for more prosperous or more desirable private developments, and partly to retain a Conservative vote in the suburban and rural electorate. Council tenants were often considered 'Labour voting fodder'. There was a general feeling that they brought inner-city social problems with them to new council estates. Therefore council efforts were further concentrated in Labour-controlled city authorities where land was scarce and expensive, and slums were worst. The Conservatives in the 1950s and Labour in the 1960s felt obliged to continue the expensive land and high flat subsidies as the only way of producing the volume of dwellings believed to be needed to tackle the worst slums through major redevelopment programmes within the city limits.

Slum Clearance

Because of the pressure during the 1950s for large-scale, fast production of council housing and because the authorities willing to under-
take big public housing programmes were on the whole the dense,
Labour-controlled city authorities, shortage of building land became
the absolute barrier to progress. The only way to get land on sufficient
scale in the cities was to demolish existing housing.

Thus in the 1950s demolition became again a main plank of the
council housing programmes, after a twenty-year respite. The policy
of large-scale demolition was sustained through subsidies to the mid-
1970s, although the public mood swung against it progressively from
the late 1960s (Figure 3.3).

The level of demolition was not hard to justify from the councils' or
government's point of view. Five million homes lacked basic amenities. At the end of the war, 42 per cent of households had no access to a
bath at all. In 1951, 69 per cent of all households either shared a home

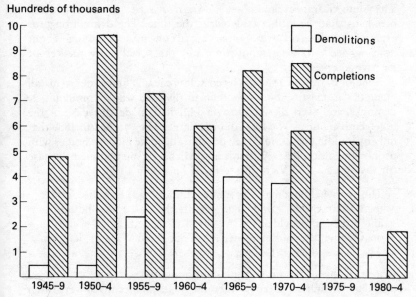

Figure 3.3 Council house slum clearance and completions, Great Britain,
1945–84.

Source: DOE, *Housing and Construction Statistics*, 1984; Merrett, 1979.
Note: Slum clearance figures for 1945–49 and 1950–54 are estimated from figures for
1945–54 inclusive for England and Wales only.
Because of a change in the way figures were recorded between 1976 and 1979, slum
clearance figures for 1975–9 and 1980–4 are estimates only.

or lacked basic amenities. Objectively, insanitary, overcrowded conditions seemed to justify demolition. But a perceptive elderly tenant from the Byker district of central Newcastle, for years a blighted slum-clearance area, observed that modern amenities could have been installed in some of the popular and structurally sound but old and unplumbed terraces: 'It's wicked – these houses have been under demolition order for twenty odd years, and you know – they could've been saved, they could've just given us a bath and hot water' (Konttinen, 1983, p. 8).

However there were many political, social and economic reasons for embracing slum clearance, rather than attempting renovation on an ambitious scale. Councils hoped through demolition and rebuilding to put an end to slum landlords. The discussion here focuses on the problems and limitations of slum clearance because they contributed in a major way to the growing problems in the public sector.

Flaws in Slum Clearance
The slum-clearance policy set in train a series of new housing problems that were ill-considered at the time. The demolition programmes themselves were often based on misconceptions about housing need, housing innovation and the social consequences of massive intervention.

A major flaw in clearance is its cost. It is cheaper and easier to install amenities in existing buildings than to displace whole communities, demolish and start again. Octavia Hill had made this case in the nineteenth century. The LCC did not agree. They argued in 1880 that only by building new could they provide adequate modern homes with proper amenities. Peter Wilmott and Michael Young argued the case for saving East End Victorian terraced houses in 1957:

> The overwhelming majority [of East Enders] want a house, rather than a flat, inside, rather than outside the East End. Should the aim not be to provide as many new and reconditioned houses as possible while avoiding dispersal? (Young and Wilmott, letter to *The Times*, 8 May, 1957)

Not until the 1970s did subsidies substantially favour rehabilitation over slum clearance, and even then the financial incentives were often too marginal for structurally sound but badly run-down houses. Although basic amenity installation grants had first become available before the war and were greatly increased in the 1960s, these were not adequate to cover major repairs, such as damp-proofing, roof replacement, replastering, or modern heating. Therefore, slum clearance continued to be the favoured economic option even after it had outlived its usefulness as a general policy. At the same time, the building industry was geared almost entirely to new building on 'clean' sites and had been for nearly 200 years. The messy and unpredictable work of rehabilitation was more suited to a small repairs firm than to a large-scale building contractor. Most were slow to adapt to the opportunities provided by rehabilitation, so the government's desire for volume production was more effectively met through redevelopment.

'Unfit'
Slum-clearance programmes were thus not sensitive to potential improvements. A large proportion of the houses declared unfit during the slum clearance decades were not actually proved to be unfit. Until public opposition to demolition emerged in the 1970s, it was common-place simply to declare properties unfit; landlords' objections were rarely upheld by government inspectors. The GLC in a house condition survey in 1967 found that 69 per cent of the properties it was demolishing in the late 1960s had been assessed as structurally sound. London alone lost 54,000 structurally sound properties in the period 1967–71. The last major redevelopment area to be demolished in Islington was the Westbourne Road area of Holloway. There, at least 60 per cent of the houses were found to be structurally sound when surveyed. In the end the four-storey terraces were demolished on social grounds based on the Medical Officer of Health's report on over-crowding, crime and prostitution. The area was demolished in the early 1970s amid a fever of enthusiasm for renovation and opposition to demolition in adjacent areas (Ferris, 1972).

It is not clear how many of the slums destroyed could not have been saved. Certainly many of the early demolition areas contained very poor housing. However, local authorities defined slums in an arbitrary way. Welwyn Garden City in assessing its housing stock claimed to have the same proportion of slums as the mining towns of the Rhondda. Liverpool, Salford and Bolton, with similar Coronation Street-style terraces, claimed respectively that 43 per cent, 34 per cent and 10 per cent of their Victorian terraces were 'slums'. Little control was exercised over slum clearance, so strong was the ambition to build anew on a massive scale (Crossman, 1975, Vol. 1, p. 450).

Councils' compulsory purchase powers were greatly increased between 1951 and 1971, making it ever easier for large areas to be swept away under the bulldozer. Councils were allowed to add areas of 'fit' housing to clearance areas in order to produce large and convenient packets of land. Some demolition areas were declared primarily because there were large gardens and councils could there-fore make a housing gain. The scale of slum clearance inevitably fed the 'mass housing' ideas of modern architects and planners. Birmingham's first postwar clearance area covered no fewer than 50,000 properties, in one grand sweep through the central city, to be followed a few years later by a further 50,000 properties. Little wonder it proceeded to build the largest concentration of tower-block flats of any city in Western Europe – over 400 blocks above six storeys. The whole approach to poor city communities was insensitive, inflexible and devastating in its impact, like its chief implement, the bulldozer.

Time-Lag in Clearance
Another element almost totally ignored by redevelopment advocates was the housing havoc created by the long time-lag, usually of ten years or more, between the decision to demolish and the completion of a new housing scheme. One area of Newham took over thirty years to redevelop (Dunleavy, 1981, p. 352). Several areas of Islington were blighted by redevelopment plans for fifteen years or more. Over the slum clearance bonanza period, areas were slowly emptied and demolished piecemeal, causing a loss of housing space and thereby generating acute housing need in the short-term and running up vast costs in terms of idle land, lost rents and rates and social disturbance. The effect on the 'slum' population was to disperse many of the people in advance of the demolition programme. This meant that by the time many city housing schemes came to fruition, the population designated to occupy them was no longer there, creating large estates for which planned demand had partially evaporated.

The huge waiting lists for council homes were often artificially created at the height of the demolition era. But slum clearance in most city areas actually caused a substantial loss of population, with up to half the previous population being 'dishoused' out of the area in the process, as the long waiting lists forced desperate but able families to look elsewhere for a home, often choosing to buy in the suburbs or move to a New Town. Even in the central Byker district of Newcastle, where there was an absolute commitment to rehouse the tight-knit old community back into the new Byker, only one-fifth of the residents actually survived the phases of redevelopment long enough to move into the new Byker estate. The other four-fifths were dispersed by the bulldozer (Malpass and Murie, 1982, pp. 129–30). The depopulation figures for the cities in part illustrate the impact of slum clearance. Over the fifty years from 1931 to 1981, the population in our cities shrank from 9.5 million to 6.5 million (Census information, 1931–81). About 2 million of those who left were directly uprooted by slum clearance.

Thus the clearance plans generated big demand, leading to pressure for high density rebuilding schemes, while at the same time displacing large numbers of the residents for whom rebuilding was taking place.

Impetus to Decline

The accelerated decline of most inner-city areas was actually fuelled by the redevelopment process. The very areas with the worst slums and greatest overcrowding were already suffering severe unemployment, industrial decay, and suburban flight by all who could escape. The postwar New Towns policy was built on this desire to move out to greener pastures. Demolition on a large scale forced an exodus of both population and small-scale industry that has not been attracted back to the cities. The slow slide became an avalanche under the impact of redevelopment schemes (Jacobs, 1962, pp. 270–1).

Dispersing Slums

The most significant element in slum clearance was the dispersal that it caused of settled urban neighbourhoods. Without romanticizing old slum streets, there can be little doubt that many of the people involved in the displacement suffered an acute sense of loss. In their seminal book, *Family and Kinship in East London* (1962), Young and Wilmott were told by the overwhelming majority of East Enders they interviewed that they wanted to stay put in terraced houses in the old streets. It is not for nothing that the nostalgia of Coronation Street has survived for twenty years on ITV as the most popular television programme among viewers. In Manchester, Liverpool, Salford, Oldham and Blackburn, it is the Victorian terraced house which is the prize council offer, not the modern flat. The irony is that in the inner area of Salford, it is quite hard to locate the few surviving streets, so dominant are the ugly modern blocks that replaced them. Today in Liverpool, tenants are voting with their feet: 10,000 households prefer to share accommodation in terraced housing rather than to live in self-contained council flats.

Planners were often quite clear about the aim and effect of slum clearance. The Chief Planner at the Ministry of Housing and Local Government stated in 1963 that 'The task is surely to break up such groupings [slum dwellers], even though the people seem to be satisfied with their miserable environment and seem to enjoy an extrovert social life within their own locality' (Burns, 1963, pp. 93–4). The social malaise which resulted from redevelopment was often minimized under a form of derision of low-income households. They were seen as unable to adapt or be grateful, 'the coals in the bath' syndrome.

In sum, a cavalier attitude to the cost of slum clearance, in both social and financial terms, and to the newly fashionable styles of postwar housing determined the ease with which over 1.5 million homes were demolished between 1945 and 1980. The replacement of old slums with unpopular new estates was made inevitable by two other major elements: the design and scale of new council housing, and the relative neglect of housing management in the face of political enthusiasm for numbers of dwellings.

The New Estates

Subsidies favoured flats over the forty years from 1930 to 1970, multi-storey flats being more favoured than low-rise developments for a period of about fifteen years up until 1967. The impact on the council stock, particularly in cities, was substantial and a high proportion (about two-thirds) of unpopular estates are large and flatted and located in city areas (see chapter 5). At least half of these are estimated to be system built. Private housing by contrast was produced in small pockets, overwhelmingly taking the form of houses built in traditional materials.

The fashion for including maisonettes on the new dense estates – an attempt at building high and dense blocks while providing a dwelling more like a house than a flat, with two floors, and therefore hopefully more suitable for families – crept in in the 1950s. The style became more and more dominant in the late 1960s as tower blocks fell from favour, until management problems, generated by lack of privacy and supervision, noise disturbance, large numbers of children on upper floors and a general dislike of the often complex and unorthodox design, made maisonettes possibly the most unpopular type of council dwelling of all. Nonetheless, substantial numbers were built and by 1981, 33 per cent of the total council stock comprised flats and maisonettes (Table 3.6), with possibly nearly half a million in the form of maisonettes (CIPFA, *Housing Rent Statistics* 1981, p. 4).

Fashion for Massive Scale
Why did the government invest so much extra money in an unpopular form of housing? The greatest single factor was the direct involvement

Table 3.6 Percentage of Houses and Flats, 1981

	Houses (%)	Flats (%)*	Total (%)
Owner-occupied	93	7	100
Local authority or new towns	66	33	100

*Flats include maisonettes built as dwellings on two floors but in a block comprising three or more storeys.

Source: General Household Survey, 1981, p. 60.

of the architectural profession in government and in big building firms. Postwar architectural fashion was firmly wedded to large-scale, dense, high-rise housing. Architects were often hired direct by big construction firms to handle large council building contracts. According to Patrick Dunleavy, who had documented the process in detail, almost every leading British postwar architect was identified with the design and production of high-rise mass housing. By the 1960s deals between local authorities, major architects and large construction firms were commonplace. In 1964, only 32 per cent of local authority dwellings were contracted through open tendering (Dunleavy, 1981, p. 24).

The whole local and central government system came to favour large-scale, mass-produced housing as foreseen by the idle visionary of modern architecture, Le Corbusier: 'We must create the mass production spirit. The spirit of constructing mass production houses. The spirit of living in mass production houses' (1946, p. 210). In the postwar atmosphere of a 'brave new world', there was an almost fanciful desire to create extraordinary environments and to experiment with unheard-of building forms. Equally there was an obsession with heavy, plain and colourless styles over which the public exercised no control. Bare, unadorned facades of grey concrete or sheet glass were the sophisticated design rage. Even guttering and window sills became obsolete for a time. The ultimate anomaly in Britain was the fixation with flat roofs (Wolfe, 1981, p. 74). 'Brutalism' was temporarily 'deified', and living in a house was transposed into 'machine living'.

Behind the government's postwar housing targets lay the new architectural mode, that of determining social contact through the physical structure of new housing, 'the streets in the sky'. The arrogance of the architectural assumptions was obvious to the general populace and only public authorities had the capital and the power to experiment on a damagingly large scale. In Britain the private sector built after the style of Le Corbusier and his ilk only on a minuscule scale. Among public bodies, the desire for large-scale and high-density estates fed off the ambitions of young architects to replace slums with a new Mecca. Tom Wolfe in his scathing denunciation of modern architecture sums up the social disaster of mass high-rise public housing in the United States:

> On each floor there were covered walkways, in keeping with Corbusier's idea of 'streets in the air'. Since there was no other place in the project [estate] in which to *sin* in public, whatever might ordinarily have taken place in bars, brothels, social clubs, pool halls, amusement arcades, general stores, corncribs, rutabaga patches, hayricks, barn stalls, now took place in the streets

in the air. Corbusier's boulevards made Hogarth's Gin Lane look like the oceanside street of dreams. Respectable folk pulled out, even if it meant living in cracks in the sidewalks. (ibid., p. 81)

The failure quickly showed up in the low demand for the big new estates, many of which were difficult to let as early as the late 1960s (Burbidge *et al.*, Vol. 1, 1981). Ordinary people did not like the style or the social consequences. One estate of tower blocks in Merseyside was blown up as redundant in 1983, without it ever having been fully occupied in its ten-year life. Another estate in Glasgow was taken down when building had only reached the second floor, because there was no demand for the type of dwellings it would offer. Alice Coleman's study of flatted estates in Tower Hamlets and Southwark spares no scorn for 'Utopia on trial' (Coleman, 1985).

Le Corbusier seized on the crowded nature of cities and argued for a nuclear view of city development, with high densities in the centre, thinning out to leafy spacious suburbs on the outskirts. His view of spacious suburbs might be viable, but the nuclear city is not, packed as he planned it to be with 'mass housing', forcing low-income families to live at densities sometimes even higher than the previous crowded slum houses. Although there are large unused areas around flatted estates reducing overall densities, the blocks themselves often have absurdly high densities, creating a caged atmosphere which the surrounding dereliction, often planned as 'leafy communal space', intensifies. Half the displaced slum-dwellers of the postwar years have been rehoused back into flatted blocks in inner cities. About 80 per cent of high-rise building is concentrated in inner areas – replicating previous slum conditions, but rationally planned on the grounds of land shortage and a modern and sanitary answer to space-starved cities. As we have learnt to our cost, the rationalism of the modernist architectural movement created a kind of human housing folly, with 100-foot-high buildings sometimes held together in large panels with only one in twenty of the requisite bolts, and unable to take a gas supply for fear of explosion (AMA, 1984, pp. 36–43; BBC documentary, 'Enquiry: the Great British Housing Disaster', 4 Sept. 1984).

Industrialized System-Building
In the early 1960s, in order to sustain an enlarged building programme, the government openly advocated new building techniques with off-site prefabrication to produce high-quality dwellings quickly, using simple assembly methods on cleaned sites. Industrialized system-building found favour among public authorities, because they believed it would relieve the housing bottlenecks. It was actively encouraged by governments, both Conservative and Labour, since it was expected to be cheaper, quicker and larger in scale:

The Minister proposes to launch a concentrated drive to increase and improve the use of industrialised methods in housebuilding for the public sector ...

The advantages for housing authorities ...

● *On numbers*: this is the only way to build the number of houses we need.
● *On speed of erection*: most industrialised techniques show worthwhile savings.
● *On price*: for flats, industrialised techniques are already slightly cheaper ... but efficient organisation of supply and demand can bring down promotion costs.
● *On design*: the use of carefully prepared standard designs will release scarce professional time to concentrate on raising the quality of layouts.
● *On construction quality*: industrialised methods facilitate quality control.

(MHLG, 1965)

None of the claims proved true. It failed to become a cheaper option for a number of reasons: the materials were more expensive, and their bulk made them awkward and costly to transport; the extra elaborate machinery needed to construct industrialized housing added to the costs; and labour costs were only marginally reduced.

Industrialized building was only rarely faster than more traditional methods, in spite of such claims being continually made for it. One reason was that the other elements in the time scale, such as clearing the site, planning and design work, took as long and the actual building time was only one small element. Other problems were the unfamiliarity with the techniques and the lack of skill of the largely casual labour force; and the intense supervision required because of the complexities of engineering – in practice, this supervision was often inadequate. Although it may have been the only building method capable of producing the volume of dwellings planned, supply was to outstrip demand in many areas and much demand was artificially generated through demolition to make room for the new buildings, so that volume of production was an invalid justification too.

Industrialized building has left a legacy of technical problems, some of which are so serious and so costly as to be unresolvable. About 3,000 flats built in the Bison system will probably have to be demolished less than twenty years after they were built. Several other standard industrialized systems are now being questioned for their safety (AMA, 1984, p. 53), and the total bill for remedies is likely to be several hundred million pounds (DOE, 1985). Often flats of concrete construction have no insulation, with the concrete panels positively conducting cold into the dwellings, generating extensive condensation and damp. Flat roofs, panel joints and open decks have leaked on many system-built estates.

Restricted Demand

There are so many elements in the design of council housing over the past thirty-five years that have led to its increasing unpopularity that it is impossible to list them all here. Unguarded common areas are known to cause insecurity and vandal damage, yet almost all council flats have such areas. Common entrances and balconies shared by six or more households are subject to heavy vandalism and lack of privacy. A high proportion of council flats are in this category. Almost all council estates have unused open space, but 'the unused is always abused' (Hill, quoted in Moberly Bell, 1942, p. 149). Bridges linking blocks, unguarded lifts, long open decks and balconies, noise-prone maisonettes, underground garages; these all require constant supervision and maintenance, a factor never built into the original plans or costings.

The biggest problem of postwar council housing in Britain has been its vast scale. No other Western industrialized country has produced public housing on a comparable scale (Donnison and Ungerson, 1982, p. 63). Councils acted as though they were building for infinite demand. yet the very rapid expansion of owner-occupation since the war in fact constantly eroded demand. Councils restricted demand themselves by their policy of building and letting predominantly for families, only recently changed. As early as 1968, nearly half the households in the country consisted of one or two persons only, while 88 per cent of the council stock was built for families (Table 3.7), a majority of dwellings having three bedrooms (DOE, *Housing and Construction Statistics*, 1974–84, pp. 67, 71).

In addition, the very areas where council house-building was concentrated were the depopulating, unpopular inner areas of declining housing demand. Demand was further reduced by building the

Table 3.7 Mismatch Between Size of Dwelling and Size of Households in Local Authority Stock in 1966 (percentages)

	1 or 2 persons	More than 2 people
Proportion of units	12	88
Proportion of households	46	54

Source: CHAC, 1969, p. 9.

Table 3.8 Densities: Persons Per Room

1911	1921	1931	1951	1961	1966	1981
1.1	0.91	0.83	0.74	0.66	0.57	0.55

Source: DOE, 1977b, Part 1, p. 26. 1981 figure is taken from the Census.

wrong product: while the vast majority wanted houses, councils were hell-bent on producing flats. The opposite was true of the private sector, which built almost exclusively houses for owner-occupation, thus fuelling the trend towards home ownership by providing what most people wanted. Many young households in the postwar years have migrated from inner-city areas and have become owner-occupiers, seeking the more salubrious suburban environment and a house with a garden. According to the General Household Survey, a large majority of the population wishes to be owner-occupiers.

National Surplus
By 1971, there was a crude surplus of dwellings over households of 200,000 (DOE, 1977b, Part 1, p. 22). Of course there were many empty dwellings in the private sector, including second homes, as well as a certain level of empty property as a result of household moves and improvement work. Nonetheless, the new crude surplus represented a fall in unmet demand, which inevitably manifested itself in low demand for badly built, unpopular council estates. Table 3.8 generally bears out this fact. The proportion of households living at above 1.5 persons per room has also dropped steadily, showing that the benefits of the greater stock of housing have reached all but a tiny proportion of the population (Table 3.9). The smaller number of households living at high density is likely to be reflected in falling demand for rehousing through councils.

There has also been a reduction in the number of shared dwellings, as shown in Table 3.10. According to the 1981 Census, around 450,000 households did not have self-contained accommodation, compared with nearly 2 million sharing households in 1951. Even so, the

Table 3.9 Percentage of Households with Over 1.5 Persons Per Room

1931	1951	1961	1971	1981
11.5%	5.1%	1.8%	1.4%	0.6%

Source: DOE, 1977b, Part 1, p. 24. 1981 figure is taken from the Census.

Table 3.10   Number of Shared Dwellings

Year	Shared dwellings
1971	300,000
1976	250,000
1981	160,000

Source: DOE, 1977b, Part 1, p. 147. 1981 figure
taken from the Census.

proportion of vacant dwellings in the total stock has expanded (Table
3.11), confirming the drop in demand. A further crude measure of
falling housing demand is the fall in the number of concealed
households, as shown in Table 3.12. (A 'concealed household' is a
married couple or a lone parent family living as part of someone else's
household.)

With the great expansion of rehabilitation programmes and improvement grants in the 1970s, the number of people without the use
of a fixed bath has dropped dramatically, and less than half a million
households are now without this facility (Table 3.13). The smaller the
number of households lacking basic amenities, the lower the demand
for council housing.

The percentage of households unsatisfactorily housed on any of the
above counts – sharing, overcrowding, or lack of basic amenities –
declined sharply over the same period from 69 per cent in 1951 to 24
per cent in 1971, and to an estimated 5 per cent by 1981. Of course,
slum clearance and massive house-building programmes did play a
major part in the reduction of housing need. The influential Parker
Morris report of 1961, which recommended minimal space standards
and amenities for all council house-building and improvement to older
dwellings, also had a major impact in bringing about higher housing
standards, although the aim of building to higher standards and
converting multi-occupied old property into fully self-contained

Table 3.11   Percentage of Vacant
Dwellings

Year	% of vacant dwellings
1971	3.2
1976	3.8
1983	3.7

Source: DOE, 1977b, Part 1, p. 76.

Postwar Mass Housing

Table 3.12 Concealed Households

Year	No. of households
1951	935,000
1961	702,000
1971	426,000
1981	266,500

Source: DOE, 1977b, Part 1, p. 19. 1981 figure taken from the Census.

dwellings often conflicted both with financial 'cost-yardstick' restrictions and with a rational internal layout of dwellings.

The combined effect of council and private housing building and renovation has been to reduce crude housing need and this in turn reduces the demand for unsatisfactory housing. But figures for demand do not take account of the growing problem of disrepair in both the owner-occupied and rented sectors which threatens to reverse many of the gains described here. In addition the level of replacement of dwellings has now fallen so low that there are indications in some areas of re-emerging chronic shortages (NFHA, 1985; Audit Commission, 1986).

The figures given here are all national totals and in no way reflect the varying conditions of different parts of the country. Inner London has for long experienced more acute housing need than other areas, and in 1971, 13 per cent of London households were still living at densities above 1.5 persons per room, though again the proportion was much lower by 1981, estimated at 5 per cent of households. On the whole, the richer areas of the midlands and south-east England have better equipped housing and lower rates of unemployment, but higher levels of sharing and overcrowding. The seriously declining areas of

Table 3.13 Number of Households Without a Bath

Year	No. of households without bath (millions)
1951	4.8
1961	3.2
1971	1.4
1981	0.5

Source: DOE, 1977b, Part 1, p. 33. 1981 figure taken from the Census.

Table 3.14   Housing Conditions in 1971 (percentages)

Area	Overcrowding*	Sharing	Poorly equipped	Unemployed
North	1.8	1.0	7.7	12.7
North-west	1.5	1.4	6.8	7.2
Merseyside	2.8	2.1	10.0	16.7
West Midlands	3.5	1.5	3.5	2.0
South-east	4.4	11.7	3.7	1.0
Inner London	12.9	32.4	12.6	1.7
Inner London 1981	7.1	7.2	9.2	12.8

*Redefined in 1981 as more than one person per room (previously 1.5).
   Source: Census Indicators of Urban Deprivation, Working note, No. 6, Department of Environment, 1975; Census data, 1981.

the north, where densities become lower as populations move away, but unemployment rates are high, have the greater poverty and more poorly equipped housing. Table 3.14 illustrates not only sharp regional differences, but also the clear relationship between economic decline and fall in demand for housing. Note the link between high unemployment and low sharing and overcrowding rates.

In overall numbers, dwellings exceeded households from the late 1950s onwards, and the gap widened steadily up until 1978, by which time there were about 800,000 more dwellings than households (Figure 3.4). By 1983 there were over one million more dwellings than households (*Social Trends*, 1985, p. 124).

The number of families awaiting council housing has fallen significantly in many areas of the country (PEP reports, 1981, 1982, 1984). The average wait for a council home for a family is down to weeks in parts of Merseyside and the north-west. Even in London, most families in housing need have some hope of a council home, although waiting time is now rising again and current cutbacks could, if continued, generate a new intensification of housing shortage. (See Chapter 5 for discussion of access, homelessness and difficult-to-let estates.) The problem has shifted to the *kind* of home that will be offered. Increasingly it is the unpopular flats on high-density estates or the prewar, cottage-style homes on run-down impoverished estates on the outskirts of towns that will be offered to incoming council applicants, as vacancies tend to arise most frequently on these estates. And the applicants will be much more reluctant now than a generation ago to accept the offer of council accommodation if they do not like it.

The result is a new kind of mismatch between households and dwellings, with increasing numbers of council homes being categor-

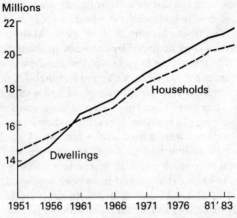

Figure 3.4 Dwellings and households 1951–83.

Source: Social Trends, 1985, p. 124.

ized as unpopular or difficult to let, and increasing numbers of
households applying to local authorities for help under the Homeless
Persons Act. While unmet demand has clearly decreased over recent
decades, council housing still has a low vacancy rate (less than 2.5 per
cent), except ironically in areas of high stress and generally high
demand (Audit Commission, 1986).

After the Mass Housing Boom

The peak years for the building of flats and for the production of high-
rise blocks were the mid-1960s. However, slum clearance and large-
scale building continued for many years after it was no longer
considered that they were the appropriate solution to the housing
problem. Slum demolition only peaked in the 1970s. The GLC's
Elthorne Estate was still being built in the late 1970s, nearly twenty
years after it was first conceived. The Byker Estate in Newcastle still
had vacant cleared land to be built on in 1982, and had all the
appearances of a building site ten years after the slum-clearance
residents were moved from the old Byker into new homes. Both these
estates replaced areas that many residents did not want to leave. Both
developments 'dishoused' a majority of people from settled communities.

The kickback from the multitude of similar schemes, the scarred
landscapes and the long time-lags produced a fever of new council

activity in renovating the fast deteriorating old stock through Housing Action Areas, a new neighbourhood-based concept in slum-renewal, introduced in the new Housing Act of 1974. Many thousands of terraced properties were acquired by councils. In Islington alone, over 5,000 street properties were bought up and renovated in the 1970s. Some slum-clearance areas were converted to rehabilitation areas and several public inquiries into demolition plans had a stormy passage in the 1970s, the later ones sometimes overturning council demolition plans and preserving old housing areas. Nonetheless, over 1.5 million new council dwellings were added to the total stock in the 1970s.

Council house-building had managed to produce well over 40 per cent of the total new stock right up to the late 1970s, partly because deceleration was harder than would have been supposed. But by 1978 the production of council housing began to drop steeply, falling far behind the private sector, a position from which it has never recovered (see Table 3.1). Figure 3.5 shows a dramatic change in the distribution of dwellings and tenures since the war. The stock overall increased by a little more than one and a half times. Private landlords halved in number; council dwellings multiplied five times, the fastest increase of any sector; but owner-occupation now dominates the national housing scene, having expanded threefold since before the war.

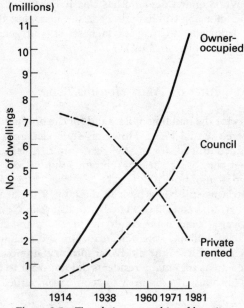

Figure 3.5 Trends in ownership of housing.

Source: DOE, 1977b.

64

Table 3.15 The Stock of Dwellings by Tenure in 1974 and 1984

Tenure	No. of households	
	1974	1984[a]
Owner-occupied	9,787,000	12,424,000
Rented from local authority or New Town	5,022,000	5,024,000
Rented from private landlord or other	2,952,000	2,238,000[b]
All tenures	17,761,000	19,686,000

[a]DOE, *Housing and Construction Statistics* 1984, p. 99, England and Wales.
[b]Includes Housing Associations and other tenures.
  Source: DOE, 1977b, Part 1, p. 38.

Thus the pattern of council housing since the late 1970s has changed greatly. While it is hard to separate the draconian cuts in public expenditure for housing construction since 1979 from other changes, clear shifts have taken place in thinking, planning and execution of housing policies among different political parties, professional bodies, central and local government. Traditional materials have come strongly back into favour. Fewer flats are being built and those that are tend to be low-rise, two- or three-storey, often sheltered dwellings for the elderly and handicapped. Sites tend to be small infill areas, and the concept of an estate is weakening, and being avoided where possible, in favour of normal streets. Rehabilitation of existing dwellings has grown in importance. It is unlikely that council housing will ever again enjoy the prestige, the subsidies and the planning acceptance that led to its heady mistakes in the postwar era.

However, the legacy is enduring with approximately 4.5 million council dwellings in England and Wales alone, of which 1.75 million are in flats, mostly on dense city estates. While owner-occupation is now the majority tenure, private landlords, in spite of all coaxing, continue to disappear and housing trusts and associations represent only a fractional though growing contribution to the rented sector. Council landlords represent a very substantial part of the national scene, housing about 15 million people and controlling vast stocks in all our major cities. They provide the major source of rented accommodation and about one-quarter of them have serious management difficulties. The contribution of local authorities to replacing industrial slums was unparalleled in Western Europe. That record was marred by the style and scale of the major estates and by the inability of town hall superstructures to adapt quickly to such rapidly expanding empires.

Chapter Four

Postwar Housing Departments

> A municipal tenant is a privileged person, living in accommodation it would be impossible to rent at the same figure elsewhere and which is in addition managed and maintained according to the most advanced ideals prevailing. (Butcher, 1942, p. 16)

Councils became public landlords without commitment, plan or forethought. They intended only to provide housing and put little effort into how they would run it. By 1939 the government was urging local authorities to put someone in charge of the stock. Only one-fifth of all councils had a housing manager or chief housing officer (CHAC, 1939). This chapter focuses on the organization of council housing departments, and the management problems of council landlords in the period of mass housing since 1946. Discussion of access and allocations is deferred to the following chapter, along with the issue of who gets the better council housing. The full scale of emerging management problems will not be examined until Part II of the book. The developments in postwar housing departments are uniquely documented in a series of reports by the Central Housing Advisory Committee to the Ministry of Housing (CHAC). The minutes of the Housing Committee of the LCC and articles in housing journals add detail from local authorities.

In 1939, a typical council landlord was organized according to the scheme set out in Figure 4.1. An enlightened housing management structure in local authorities with slum-clearance problems and large new estates might be organized more along the lines shown in Figure 4.2. We have discovered no local authority at that time which had a fully integrated housing management structure to cover all dealings with tenants. Nor could individual representatives of the landlord exercise control over any other part of the landlord service (such as repairs) in their dealings with the tenants.

Housing management, as conceived by the Society of Women Estate

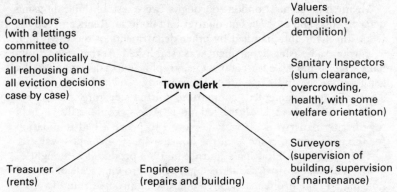

Figure 4.1 The organization of local authority housing services (based on CHAC, 1939).

Officers, was, according to available records, not practised within local authorities. At best a few threads of welfare work were woven into a complex town hall structure in the face of major problems with families from slums, or a particular estate was singled out for special local treatment because of its social and management problems.

The War and After

At the outbreak of the Second World War, a few housing departments existed, like the LCC. But the war led to severe cutbacks in the estate-based services like repairs and caretaking. Under the impact of staff shortages, the LCC itself handed over much of its rent collection to private agents, and amalgamated the management of several large estates under one non-resident superintendent. This probably hastened the end of the resident management service to the large estates and increased the already remote scale of operation.

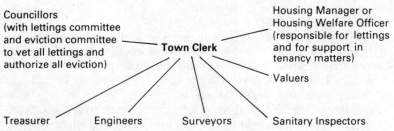

Figure 4.2 Housing organization in local authorities employing a housing manager (based on CHAC, 1939).

Meanwhile some London boroughs were establishing housing departments, and by 1946 one-quarter had done so. Rents and repairs were still invariably handled by other departments of the town hall, even where a housing department was established. At that stage, town halls were responsible for compact geographical areas, something of a genuine parish, and each council, on average, owned 1,400 houses. Therefore the fragmented, compartmentalized structure, inadequate as it was for good landlord–tenant relations, could still be held together by paperwork. It was, however, to prove a bad foundation for the problems to come with the housing spurt of the postwar era.

The Institute of Housing's journal in 1942 produced a thoughtful analysis of the way forward in the light of the growing scale of council housing and the problems of often confused, uprooted slum-dwellers in the face of an unidentifiable landlord. It was argued that maintenance should be firmly in the control of the housing manager; that mixed housing should be built in small groups of dwellings; that selection and training of good staff was vital; and that

> The ordinary tenant ... likes to have a quick and easy contact with some person in authority capable of giving a quick and clear-cut decision, and is moreover not at ease if contact can only be made after a journey to a somewhat grandiose building. For this reason some enlightened authorities have decentralised management into local groups in charge of officers with delegated powers to deal with all matters of a difficult or technical nature to whom the tenants have easy and local access. (Butcher, 1942, p. 15)

This demand for a localized service was instigated primarily by the needs on the one hand of disorientated new occupants of council housing, and on the other of housing managers facing a complex battery of responsibilities on large estates. However, it was very much the exception to the rule.

The Government's 1945 Report
In 1945, the Central Housing Advisory Committee produced for the government a second report on the management of municipal estates, giving the clearest insight available into the problems of local authority landlords (CHAC, 1945, p. 7).

Many municipal organizations contributed advice to the 1945 Committee. The LCC and most urban authorities with more than 1,000 dwellings, supported by the Institute of Housing, advocated the appointment of a housing manager to each local authority. The rural districts, with far less stress, felt less need to organize management into a single department. The Municipal Treasurers and Accountants inevitably thought that rent collection should be kept separate from other aspects of management, firmly under their own wing, and that 'business or work' time should not be uneconomically used on integrating welfare with management. The Sanitary Inspectors' Association argued that their members were well placed to become effective housing managers. The Municipal Engineers argued with regret that rent collection had taken precedence over other aspects of housing management, such as maintenance.

To the reader forty years on, the evidence of the municipal experts gives ample testimony to the piecemeal and even chaotic approach to estate management through the conflicting roles of different 'professional' departments and specialisms. Most local authorities claimed in their evidence that housing management problems could be solved by more comprehensive and more rigidly enforced procedures in each department. Because operations were increasingly tied up at the centre in an attempt to solidify and clarify procedures, the ground level jobs of caretakers, rent collectors, welfare visitors and repairmen became more and more remote from decision-making and therefore more ineffective. The gap was not just between landlord and tenant, but between estate-based menial workers with little responsibility or supervision, and the operational and 'professional' base firmly lodged in the town hall. The 1945 report concluded that 'the varying needs of many thousands of individuals cannot be reduced to a mathematical formula' (ibid., p. 19). The government's advisers could on balance see the need for radical developments in housing management, but they failed to give shape to this general sense of going down the wrong path.

The report concluded that tenants were to blame for many problems because of a 'deterioration in tenants' care'. This was associated with the war and the encouragement of animals in backyards for food, coupled with the removal of metal fencing for munitions. Anxiety was expressed that pigs and fowl should be banned as soon as food supplies increased. Such a ban in practice did little to reinstate a sense of control, purpose or order among individual householders, in the face of absentee landlords.

Over the early postwar period, the LCC underwent a series of management changes. It finally responded to the CHAC recommendations to make housing management more personal, by spreading door-to-door rent collection in the place of resident superintendents. This method reduced arrears and improved contact with tenants, it became very mechanical with each collector covering about 800 dwellings a week. It also led to the closure of several estate offices. Over the same period, some housing functions were handed over totally to other departments in response to the demands of the scale of operation. A separate Works Division was established; so were an Acquisition Division, Rating and Statistical Division, Administration and Establishment Division. Housing architectural work was handed back to the central Architects' Department. In addition, valuers, engineers, the Chief Officer of Supplies, the Comptroller of the Council and the Medical Officer of Health were variously involved in parts of the housing service. The Housing Department itself had reduced its functions to allocations, welfare, caretaking, arrears pursuit, and repairs ordering. Eleven different departments at County Hall were thus directly responsible for fragments of estate management. The most serious setbacks in housing management within the LCC came about when resident superintendents were completely withdrawn after 1948. This change was coupled with wider social developments leading to 'a general growth in vandalism and hooliganism' (Macey and Baker, 1982, p. 457).

The war could be blamed as a major cause of the social problems which continued to mount on the poorer estates. At a big housing conference in Scotland in 1948, vandalism was highlighted as a serious problem, echoing the CHAC reports' anxiety over lack of 'tenants' care'.

> There is still an evident lack of social conscience on the part of the general community towards communal property. Trees and shrubs, flowerbeds and playing field apparatus are still being destroyed to an alarming extent. (*Housing*, April 1948, p. 7)

In addition, gardens were reported neglected, in spite of food shortages, rationing and the drive to vegetable growing, and packs of dogs roamed uncontrolled. Little was it dreamt that in the 1980s many of those vital garden fences, establishing dominion and control, would still be missing, and back wastelands would still be the preserve of packs of stray dogs.

The Institute of Housing and the Development of Housing Management

The demand for housing personnel in local authorities was accelerating and systems were constantly modified to keep pace with the demands of expanding rehousing programmes.

In the late 1940s there was a severe labour shortage and major difficulties in recruiting qualified staff into local government. Many recruits were untrained and had a minimal educational background. Job structures were consequently routinized and narrowed, and areas of discretion as far as possible eliminated. The LCC was forced to reduce its entrance requirements from the equivalent of two A-levels to two O-levels over this period, a far cry from the prewar recommendation that only graduates should be recruited for the job of estate manager.

Throughout this period, the most serious misconception of both government and local authorities was the belief that slum demolition and rehousing was solving most social problems, thereby removing many social needs in one 'simple' operation.

The Institute of Housing was continuing to recruit members and to engage in the housing debate. Although full membership of the Institute was still in the region of 262, associate members and student members boosted the total to 1,612 by 1949. The Society of Women Housing Estate Officers, with 250 members, was finding it hard to recruit suitable candidates for its rigorous training. They played an accommodating role in local authorities, trying to make the system bend to the requirements of housing management. On this, almost everywhere, they fought a losing battle.

The Institute of Housing had lower recruitment and training standards than the Society of Women Housing Estate Officers. The Institute still held that welfare and the 'women's side' of housing management should not be confused with the main council job of keeping the technical side operating smoothly. It also argued that in more affluent postwar conditions, intensive management was normally no longer necessary. The Society continued to argue that high-density, communal housing presented special management problems and that 'group management', where each manager was responsible initially for all aspects of the landlord–tenant contact, was more effective than the prevailing 'sectional management' where functions such as rents, lettings and repairs were separately run within the town hall and often not controlled by a housing manager at all (*Housing*, April 1948, pp. 5–9; Rowles, 1959, pp. 38–47).

The Government Report on Flats, 1953

A special sub-committee of CHAC in 1952 considered the problems of flat-living, because special management needs were generated by this peculiarly communal form of housing. While making many clear recommendations in favour of resident caretaking, supervision of common facilities, such as laundries, liaison with tenants' representatives, and rehousing families with children in houses rather than flats, the report did not challenge the basic assumption that flat-building was necessary. Nor did it propose a radical reorganization of management to encourage local, estate-based offices. It argued consistently that local authorities should avoid 'an ongoing maintenance commitment', and yet by CHAC's own definition flats required long-term, continual management and maintenance. At the time of the government's report, councils were building about 100,000 flats a year. Yet the members of the committee barely addressed the major problem of long-term, coherent management and maintenance of an increasingly difficult stock, while recommending that pets such as rabbits and pigeons should be encouraged and that creepers be planted up the bare walls in order to help tenants keep in touch with nature. There was a strong sense that the government and its advisers were running behind a scale of problem they barely perceived (CHAC, 1953a, p. 31).

The whole issue of flat-building, and the subsidies to encourage it, was not raised by the membership of the committee; nor was the question of funding the additional management costs of flatted estates. According to the LCC, it cost more than twice as much to manage and maintain flats than cottages (Table 4.1).

Many ideas, such as 'consultation with responsible representatives of the tenants through their own organisation', or proper rubbish disposal, were caring but ill thought out. Others were simply idealistic, such as collective tenants' gardens making use of the surplus open space, or unrealistic, such as the introduction of cleaning rotas. There was nothing wrong with these ideas in themselves if they could be organized and supported by a local management structure. The committee did not come to grips with either the scale and cost of the problem or the impossibility of applying local tenant-oriented solutions without an intensive local management presence. Resident caretaking was the only vital link, but caretakers had no management authority and no control over the main services such as lettings, repairs or cleansing. The failure of local authorities to raise these basic problems with the committee is ample proof of their ignorance of the problems they were generating. The implication is that none of these issues were being addressed by local authorities. The report reveals a singular blindness to the government's headlong propulsion into large-scale flat-building without a concept of the public landlord's role or structure.

Table 4.1 Unit Cost of Supervision and Management (£)

	All dwellings	Cottages	Flats
1950–1	4.9	3.4	7.9
1951–2	5.4	3.7	8.8
1952–3	5.7	3.9	9.3
1953–4	6.3	4.0	10.8

Source: LCC, Housing Committee Report, 28 July 1953.

The Government Report on 'Unsatisfactory Tenants', 1955

The postwar boom, leading to relative affluence and full employment, did not do away with the question of 'unsatisfactory tenants', and in 1955 CHAC was again publishing on this taxing subject (CHAC, 1955b).

The scale of the problem was estimated to be very small – only 0.1 per cent of tenants being considered 'problem families' and 5 per cent requiring fairly constant support or 'supervision'. The advice was sound: tackle arrears early and firmly; do not cluster anti-social families together; give practical help rather than 'mere advice and verbal encouragement'. The main realization was that 'mere provision of a house is usually not enough'. However, this admonition was never taken sufficiently seriously and many social workers still believe that housing conditions alone are the main cause of a family's problem. In fact, it is possible to argue that the uprooting and rehousing of disturbed families within poor communities through slum clearance, coupled with the greatly increased material commitments of a new council house and the total change in housing environment in some cases, pushed a precarious family over the brink (Young and Wilmott, 1962, p. 2; CHAC, 1956, p. 2). The fact that the landlord structure was remote, unclearly organized and uninvolved in the wider social dimensions of rehousing, catapulted a small number of families suffering social breakdown into centre stage.

Housing Management Shifts Gear

By the mid-1950s, waiting lists were growing everywhere in the wake of the postwar marriage and baby boom, slum-clearance programmes were starting up, and the proportion of flats to houses being built was rising. Average densities were lower than prewar levels and more communal spaces were provided, requiring additional care and cleaning. But the blocks themselves were as dense or denser, as high flats became more fashionable. In 1955, the LCC alone received half a million inquiries about the waiting list, and the expected wait for a dwelling was seven years. In the following year, the waiting list was frozen. Under this pressure, beleaguered housing officials scrambled to make the system fit new and expanding demands. Allocations became the critical area of housing management. Ingenuity was taxed, corners were cut, and applied management at estate level was rarely the primary concern or even a topic of debate. For many years, the only direct contact between landlord and tenant had been the rent collector. Yet because of the rapidly expanding stock, the rent collector was increasingly seen as a person of limited ability and application, hired to cover as many doors as possible, as fast as possible, and his function was constantly being narrowed (Collyer, 1957, p. 111). Partly because of this and partly because management problems with the central bureaucracy were growing, further attempts were made at streamlining by reducing rent collection to fortnightly rounds (Harris, 1957, p. 118). The limited contact was becoming widespread, and with it came higher arrears and general neglect of detailed 'chasing', whether of arrears, cleaning or repairs. With the limited contact also came a further disparagement of the rent collector's role and of the vital connection between landlord and tenant.

Simultaneously, because of the political importance of rehousing on the vast scale that was now under way, housing departments as such were becoming more fashionable. Single-point 'management' was openly advocated, but the entire debate focused on the creation of a unified housing department within the town hall, as opposed to fragmented, multi-department management, as previously practised.

However, the emerging housing department rarely incorporated repairs and often did not take over rent collection. Therefore, there was a large gap between a 'single-point' housing department, with functions divided and delivered separately, and the 'single-point', estate-based manager responsible for a small group of dwellings and the well-being of their occupants. Because of this gap, enlightened housing managers argued that decentralization to districts, which was just beginning, was only workable in an integrated housing department capable of delegating total housing reponsibility to a district (Butcher, 1942, p. 15). A decentralized office, within which decisions constantly gravitated back to the centre, would not resolve the basic management problems. Unfortunately, most efforts at coherence were concentrated at the overgrown centre.

The 1959 Report on Housing Departments

In 1959, CHAC attempted to address the central problems of housing departments. CHAC conducted a unique inquiry into the organization of housing departments in fifty-seven local authorities, and found that fewer than half, only twenty-seven, had a separate housing department, responsible for most elements of housing management. The other thirty authorities varied from eleven with no housing manager at all to nineteen with a housing manager usually responsible for a limited part of housing management, such as lettings and welfare, based in another department (CHAC, 1959, p. 3). Just under one-third of the authorities gave housing managers responsibility for repairs. Only just over a half collected the rent. More than half the local authorities listed the Treasurer, Surveyor or Chief Public Health

Table 4.2 The Number of Local Authorities where the Housing Manager Performed Each Function

Applica-tions	Alloca-tions	Rent collec-tion	Ordering repairs	Execut-ing repairs	Super-vision of estates	Housing welfare	Total
45	43	30	36	18	45	42	57

Source: CHAC, 1959, p. 7.

Inspector as in charge of housing . Table 4.2 indicates the way housing functions were divided.

The inquiry found that almost all rent collectors also took repairs orders, thereby underlining the point that the personal contact between tenant and rent-man brought its own positive management benefits, however limited the rent collectors' role was now considered. This was in spite of the fact that rent collectors were often controlled by another department, such as the Borough Treasurer's.

As a result of the survey, CHAC at last argued strongly and clearly for detailed, unitary, localized management, including door-to-door rent collection, local management control of repairs, close co-opera-tion between landlords and tenants, and the need for training of managers, as well as recommending input from tenants and managers into design. However, the new report stressed the virtual autonomy of local authorities and offered no coherent strategy for dealing with the new scale of public housing provision. 'Local authorities have complete freedom to manage their estates as they think best' (ibid., p. 3).

No consideration was given to recruitment of staff, training pro-grammes, budgeting, repairs, apprenticeships or any of the other critical issues facing local authorities. The approach of the 1959 Housing Advisory Committee contrasted sharply with the govern-ment's approach to training, recruitment, inspection, budgeting and management within the health, education and social services. The Ministry of Housing, throughout this period, employed only one civil servant to advise nationally on housing management, yet the stock by the late 1950s represented nearly 4 million dwellings and an investment then worth approximately £12 billion.

The 1959 report, while raising these key issues, misfired in several directions. For example, it endorsed the spreading practice of fort-nightly rather than weekly rent collection, while arguing that payment of rent was the primary link between landlord and tenant; it did not challenge flat-building nor address the serious problem of supervision on large flatted estates; it made a big play of management costs, arguing that tenants should take over internal redecoration, which was bound to increase difficulties in re-letting and have greater impact on poorer tenants. It did not question the general philosophy of large-scale mass housing, based on drastic redevelopment policies.

There was one vital point in the 1959 report that was seriously debated for the first time: the general appearance or environment of estates. The report found instances where 'the general level of maintenance of open spaces and verges falls considerably below the quality of the houses and the efforts of the tenants themselves' (ibid., p. 23). CHAC recognized that this lamentable decay lay not at the tenants' door, but at the landlord's, underlining the drastic splits within local authority management: 'The local authority should have an agreed policy' with arrangements for 'co-ordinating the work of general maintenance and the supervision of the estate as a whole' (ibid., p. 23). It was clear that such common-sense liaison and on-the-ground organization did not normally take place.

The Committee, with singular lack of wisdom on the multiplying social problems, found a hidden advantage in the proliferation of flats, as 'it becomes easier to offer to tenants who either cannot or will not cultivate a garden, transfers to more *suitable accommodation*' (in other words, from houses to flats; ibid., p. 24). The painful fact that flatted estates were far harder for the local authority to maintain by virtue of the *communal* space that the landlord, and not the tenants, was directly responsible for was ignored. The reality that tenants with an untidy garden were likely to cause more nuisance if their untidiness spilled over to communal balconies, staircases and courtyards was also overlooked. The government openly endorsed pushing less ambitious, less coping families into flats on the grounds that they would cope better without the added burden of a garden. This view was only a short step from the widespread view of many ward councillors in the mass housing era that 'bad' tenants should be rehoused on 'bad' estates, thereby weaving another whole strand into the development of unpopular estates.

The government was equally shortsighted in its attack on the other glaring environmental problem, car-parking. Because so many prewar and flatted estates had little or no parking facilities, grass verges and front gardens were often converted to that use. The report therefore recommended universal car-parking provision: 'It is better to make over-provision than under-provision' (ibid., p. 27). Planners, architects and developers roundly adopted this advice, leading to the gross over-provision of unusable garages on flatted estates and the current spate of demolition of multi-storey car parks and plans to concrete in many virtually abandoned underground garages (see chapters 6 and 7).

Advice on welfare was equally misdirected, separating out housing functions from social support. Local authorities 'should not give the impression that they are running a "secondary welfare service" for council tenants' (ibid., p. 28). In any case 'the need for specialised welfare work as part of the landlord's function has decreased' (p. 33). The report concluded with a proposed pact between landlord and tenant: 'There must be a real understanding of human needs by the landlord and a willingness on the tenant's side to take his share as a responsible tenant and neighbour' (p. 9). The underlying ingredient to this pact was in almost every case still missing – a local management organization through which access between landlord and tenant was possible, and without which no trade-off of responsibilities could be established.

The report advocated local management where possible or suitable, particularly in large authorities: 'that such offices, and in particular the presence of a resident officer, are welcomed by tenants was made clear in evidence we received from tenants' organisations' (ibid., p. 9). However, the changed social conditions of the postwar era were assumed to dictate a generally reduced need for housing management. CHAC was therefore speaking with forked tongue, making it easy for the prevailing wisdom to continue.

The report was generally complacent and unchallenging, assuming that all was reasonably well in municipal housing:

> These changes have . . . resulted in the community now accepting increased responsibilities. In addition there have been great advances in design, both of individual dwellings and estates due to increased interest in and study of all aspects of housing; there have also been modifications and improvements resulting from technological advances, in the construction, fitting out and servicing of dwellings. (ibid., p. 1)

The Central Housing Advisory Committee suffered from the attempt to represent the views of the main housing professionals within the local authority world, and from the fact that it had no political clout because of the government's limited statutory role.

Cullingworth on Housing Departments

Barry Cullingworth chaired the Housing Management Sub-Committee of the Central Housing Advisory Committee for the ninth report 'Council Housing, Purposes, Procedures and Priorities' in 1969. His earlier study of housing and local government (Cullingworth, 1966) had examined the haphazard and inconsistent growth in housing management.

Cullingworth's analysis revealed that housing departments employed one member of staff for fewer than every fifty properties, including all repairs and maintenance workers and all other manual staff employed on estates. This was a higher ratio than the philanthropic housing trusts and should have allowed a local authority to manage all its stock intensively along the unitary lines developed by Octavia Hill. However, a further detailing of the jobs covered in Bristol's Technical Services Department illustrated the structural problems of local authority staffing.

> The Technical Section is not formally subdivided as is the Administrative Section, but its responsibilities are equally as extensive and varied. The staff includes 19 Technical Assistants, 7 Bonus Surveyors, 4 Housing Inspectors, 3 Administrative Assistants, 25 Clerical Assistants, 8 Maintenance Superintendents, 10 Foreman, 9 Depot Assistants, 9 Storekeepers and 623 Building Trade Operatives. (ibid., p. 95)

Bristol Housing Department was responsible for no less than sixty-six estates, with an average of 560 dwellings on each. The case for decentralization and estate-based management could not have been stronger, and yet it was not even considered by Cullingworth or by Bristol itself.

The outline structure of Bristol Housing Department in the 1960s, a relatively clear and integrated service compared with Leeds and the GLC, the other examples given by Cullingworth, illustrated a large, modern, sectional housing department, comprehensively organized (Figure 4.3). It was a model for the great leap forward of the 1970s, when most housing departments burst their seams.

Developments in the LCC

By the early 1960s, the LCC was operating on a massive scale, owning 110,000 dwellings, processing and completing 21,000 allocations in 1964 alone, and employing one estate officer (i.e. manager) to every 310 dwellings. The overall staff ratio in the housing department, including repairs workers, was by now well under one to thirty dwellings. In 1964, the LCC was reorganized into the Greater London Council with a strategic housing role, expanding its activities even further and serving to intensify the difference between outer and inner estates, as well as enhancing the complexity of the internal organization. The LCC was double the size of Bristol and several times more complicated. At the same time, the London boroughs were reorganized into much larger and more dispersed areas, against serious

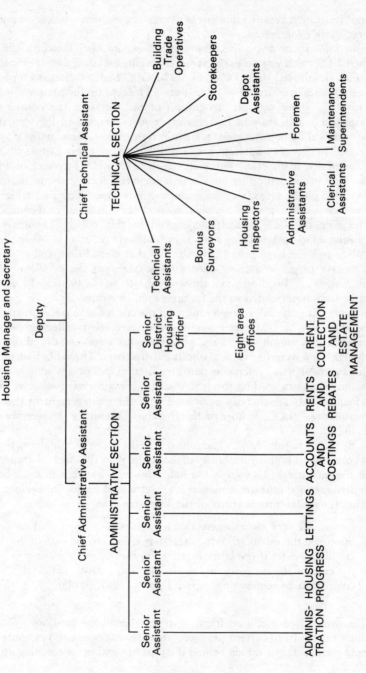

Figure 4.3 Management structure, City of Bristol Housing Department in 1965.

Source: Cullingworth, 1966, pp. 93, 95.

staff resistance, creating housing management problems on a scale not previously experienced.

In 1967, there was a special investigation into hooliganism within the GLC, which was on the increase, especially on large, flatted estates which dominated the GLC stock. (The GLC had 360 flatted estates and 44 cottage estates. The latter were all located on the periphery of London.) There was no recognition of the fact that the constant population upheavals of the previous twenty years, and the virtual withdrawal by housing management into the centre, were in any way related to the accumulating social problem. The report expressed a sense of defeatism – sanctions were felt to be limited. The police could not help in prevention because at that stage the police only patrolled so-called public areas, thereby excluding most council estates, which were considered private housing areas. Public housing authorities, including the GLC, widely acquiesced in this policing anomaly, causing up to the late 1970s a major breakdown in contact between the police and the large urban communities that were being transposed into ever bigger and more alien estates. Many of the problems of ultimate social breakdown on the worst estates in the 1970s and 1980s must have been related to the failure to police estates.

The next year, following a report on the cost of management, staff numbers at the GLC were severely restricted, rent collection was reduced to a monthly cycle and giro payments were introduced even though they were found 'not wholly satisfactory'. The GLC housing management was under constant attack from politicians and community activists, leading to a proposal to 'bring forward schemes in which tenants are directly associated with the management of their own estates' (LCC, *Report of the Housing Committee*, 1 December 1970).

By this time John Macey had joined the GLC from Birmingham, the second largest housing authority in the country. In 1961 he had argued in the Institute of Housing's journal, *Housing*, that repairs must be fully integrated into the management service, and he quoted evidence from the philanthropic trusts of the Victorian era:

> Experience very soon showed that tenants readily responded and improved their own attitude to rent-paying and to the care of the landlord's asset *if the latter himself showed a proper interest* in the care of the property and dealt with the tenants' reasonable complaints or requests for repair. (Macey, 1961, p. 145)

This was, of course, a profound statement about the landlord's role but a far cry from current practice, where management and maintenance were usually running behind the problem and never catching up.

Public landlords either did not accept or failed to deliver on the notion of meticulous management.

However, in 1965, in the first edition of his important book on housing management, Macey argued that while the intensive and unitary system of management was clearly the most effective, it was no longer necessary, except in special circumstances, because of the declining social problems: 'In pre-war days when there were far more problem families ... it was a popular system ... such an intensive system of supervision, which is necessarily expensive, would now be justified only very exceptionally' (Macey and Baker, 1982, p. 337). He acknowledged that with resident staff, including repairmen, 'the relationship between landlord and tenant is much better than under any other system' (ibid., p. 338), and that 'the comprehensive door-to-door system of collection and management is probably the best combination for economy and efficiency *for authorities with large numbers of houses*' (ibid., pp. 374–5).

Macey believed that with 2,500 dwellings or less, a local authority could run an economically viable, unitary service on the ground, including repairs. What he did not address fully either in the Institute of Housing, in his book or during his tenure at County Hall, was how to disaggregate the housing service in practice. His sense of fairness and desire to co-ordinate housing activities at the top would not allow him to relinquish central control of a broad-fronted housing service. Therefore, his powerful advocacy of local management entities, including repairs, was not developed into a practical system, and the new GLC continued to withdraw and centralize its services, finally even removing resident caretakers and local repairmen in the early 1970s. Macey rejected his own preferred method as too labour-intensive and socially outdated. While weak government reports appeared to fall on deaf ears, John Macey's Housing Management blueprint missed a critical moment in the history of housing and his tenure at the GLC intensified the trend towards a highly functional and central 'professionalism', while nowhere elaborating procedures for a local integrated service. The role of trade unions in hastening this process within the large authorities was held to be crucial.

By the time John Macey retired from the GLC in 1971[1], there were 10,000 employees in the housing department, and within a decade of the establishment of the London-wide authority, the dismemberment of its housing department with the transfer of estates to the London boroughs was set in train, only to burden the already large London borough landlords with major acquisitions of difficult-to-manage, flatted GLC estates. The problem was being transposed yet again.

Management Cuts

Meanwhile other pressures were at work within the arena of public housing management, mainly the desire to minimize the cost and staff commitment of an exploding service. The influential Metropolitan Boroughs' Committee produced in 1963 a series of recommendations on how to cut the costs of management in line with the local authorities' general feeling that housing management could work perfectly well for the majority of 'normal' tenants remote from tenants themselves and with a minimum of contact. It advised on how housing departments should save money on basic services.

Some of the recommendations were as follows:

- Rents should be collected fortnightly or less frequently.
- Door-to-door collection should be linked with other work or discontinued
- Visits should be made for less than three weeks' arrears.
- Certain work should be made the responsibility of the tenants.
- Responsibility for the elderly should be placed on caretakers, rather than managers.
- Daily supervision of caretakers should be discontinued.
- Some cleaning should be carried out by tenants and the use of mechanical equipment should be extended.
- Visiting cleaning gangs should replace residents.
- Motorised transport should be provided for (caretaking) patrols (cf. Panda policing).
- Typing pools and mechanised dictation should replace personal clerical support.
                    (Metropolitan Boroughs' Committee, 1963, pp. 71–5)

Each of these recommendations represented a retrograde step into the centre and a withdrawal where it hurt most. The Metropolitan Boroughs' Committee was very much swimming with the tide, but these measures, often appearing perfectly logical as a paper exercise, led to the widespread disappearance of the vital personal contact and supervision that made rented housing viable. Maybe the crucial error was to imagine that the landlord could withdraw as long as tenants were coping and well housed, on the grounds that they would act like owner-occupiers and actually take charge of their property. It was possibly forgotten that the legal relationship between landlord and tenant would not be so readily abdicated on the tenants' side, without the actual security of ownership. Local authorities broadly followed the recommended cuts in service.

Management problems continued to grow and in 1968 the Scottish Housing Advisory Committee noted that local authorities 'have generally failed to accord to management the importance and priority it requires if a satisfactory service is to be provided' (*Housing*, March 1968, p. 32). It was found that, in Scotland, housing managers were only responsible for about half the key functions of management. Local management was not even mentioned.

A New Turn for the Institute of Housing

The Institute of Housing had undergone fairly radical changes in the twenty years since the war, of which the merger in 1965 with its rival, the Society of Housing Managers, was an important part. The Society, in the postwar conditions of mass public housing, first decided to admit male members in 1948, then lowered its recruitment and admission standards to cope with the demand for housing personnel and the shortage of applicants. Finally, it amalgamated its examinations with the Institute's in 1962 at a level generally held to be more basic than the Royal Institute of Chartered Surveyors, through which it had previously passed its members. In 1965, the two organizations merged completely, under the new title of Institute of Housing Managers, later to be renamed the Institute of Housing with all reference to management disappearing and symbolizing a new sense of the profession. Management, in the women's sense, had never been acceptable to the men, and this was enshrined in the new organization's examinations, with their emphasis on building, planning, the law, housing finance, local and central government history and structures, and a reduced role for the applied duties of rent collection, repairs, and the integration of social support into business management.

However, the Institute's membership was more alive than ever to the debate on housing management organization, probably influenced in part by the active women members who were now more centrally engaged as a result of the merger. In 1968 in the Institute's yearbook, a radical new line was taken:

> All aspects of housing management should be in the hands of one person . . . [who] should be responsible for the collection of rents . . . This contact with the tenants has a very considerable influence on the standard of an estate. (Institute of Housing, 1968, pp. 6 and 166)

Such contact had influence not because it was a means of 'upgrading' tenants, although some pressure could be brought to bear on individual households with problems, but because it was the vital channel for delivery of prompt and effective landlord services. It was the sign of a responsible landlord, determined to take care of his property and to look to the welfare of his tenants. A good estate was always primarily a function of a good landlord: tenants feel collectively unable to enforce communal standards in the face of landlord neglect and a paucity of service. The Institute advocated that 'The housing manager should order all repairs and approve completed work' (ibid. p. 16). It totally shifted the emphasis from professional departments at the town hall to housing managers on an estate, and from separate technical departments to integrated repairs services. It also shifted from the idea that bad tenants cause decay in otherwise 'good' areas to the landlord being directly responsible for the housing service.

Reorganization and the Comprehensive Housing Service (1974)

Local government history was about to take another sharp twist which was to have a devastating impact on the already weak and complex structures of housing managment. In 1974 the government reorganized all local authorities into new, amalgamated and much larger units. The number of local authorities in England and Wales was chopped from about 2,000 to 400, in the name of streamlining and simplification. Many mergers did not make sense geographically, and local government in many places is still grappling with the organizational nonsense that was created in 1974, with town hall functions often split between different historic administrative centres. Worst of all, housing departments often tripled in size overnight, in a few cases rationalizing a small and scattered stock, but in most urban areas taking the landlord a large step further away from the tenants. Council housing stock jumped from an average of 1,400 after the war to 14,000 in 1975 in each local authority. The city authorities were often more than double this size.

Many housing departments ended up with subsidiary town halls, often located several miles from each other with different functions based in each. Therefore, there was no longer simply the historic confusion and the rapid expansion of difficult-to-manage estates, but the unwieldy structures and scale of amalgamations.

The Comprehensive Housing Service

As the public stock expanded, the complexity of building styles increased and populations on the less popular estates became more universally poor, so councils moved towards a unified housing service, with some sense of urgency. Unfortunately an integrated but centra-

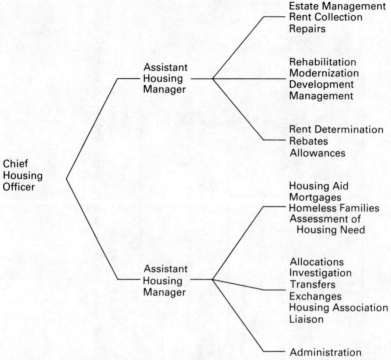

Figure 4.4 Management structure of a district council (under 5,000 dwellings) as recommended by Housing Services Advisory Group.

Source: Housing Services Advisory Group, 1978, p. 19.

lized system was no longer adequate because of the scale of public housing and the 'sectionalism' of local authority administration.

The Housing Services Advisory Group – a government-sponsored committee, which took the place of CHAC in order to make recommendations about the organization of the housing service – in 1978 produced its housing blueprint for the government and local authorities, called *Organising a Comprehensive Housing Service*. This was welcomed by progressive housing managers within local authorities as a major step in giving some coherence to fragmented housing management. The scale of operation, however, made coherence difficult in practice. What was commonly called the Comprehensive Housing Service comprised a central housing directorate covering housing policy, development, housing management, private sector matters and advisory issues. It was responsible for an average of 14,000 properties,

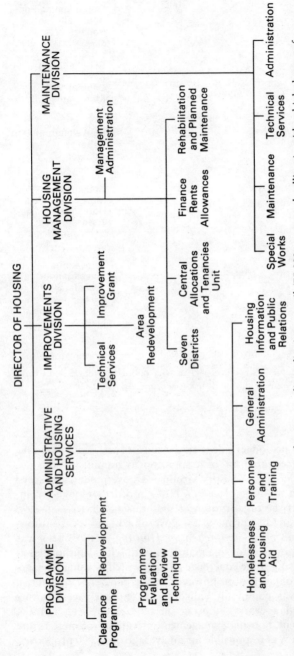

Figure 4.5 Management structure of a metropolitan district council (75,000 or more dwellings), with a high degree of area decentralization, as recommended by Housing Services Advisory Group.

Source: Housing Services Advisory Group, 1978, p. 21.

rising to 38,000 in the metropolitan authorities. The Comprehensive Housing Service often served to reinforce centralized and functional organization at the expense of what few remnants existed of local management.

The Housing Services Advisory Group recommended a structure for the Comprehensive Housing Service which belied the unified approach altogether by putting each area of housing management under a different section leader, while putting a single 'Director' in charge of the overall service. Figures 4.4 and 4.5 illustrate the typical unification and division of responsibilities.

Repairs and Other Parts of Housing Management
The execution of repairs was not normally included within a comprehensive housing department and was almost always handled by a separate directorate or division for whose services the housing department became the so-called client. There was no leverage in the market sense because the repairs organization enjoyed a monopoly within the local authority.

Nor was there leverage in a hierarchical sense internally, since repairs were usually run by a department as powerful as or more powerful than housing. More importantly, technical services, including repairs, commanded the lion's share of housing budgets, and called the shots. The Local Government Planning and Land Act of 1980 forced local authority repairs organizations into direct competition with private building contractors for a majority of their work. It did not alter the controlling position of technical departments in relation to housing services, since contractors worked for the repairs organization while the housing department was the 'customer' or 'client' for services received.

Repairs have increasingly been ordered by telephone or at district and central offices, as contact at estate level has shrunk. Lettings too almost invariably continued to be run centrally on a tight rationing system in spite of evident changes in demand and the decline of slum clearance. Arrears continued to be followed up locally, but rent accounts were handled centrally, often in finance departments. So estate managers have usually been left with no effective role within the newly 'unified' service.

A modern housing department put a typical London housing director in charge of 20–40,000 properties, with some 500–1,000 staff and at least £400 million of public investment in the stock itself. Many ladders of responsibility were involved in holding such an operation together, and at the bottom of it there was a collection of poor, badly designed or located estates, which the Director could not readily deal with and, in many cases, had not even had time to visit. Therefore to

87

regard the Director of Housing as the person who could ensure the unified delivery of all services to a particular tenant on a particular estate through a single operation, called the 'Comprehensive Housing Service', was to whistle in the wind.

The Housing Services Advisory Group was so concerned to advance the unification of housing functions in a single department that it paid no regard at all, and gave not even a passing reference, to the urgent need to address the size and scale of the public housing stock, and the economic and management viability of an operational unit of the size it was proposing. It ignored the question of estate-based management altogether. It even stated quite categorically that repairs could not be considered a 'core service' of housing management, while every previous government report had stated it to be one of the pivotal services (Housing Services Advisory Group, 1978).

Conclusion

The notion of a Comprehensive Housing Service upgraded the town hall status of housing departments at the expense of the basic jobs on the ground.

Housing is historically in an anomalous position in local government. The Secretary of State and the Department of the Environment (previously Ministry of Housing) have virtually 'no jurisdiction in regard to the management of the local authority's housing stock' (Macey and Baker, 1982, p. 51) except for limited responsibility under the Acts of 1957 and 1980. There are few enforceable standards and the government plays a purely advisory role in the running of the housing stock. Yet the stock is worth nationally £100 billion at replacement cost (Audit Commission, 1986).

Nor are local authorities directed by statute to set up a housing committee with the specific task of running the housing stock owned by the local authority. There is no requirement to appoint a housing manager. So not only is the government not responsible, it has apparently not laid down a framework for local government to carry out its duties as a landlord either. In fact, not until the Housing Act 1980 did local authority tenants enjoy such basic rights as security of tenure, and some local authorities have only set up housing departments at all since 1982.[2] This compares sharply with the political and legal framework concerning almost all other aspects of local government, and with private sector housing, which is infringed with numerous Rent Acts and public health laws. It was not the lack of control or decision-making, but the lack of a basic frame of operation that made it so difficult for local authorities to perform as landlords.

It is unclear why the Institute of Housing in its early years failed to advocate the establishment of a unified housing department within the town halls. At a stage when local authorities were relatively small landlords immediately after the war, it would have made sense and would have given some direction to developments. Only after management problems assumed overwhelming proportions and the preoccupation with building declined did serious attention focus on management. By then, it was too late to resolve the problem within the central framework. Weak management and maintenance organization, the problems of poverty and social uprooting, unfavourable design and large-scale estate development all fed each other at the least popular end of the housing scale, just as they had done in the old, privately rented housing market.

While Alice Coleman acknowledges only in passing the significance of housing management in the development of unpopular estates, compared with the impact of design (Coleman, 1985), Octavia Hill's Victorian predictions no longer appear as outmoded as they seemed:

> These [new estates] will rapidly become as forlorn and rowdy as their old haunts, unless something of thoughtful rule be established in them. And the huge blocks of flats will equally need the presence of trustworthy leaders and human government. (Hill, 1901, p. 176)

More recently, through the Department of the Environment's Inner Area Study in Lambeth, Jean Cox observed: 'In general the quality of the environment seems to depend more on the way the estate is maintained and cared for than on the standard of design' (1977, p. 130). The most recent observation came from the Audit Commission's report on local authority rent arrears, where it is asserted that arrears were partly accounted for by the style of management, as well as by the incidence of deprivation.

> The importance of management performance . . . far outweighs the impact of external factors . . . Good management can affect the local situation, even in the most difficult circumstances. More successful authorities . . . often have arrears 50 per cent or more below the levels of authorities facing similar socio-economic conditions. (Audit Commission, 1984, pp. 18–25)

The current crisis among large, remote local authority landlords has grown from this chequered history. The results are multiple and do not derive in a simple progression from the developments we have highlighted. However, four salient problems appear directly linked to the late emergence of coherent housing departments:

1 Vastly expanded rent arrears in line with the withdrawal of the door-to-door service (Duncan and Kirby, 1984, pp. 98–9).
2 Centralized and expensive repairs services that are often slow and unresponsive to tenants and *very* inefficient in terms of productivity, completion times, preventive maintenance and so on (Federation of Hackney Tenants' Associations, 1982; Parliamentary Commission for Administration, 1983; Wolmar, 1983; Stanforth *et al.*, 1986).
3 Housing managers, usually untrained, with an assortment of parts of jobs and no overall control of responsibility (Legg, 1981).
4 Distant if not hostile relations between tenants and the landlord and a common desire among tenants to keep moving (more than among owner-occupiers) (Andrews, 1979).

While local authorities drew together the disparate landlord services within a large, multi-purpose political bureaucracy, housing trusts and associations continued to develop and deliver a locally focused and integrated form of management. The generally smaller scale of housing associations and the screening of tenants to exclude the most difficult cases certainly made their job easier. In addition the organization of management and maintenance subsidies was clearly delineated and the single focus of effort was to provide a high standard of management and maintenance for tenants. With hindsight, both direct management and maintenance subsidies and unitary management organizations could have made the job of public sector housing management a great deal easier (NFHA, 1985).

Notes to Chapter 4

1 John Macey continued to be active in housing management long after retiring from the GLC and he has been a major force in the Housing Trusts, defending and extending their intense involvement on the estates in local, tenant-oriented management, as well as advising and supporting new housing management initiatives. He retired as Chairman of the Samuel Lewis Trust in spring 1985.

2 Tower Hamlets established its housing department and appointed its first Director in 1982. In the Rhondda Borough Council, the Borough Treasurer is still largely responsible for housing management in 1987.

Chapter Five

Housing for All or Housing of Last Resort?

Unnecessarily rapid decay of the housing stock will be proportional to the degree of social segregation which obtains.

(Reade, 1982, p. 331)

The decision as to who deserved what council housing has always been the most difficult and sensitive area, and one which in the end defied resolution.

By the 1950s, the institutionalized sifting of applicants was firmly entrenched and most local authorities were judging applicants twice over: were they eligible for a council home? What kind of council home did they deserve or best suited their style of life? A whole battery of assessments, points, home visits, gradings, quality offers, rights of refusal, picking and choosing grew up, which not only eventually snarled up the lettings process into a laborious and lethargic maze, but also categorized tenants in a way that no self-respecting welfare or private system should, solidifying sub-class divisions far more intensely than the old slums ever had, and creating communities at the bottom of everyone's aspirations, which inspired only a desire to escape.

The following analysis is based on the author's long involvement in the lettings processes of Islington and the GLC, on visits to nearly 100 local authorities and housing associations between 1979 and 1986, and on the fragmented and partial accounts available officially. Few local authorities have been open, until very recently, even about such basic matters as how they operated their points system. Much of the account below is derived from first-hand experience rather than second-hand sources. The pattern of sifting, grading and sometimes segregating applicants was found to be almost universal in the housing departments contacted (Burbidge *et al.*, 1981, vol. 1, p. 35; Power, 1984, p. 8).

In earlier chapters, the changes and developments in who should be entitled to a council home have been outlined. The actual policies governing selection for particular dwellings do not appear to have been documented. Right up to the Second World War, access to any kind of council housing was considered a huge step up the ladder, and although stigmatized estates were emerging, the incipient lettings problems were not recognized until well into the 1960s.

The postwar Labour government of 1945 was committed to council housing for all, as a universal service, and the 1949 Housing Act removed the obligation on local authorities to house only the 'working class'. But the 1957 Housing Act stressed that 'Local authorities must give reasonable preference to persons who are occupying insanitary or overcrowded houses, have large families, or are living under unsatisfactory conditions' (Macey and Baker, 1982, p. 297).

Because of the massive slum-clearance programme that was by then gathering steam, in practice councils had very little choice in who they rehoused. Between 1960 and 1975, 1,100,000 homes were demolished and 1,600,000 new dwellings were built by councils. Many of the demolished dwellings contained more than one household. It is therefore easy to see that most new dwellings in that period were required simply to redress the balance of demolition. Some new dwellings, however, were used to rehouse existing council tenants wanting rehousing from older council property in order to make room for 'poorer and less deserving' families in inferior dwellings. This was generally considered a realistic way of allocating very different qualities of property to families with often very different standards of behaviour and housekeeping. However, many of the new estates were built to high density in the form of unpopular flats, and residents of old, decayed areas often proved reluctant to move. A pecking order of rehousing was developed, with the more skilled getting a better deal from the council, which still had complete autonomy to allocate to whom it chose the more popular dwellings within the stock. Lettings priorities had become a central housing issue as the scale of building continued at a high level.

Need and Merit in Allocating Housing

Councils accepted responsibility for the needy while attempting to maximize the use and value of a varied stock. Applicants were assessed usually through a points system that gave priority for overcrowding, lack of amenities and sharing a dwelling. But points were also given, often disproportionately, for length of residence, which often positively militated against need. Large numbers of tenants were not eligible for points at all, either because they had not lived within the local authority area for five years, or because they occupied furnished rooms and were therefore categorized as transient, regardless of how long they had lived there. For decades, both these restrictions disqualified all immigrants and all new city dwellers from rehousing. Points only began *after* you were deemed eligible by the particular local authority. These restrictions also usually applied to slum-clearance and demolition areas, thereby ensuring that the most vulnerable families often could not be helped but were shunted on from one redevelopment area to the next, as the supply of rented housing in more salubrious areas declined in the face of rapidly expanding owner-occupation.

Once accepted as eligible, tenants were graded according to suitability or merit, usually by a home visitor who assessed tenants' housekeeping standards, quality of child-care, rent-paying ability and general competence. Ironically, the home visit to assess need in a very personal way was the tool whereby poorer, more needy households were often designated unsuitable for better housing. The most vulnerable households were thus often rehoused into the least suitable property, leading to strong social segregation according to the popularity of estates and the merit of the applicants (Corina, 1974).

The Oldham Community Development Project did a comparative study of allocations in several northern cities dating back to 1950, which demonstrated that grading of tenants and social segregation in rehousing were widely accepted practices (ibid.). There were in fact objective reasons why the sifting and ranking went on in spite of a commitment to rehousing according to need. Each applicant faced a conflict between timing and quality in the offer he was prepared to accept (Smith and Whalley, 1975). Time pressure induced the most desperate families to take what they could, quickly, according to availability. Quality aims led waiting list applicants and more determined, less vulnerable households to wait for good offers.

For people in need of rehousing from council clearance areas and rehabilitation programmes, timing and quality pressures combined to give them first claim. Studies conducted in the GLC (1976) and in Birmingham (Lambert, Paris and Blackaby, 1978) both found that 'good' rehousing cases from demolition areas had the pick of the property on the shortest time scale. Usually rehousing cases were allocated the best property quickly unless they were a 'poor quality tenant' or a 'low-grade' applicant, where their vulnerability would lower their resistance to acepting inferior accommodation. The councils' need to empty condemned property ensured favoured treatment for residents of demolition areas. Vulnerable, needy households were offered the worst, quickly. Their access was determined by their need, but their need and therefore their desperation enabled councils to put them in the worst property. Those that could wait, but were eligible for rehousing, could pick and choose and ended up in property they liked, often after a considerable wait. Tenants of private furnished property were normally simply evicted before the council took over (North Islington Housing Rights Project, 1976).

John Lambert (Lambert, Paris and Blackaby, 1978, pp. 48, 62) described vividly the complex structure of rules to regulate need through merit, allowing for pressure, favours and special pleading, underlining 'the personalised and individualistic nature of the wait in the queue'. As many as five different departments would be involved in the lettings process in Birmingham, the biggest housing department in England, after the GLC. Different demand groups would 'bid' for dwellings, with the homeless, the poor and the non-white faring invariably worse than others.

Thus need and merit acted as the shaky and conflicting criteria of fairness in the allocation of council housing even though need became widely accepted as the main criterion of access, and merit the principal criterion of allocation.

Housing Managers' Allocation Problems

In their book on council house management, John Macey and Charles V. Baker (1965) grappled with the problem of how to allocate the council stock to applicants, recognizing that some estates were much more in demand than others and that tenants, given the choice, would always opt for the most popular estates, thereby creating a lettings bottleneck. They therefore weighed up who 'deserved' good housing and how less popular homes should be best used. The approach advocated by Macey and Baker was based on widely accepted current local authority practice and long experience. Their overriding aim was to be fair, and their formula has been regarded as a blueprint by many housing professionals for twenty years.

Market Rents to Determine Who Gets What

Macey and Baker did not enjoy sitting in judgement over tenants struggling to improve their housing situation. But they were intensely conscious of the conflicting claims of different households and wanted to establish a method that would eliminate accusations of favour and privilege. They concluded that rent levels should dictate broadly which tenants chose the better or worse housing. This idea has commonly been rejected on the grounds that it would intensify socio-economic segregation. It also failed to address the problem that many council tenants could not pay anything approaching a realistic rent, made worse by the growing phenomenon of very high levels of unemployment, with 65 per cent of council tenants nationally in receipt of Housing Benefit (DOE, 1985). However, their proposals on rents were echoed in the Inquiry into British Housing (NFHA, 1985).

The market-oriented approach to rents of Macey and Baker was not widely adopted. Rents have been fixed by a combination of non-market calculations, leading to sometimes absurd anomalies. For example, in the city of Liverpool, rents for flats in some highly stigmatized blocks were higher than in the adjacent houses with gardens that could be let many times over. The actual construction and debt repayment costs, as well as perceived standards of amenity for modern flats as opposed to old houses, were so much higher that this influenced rent levels. Although the very low cost of prewar cottage estates has been used to offset the cost of modern flats through a system of rent-pooling, tenants still usually pay more for the less popular modern estates. Therefore, council rent structures have not been related to the popularity of or demand for particular dwellings. Instead of *low* rents attracting poor tenants to lower quality housing, relatively *high* rents for unpopular flats have driven away many potential applicants, making unpopular housing even more difficult to let. As a result, low priority applicants on supplementary benefit, who have therefore not had to take account of rent levels, have moved into relatively expensive unpopular flats. This has resulted in concentrations of dependent and vulnerable households living in high-cost, but highly unpopular blocks, leading to severe stigmatization.

The socio-economic segregation that Macey and Baker's 'market' approach would have encouraged has thus happened in places through the reverse process, with undifferentiated council rents tending to drive away from the least popular estates wage-earning tenants and encouraging a concentration of welfare recipients for whom rent levels are not a deterrent. Although Housing Benefit, introduced in 1982, aimed to make rent levels irrelevant to the allocation of housing by enabling low-income households to be offered good property at high rents, it is not clear that it will help other lettings on stigmatized

95

estates, unless rents there are kept down to encourage wage-earners. Rent levels are a crucial issue for wage-earners who have to pay full rent and rates. They will expect to pay significantly less for poorer quality accommodation. Meanwhile rent levels have not been used as an objective, if economically discriminating, method of determining access to better or worse council housing. Macey and Baker did not in any case believe that ability to pay alone should determine allocations. Because rents have been virtually unrelated to the quality of dwellings with no consequent trade-off between cost and quality, the administrative mechanisms for allocating council housing have been all the more important. There is certainly an argument that rent levels should to some extent reflect the quality of the rented dwelling in fairness to the 35 per cent of tenants who do pay the full rent.

Fairness in Allocations

Macey and Baker argued in 1965 that good, reliable tenants should be offered the best property and 'unreliable' tenants the worst on grounds of justice and prudent management. 'Apart from the avoidance of trouble to the management, it will usually accord more nearly with the popular idea of fairness that good behaviour should receive some reward' (Macey and Baker, 1965, p. 215). Although this dictum might ring true, the GLC (Parker and Dugmore, 1976, p. 61) found that over 90 per cent of applicants had no history of rent arrears and 80 per cent were deemed suitable for the best property. Even if Macey and Baker's notion of just allocation were accepted and applied, council applicants, the vast majority of whom were assessed as 'good and respectable' in the council's terms, would be competing for the small proportion of council property that was most desirable, at least in the major cities where unpopular flats formed so much of the council stock. Therefore the reward of the best offer became highly subjective and personalized with lettings officers selecting from among the majority of 'respectable' tenants which ones should actually get the minority of 'good' offers.

Macey went on to recommend that homeless families should be allocated according to their circumstances. If homelessness was seemingly the families' own fault, such as wilful rent arrears leading to eviction, they should be offered inferior property.

> In cases, e.g. those where eviction is the result of wilfully running up arrears without reason, it would be folly to provide the family with a better home than the one they have lost.

There needs to be a carefully considered and firm policy for allocations to the homeless. While it is very undesirable to use the long-known deterrent of splitting up families, it may be necessary to acquire some older, less popular housing, for those whose claims on the resources of the authority are weakest ... housing can only be given to one group at the expense of other, often more deserving families. (Macey and Baker, 1982, p. 311)

Macey and Baker observed at the bottom of the housing ladder a group of households whose seeming fecklessness and inability to manage their affairs made them suitable only for low-grade council property. In this way social stratification became institutionalized in council housing departments even though prewar government reports had recommended the dispersal of 'uncoping' households among coping tenants so that they would get help and support (CHAC, 1939).

The decision of which people to place on the worst estates was not taken lightly. Macey and Baker attached great importance to home visiting in assessing the suitability of an applicant for particular types of property:

The applicant's suitability from this standpoint is usually judged by a visit to his present accommodation ... Trained housing assistants can distinguish between untidiness and dirt due to adverse conditions, and that which is due to poor standards of home care. *There is rarely any real excuse for lack of personal cleanliness.* The current rent book will indicate the applicant's attitude in the matter of meeting his financial obligations, due consideration being given to the validity or otherwise of any explanations put forward as the reason for any arrears shown ...

... It is desirable, but not always possible, for assistants engaged on the 'office' side of lettings work to have had a good deal of experience of seeing people in their own homes, and learning to judge both their good and their bad qualities.

It will be appreciated that the personal suitability of the applicant and his wife are a guide in the type of dwelling to be offered. (Macey and Baker, 1965, p. 215)

Home visits were standard practice in the GLC, Birmingham and many other local authorities. Councils could not think of a better way of 'assessing' applicants, although the original idea of visiting applicants was to *help* them make the move from terrible slum conditions into a brand new home (CHAC, 1939).

Transfers from Old Property

Macey and Baker proposed two important uses of the diverse housing stock in order to implement their allocations policy. Both had disastrous social consequences. First, they proposed that old property should be kept available for the very poor on the grounds that they could not afford better. Secondly, they advocated maintaining as many prewar council properties as possible available for 'low priority' applicants by rehousing existing tenants and high priority applicants to better dwellings. The use of transfers as a social ladder had the great advantage of giving dissatisfied and aspiring applicants a leg-up into the bottom of the council sector. However, it failed to allow for the fact that the very process of sifting and shifting was to undermine the stability of estates which had often only existed for a generation, by advertising the fact that the 'better' families moved off. It generated a disproportionate desire to leave old for new, and inspired a sense of failure and captivity in those who did not succeed in gaining a transfer.

The bitterness generated by the failure was in turn often meted out to new incoming tenants who were blamed for 'dragging the estate down'. Indeed they often were poorer and more disadvantaged than the successful 'leavers'. In that sense a liberal transfer system within the council sector bedevilled the chances of older and less popular estates maintaining their own sense of identity and anchorage. The result was an ugly decaying spiral.

Transfers have worked in very much the same way as the right to buy is now working. In fact transfers have facilitated the exercise of this among more ambitious and better housed council tenants. The scale of transfers in the last twenty years has accentuated the contrast between old and new estates, flats and houses, reputable and disreputable estates, by constantly generating the aim to move on. It has also undermined among residents the commitment to improve conditions. It has left a constant vacuum at the bottom of the scale since families only ever want to transfer upwards.

In the late 1960s, while the supply of new council accommodation was still plentiful, a decline in the number of new redevelopment or demolition areas set in. Because of the drop in rehousing cases from demolition areas, new property became available for other categories of applicants and there was an acceleration in the transfer of existing council tenants into new council property, accentuating all the problems at the less popular end of the stock. Already by the end of the 1960s, nearly half of all lettings were to transfer cases (CHAC, 1969, p. 20).

A close investigation of local authority policy and practice in the 1970s showed that:

> The decision common to all authorities studied to give priority to transfer applicants in the allocation of houses has tremendous effect. This decision apparently influences the type of waiting list applicant who will be housed by determining the type of property available for letting to new tenants. (Niner, 1975, p. 68)

Inevitably, the less popular property made available to first-time applicants through transfers attracted less ambitious, more needy households. Councils had broad discretion and a minimum of legal obligations over transfers. Because transfers counted for so many moves in the council sector and tended to be moves to better property, the sifting process was intensified. This was simply a reflection of the dissatisfaction of many tenants with their existing accommodation.

By the same token, if a large part of the property let to first-time tenants is of poor quality, then council occupancy is constantly getting off to a bad start. It becomes hard to generate a sense of pride or purpose and the general objective of a council tenant becomes to get out or move up. The degree of social grading in the council sector thus becomes more and more intense, with transfers both a cause and a result.

There are now serious practical limitations on transfers that are working in favour of a more integrated and businesslike approach to poorer estates. A large-scale transfer system is only possible if there is a constant supply of vacant and popular property. Because very little new council housing is now being built, transfers are declining and are made available only to the most eligible and 'deserving' tenants. This has intensified the pecking order at the top end, but the population stability it is generating on the less popular estates could force other improvements to take place (DOE, 1981, p. 13).

It is ironical that transfers generated such mobility among council tenants that they moved more often than owner-occupiers. This was particularly true of tenants on unpopular estates. 'The public sector has in fact developed into a fairly fiercely competitive status system' (Reade, 1982, p. 36).

Macey and Baker thus endorsed the prevailing wisdom that good housing should go to respectable and deserving tenants and that the least desirable, poorest housing should go to corresponding households. As long as someone had to sit in judgement over who got what, it was hard to come up with a fairer notion. Their book, *Housing Management*, validated judgement over poor people's access to 'welfare housing'. Long before it was ever recognized as such, council housing had become a gateway. For some it was a way up, for others, a further step down. How your fate was sealed mainly depended on the all-important lettings officer.

Cullingworth's Report on Allocations and Management

While problems of social segregation were accumulating within the council sector as a result of discriminatory allocation procedures, government and enlightened housing experts were still focusing their energy on the issue of access to public housing as such. The Seebohm Report (Report of the Committee on Local Authority and Allied Social Services, Cmnd 3703, 1968) pressed hard for council housing to be allocated according to much wider social considerations and this was taken up in the following year by Barry Cullingworth.

The 1969 Report of the Housing Management Sub-Committee of the Central Housing Advisory Committee, of which Barry Cullingworth was Chairman, made a number of important recommendations on the management and allocation of council housing.

Date-Order Access

Cullingworth attacked the accepted system of grading tenants according to their suitability for better or worse property. He argued that this was unnecessary for the allocation process. Instead, he advocated date order for access. But by 1969 much of the council stock was already highly unpopular and difficult to run. Unless tenants lost all rights to choose where they lived, date-order lettings would enable applicants under least stress to hold out for the best property, since they could wait the longest. However, his stand against merit or a points system was more radical than was obvious at the time. And no one has since come up with a fairer allocation system.

Open Waiting Lists

Cullingworth's other important and contentious recommendation was that waiting lists should be open to all-comers and that residential qualifications should not be a bar to a council tenancy any more than they were a bar to owner-occupation. This should be coupled with a publicly declared system of allocation.

It is possible that had these two recommendations been widely followed, council housing would have become an open door to the whole community, as were other social provisions such as schools. Social polarization through allocation might then have been less severe, because open allocation on a straight date order and the critical exposure of selection and allocation to public examination would have shown up the problem of segregation and discrimination much earlier.

By raising the vital areas affecting access to council housing, the Cullingworth report was representing the government's concern with councils on the one hand excluding needy groups and households, and on the other creating social or racial ghettos. But the report did not tackle satisfactorily the issue that was already at the forefront of housing managers' agendas – how to avoid unpopular estates being matched with impoverished populations, once *access* to council housing itself had been assured. Cullingworth did endorse the approach that was long overdue if council estates were to be saved from the same fate as the slums they were built to replace: 'Local authority houses and flats represent a considerable part of the nation's wealth and it is the responsibility of local authorities to treat their management as an important business enterprise' (CHAC, 1959, p. 1).

Cullingworth moved the debate a long way forward from the conventional wisdon of Macey and Baker. His recommendations were not backed by housing legislation, and council housing is still largely bedevilled with assessments and judgements of fairness, following the same historic system that the Cullingworth Committee aimed to dismantle in 1969.

Access for the Most Disadvantaged

While advocating an open and non-selective allocation system for the bulk of applicants, Cullingworth argued strongly for the most vulnerable and sometimes problematic families to be given absolute priority for a council dwelling, but with the important proviso of built-in social services support. He later countered the accusation that he had been advocating the ghettoization of council housing. The size of the council sector was such that much more responsibility could be taken for the most needy without the whole public sector becoming stigmatized.

Cullingworth did not, however, allow for the fact that the least able tenants he was trying to persuade councils to help would end up on the least popular estates. Social ghettos were created within the council sector by virtue of the most desperate cases gaining access according to the prescription of the Cullingworth report, but being allocated on the whole only to less suitable estates where there were already apparent social problems.

Nor did he consider satisfactorily the implications of rehousing in blocks of flats families whose behaviour was such that they could not cope with community life on high-density estates. Most council dwellings were on communally designed estates which stripped a family of privacy and drew attention to and accentuated the nuisance caused by anti-social behaviour. Cullingworth overlooked the nature of many public housing estates in his advocacy of access for the tiny minority of families who could not cope with normal life. While arguing for special *social* support for such families, he failed to identify the special *housing* requirements of specially disoriented households.

Dispersal of Racial Minorities

Although Cullingworth did not recommend the dispersal of uncoping families across the range of stock, he did recommend with great force the dispersal of Commonwealth immigrants to avoid racial ghettos. His recommendations on this were no more adhered to than the 1939 recommendations for the dispersal of 'problem' tenants. Colour became enmeshed with other elements of discretion and discrimination in the allocation of coucil housing, and Cullingworth's report will stand out as a farsighted failure to influence practice.

Discrimination in the GLC

Although a decade has elapsed since the GLC study *Colour and the Allocation of Council Housing* (Parker and Dugmore, 1976) was conducted, it is still a landmark in its penetration, its self-criticism and its carefully documented explanation of the lettings process, which has produced, not just in London, but virtually country-wide, a hierarchy of estates and a pecking order of households in the queue for a council home.

The GLC lettings survey in 1976 described the grading process as it had grown up over the years of priority lettings, dating from about a century before.

> The first stage of the lettings process involves the applicant being visited by a welfare assistant, who assesses the prospective tenant's suitability for different types of property by looking at their rent record and judging their domestic standards. (ibid., p. 3)

This was inevitably a subjective process. Income and economic security played a large part in a family's reliability, standards of housekeeping and general ability to cope. Race also played a part in grading according to the GLC survey. Black tenants were on average less often assessed at the highest grade than white. This was partly due to much greater overcrowding and poverty among immigrants and larger numbers of children. It was also a result of cultural differences and possibly of prejudice. Even so, 75 per cent of non-white applicants compared with 87 per cent of white were assessed at the highest grade, thereby guaranteeing a matching problem between a majority of *suitable* tenants and a majority of *unpopular* estates.

The GLC's complex system of matching tenants and property illustrates the highly bureaucratic and judgemental nature of grading by merit, as well as the severe lettings problems posed by a largely unpopular stock of dense flats on big estates. Whereas most applicants were assessed at the most favoured grade, most dwellings were assessed at below the most favoured grade, and so the grading of tenants and property was only the first step in an attempt to match the two.

Each property and applicant were given a 'lettability range' of 1 to 19, which determined the quality of property offered. The GLC developed a measurement of popularity for the full range of its dwelling-types, taking account of age and type, that may indicate broadly the popularity of the council stock nationally. The main categories in order of popularity were:

(1) Post-1964 house
(2) 1955–64 house
(3) 1945–54 house
(4) Interwar house, post-1964 flat, pre-1919 modernized house
(5) Pre-1919 house, 1955–64 flat
(6) 1945–54 flat and interwar modernized flat
(7) Interwar unmodernized flat and pre-1919 modernized flat
(8) Pre-1919 unmodernized flat

(Parker and Dugmore, 1976, p. 19)

This ranking order of popularity is based only on physical type and does not allow for social or management factors that can distort the scale.

Flats are now widely recognized as less popular than houses for many types of household. Unfortunately, since 1964, almost as many flats as houses have been built in the council sector nationally (DOE, *Housing and Construction Statistics* 1974–84). Tenants' dissatisfaction was intensified because most applicants lived in houses prior to becoming council tenants, thereby linking dissatisfaction with the new flat and with loss of the old home.

John Lambert, in his study of Birmingham's housing department in 1978, found that council employees, responsible for letting the large number of flats available, had to exert considerable pressure on applicants not to hold out for the rare but popular offer of a house. 'There was understandable pressure on housing visitors to find prospective tenants for the many flats which the Council possessed' (Lambert, Paris and Blackaby, 1978, p. 79). Similarly, a survey conducted in 1975 of slum-clearance residents in Hull (Gregory, 1975, p. 79), came up with the staggering figure that only 2 per cent of the applicants said they would accept offers of accommodation in flats or maisonettes. Over 96 per cent would hold out for a house, However, in practice many applicants would end up in flats because of pressure from lettings officers, by virtue of the number of flats available for letting during the slum-clearance period.

Flats have been demolished in Liverpool, Knowsley, Birkenhead, Glasgow, Tyneside and London because of the difficulty of persuading tenants to live in them. In very few cases were the flats demolished because they were structurally unsound. Two-thirds of the unpopular estates in the recent Department of the Environment study of estate-based management (Power, 1984, p. 10) were comprised of flats, even though they form only one-third of the total council stock.

Obviously, if over 80 per cent of applicants were given the highest grading initially and only about 10 per cent of the stock was in the most popular category, then the lettability range given to tenants was determined by more subjective and discriminatory factors. The GLC report (Parker and Dugmore 1976, p. 69) clearly established that, based on the home visit which determined the type of offer made, the most economically and socially disadvantaged were concentrated on the old flatted estates, the least popular lettings offer (Table 5.1).

With such a complex set of allocation procedures, it was hoped to reduce areas of discretion to a minimum. Yet the report admitted that 'owing to the flexibility of the system, it was quite possible for identical applicants to be given different lettability ranges' (ibid., p. 59). The object of grading and matching was to ensure that unpopular property was let and the value of good property was maximized. Yet in spite of grading and matching, 'desirable properties let quickly: whereas unattractive, old flats can be unlet for months' (ibid., p. 59).

So in the area of highest housing demand in the country, some property became virtually unlettable and the complex system of grading failed to solve the problem of allocations. Tenants low down the grading scale resisted the allocations system even where they had little hope of finding their way to a better offer. The GLC's experience

Table 5.1 The proportion of households from disadvantaged groups in the GLC sample allocated to older flats

Head of household	Proportion allocated an older flat
Homeless	43
Non-white	45
Unskilled	21
Under 30	42
All other applicants	15

Source: Parker and Dugmore, 1976, p. 63.

seemed to indicate that the very complexity of grading, lettability ranges and matching so downgraded the poorer estates and refined and slowed down the system as to make it unworkable. Any tenant who could resist, did so.

For adversely graded families in Birmingham, condemned property was used systematically until the late 1970s, when the last redevelopment areas were demolished. The lettings files of these families were labelled 'recommended for older property only' (Lambert, Paris and Blackaby, 1978, p. 50). In Glasgow, very large areas of city council housing have become unlettable and about 8,000 unpopular council dwellings, some relatively new, have been demolished since 1975 (City of Glasgow Housing Department, Annual Housing Review, 1983, p. 38). Adverse grading enhanced the unpopularity of certain estates. Similar tales could be told in Manchester and Liverpool. In Newcastle and Islington, the worst blocks of flats were earmarked for 'unsuitable' tenants. Eventually these blocks too were fit only for demolition.

The object of grading was to classify estates on a scale from most to least popular and to do likewise with tenants. Grading did not work as a means of ensuring proper use of the council stock. On the contrary, it so stigmatized estates at the bottom end of the process that their decay was hastened. The policy of grading and then allocating, not according to need, but according to perceived social disadvantage, including homelessness, colour, unskilled work or no work, created hostility to the stigmatized estates, low demand, empty dwellings, and consequent social disarray on the least popular estates: 'the breakdown of the system of social controls which normally exists in those residential areas with which their residents identify' (Reade, 1982, p. 37).

Racial discrimination is more insidious in its long-term effects than other forms of discrimination in council housing, because it marks people by virtue of their skin colour only. No effort on the part of the person can change the fact of colour. The GLC (Parker and Dugmore, 1976) analysed in great detail the relation between colour and allo-

Table 5.2 Housing Offers to White and Non-White Applicants (percentages)

	Non-white	White
In flats rather than houses	92	73
In pre-1945 property	45	25
Above tenth floor	6	3
Inner London (rather than Outer)	91	63
On cottage estate	4	25

Source: Parker and Dugmore, 1976, pp. 20–1.

Table 5.3   Racial Disadvantage and Quality of Housing

	White	Black
Unskilled		
Average quality* of housing	5.3	6.4
% in older flats	28%	57%
Unemployed		
Average quality of housing	5.8	6.2
% in older flats	48%	56%
All applicants		
Average quality of housing	4.6	5.8

*Quality is measured on a scale of 1 (highest) to 8 (lowest).
Source: Parker and Dugmore, 1976, p. 31.

cation. Its findings coincided with other less comprehensive studies of discrimination (Burney, 1976; Lambert, Paris and Blackaby, 1978; CRC, 1984). All other factors causing low-grade allocations, such as homelessness, low income, poor previous housing conditions, female head of household and family size, were controlled for and the writers still concluded: 'Differential allocation cannot be completely explained by the measurable aspects of the lettings process' (Parker and Dugmore, 1976, p. 62). Racial discrimination was the explanation for the constant over-representation of racial minorities in the least popular dwellings.

The findings of the GLC were clear and disturbing. Non-white applicants compared unfavourably with white on all aspects of housing type, as Table 5.2 shows. The unskilled and the unemployed fared worse than other socio-economic groups, but within them non-white applicants were much the worst (Table 5.3). The GLC found that as many as 45 per cent of all new lettings in older flatted estates were to households with a non-white head, causing the emergence of racial ghettos on some estates.

Not surprisingly, non-whites were much more dissatisfied with their housing than whites as a much smaller proportion was rehoused in the area of their choice or in the type of property they wanted. A particularly striking finding was that 84 per cent of non-white households had no friends or relatives in the area they were rehoused in, compared with 64 per cent for whites. Councils often countered allegations of racial discrimination with the argument that 'they like to live together'. This view was not borne out by the GLC survey. The GLC survey did conclude, however, that 'non-white households were more resigned to dissatisfaction' (ibid., p. 51).

The London Borough of Islington lettings survey in 1976, the

Runnymede findings in 1975, and the recent CRE report on Hackney (1984) all showed unexplainable concentrations of households from racial minorities on the worst estates. The survey of estate-based management offices conducted in 1982 (Power, 1984) by the Department of the Environment showed that in all areas in the survey with an ethnic minority population of 10 per cent or more, the most unpopular estates in those areas had a disproportionate concentration of households from ethnic minorities.

A series of factors in many allocation systems offers opportunities for racial discrimination (Smith and Whalley, 1975, pp. 77–80):

(1) residential qualifications for the waiting list;
(2) poor communication between the town hall and members of racial minorities;
(3) assessment of housekeeping standards;
(4) shortage of larger dwellings which are more in demand among racial minorities;
(5) greater housing need among minorities creating much more pressure to be rehoused in areas of less choice.

Cullingworth, in 1969, foresaw the possibility of racial concentrations developing within the council sector. The GLC survey bore out his fears. Prior to council rehousing, non-white applicants to the GLC were spread fairly evenly through eight inner London boroughs. After rehousing by the GLC, they were largely concentrated within the four boroughs with the greatest proportion of prewar council flats (Parker and Dugmore, 1976, pp. 34, 39, 40). Racial concentrations on the worst estates have reinforced their stigmatization, heightening white prejudice by linking the presence of black people with the worst conditions.

Homelessness and Empty Council Dwellings

In spite of increasing vacancies and the emergence of difficult-to-let estates, access to council housing was not made easier in time to avert the growing problem of homelessness.

Cullingworth, in his essays on housing policy in 1979, pointed out that 'It is possible to have a general surplus of housing accompanied by acute need which market forces and public policies do not meet' (Cullingworth, 1979, p. 35). Thus there can be high vacancy rates in dwellings and high numbers of homeless. The explanation is clear: 'The homeless do not have easy access to available accommodation ... its very existence by definition points to a particular housing shortage' (Cullingworth, 1979, pp. 36–7). It has not paid private landlords in cash terms to let to otherwise homeless families and it has not been an obligation on local authorities to give vulnerable households sufficient priority within normal allocations procedures to prevent the problem of homelessness arising. Yet generally the number of empty council dwellings matches or exceeds the numbers of families received into local authority accommodation as homeless, especially within the city areas where most homelessness occurs. The Audit Commission has shown that in London in 1983, there were 5,500 homeless families being accommodated in temporary accommodation, at a cost of £18 million, while there were 30,000 unlet council homes within the same local authority areas (Audit Commission, 1984, p. 7). Although many of these dwellings are not fit to let and require large sums to be spent on them, a large number are ready for occupation and are held up in the administrative systems of lettings departments (Audit Commission, 1986, p. 37).

'Homeless' families are, however, rarely homeless as such. They are either under threat of homelessness or they are in temporary accommodation arranged by the council. Therefore in some senses 'homelessness' is a misnomer, applied to the most desperate families forced to throw themselves on the mercies of the council sector for want of any alternative.

The concept of homelessness covers two housing allocation problems. First, there is the problem of access to housing by homeless families and vulnerable households (Parker and Dugmore, 1976). Because of restricted access, these groups are disproportionately squeezed into the homeless category, which is their only avenue to a council home. Since the Housing (Homeless Persons) Act of 1977, homelessness has provided obligatory access to temporary accommodation at least for certain categories of homeless households. Because of restrictions on capital spending, hard-pressed local authorities have been able to put families in temporary accommodation (largely paid for by the DHSS) while finding it difficult to renovate their unusable stock.

Secondly, there is a problem of moving homeless families from temporary to permanent council accommodation, the issue being what housing they should be entitled to. On the whole, homeless families are allocated as a policy to the least desirable accommodation. Even where it is not policy, the pressure to rehouse a homeless family into permanent accommodation leads the council to offer them the most readily available and therefore least desirable stock for which there is little competition from other groups. As long as the homeless are rehoused on an emergency basis, they will continue to be treated differently from less pressured households, and they will be expected to accept whatever is offered as proof of their genuine need.

Stigma of Homelessness

Councils, through eviction of troublesome tenants and tenants with large rent arrears, actually cause some homelessness and exacerbate the identification of homelessness with families in difficulty. Conditions in temporary accommodation, to which homeless families are usually admitted, are often quite appalling. In 1980 Islington was rehousing families in an old seamen's hostel in Stepney, which had previously been closed down, while it had 4,000 empty council dwellings within the borough. Conditions in the hostel made family privacy and stability extremely difficult. The same applies to the very expensive solution of bed and breakfast accommodation, commonly used by many London boroughs. The cost causes intense bitterness among properly housed rate-payers. Families in this plight are accelerated down a social spiral, validating discriminatory lettings as they go. The existence of homeless families alongside empty dwellings somehow implies inadequacy on the part of the homeless. Why couldn't they get a home like everyone else?

There is abundant evidence that previously homeless families are disproportionately concentrated on the least popular estates. On the least popular estates in one London borough, up to 80 per cent of offers are made to homeless families. In a hated tower block in another London borough, almost all lettings in one-bedroom flats at one stage were to one-parent, black, homeless families. The five Home Office Community Development Projects revealed very big concentrations of homeless families on the least popular estates (Corina, 1974). Unless more popular accommodation was actually reserved for the homeless, this would be inevitable, because of the pressure they were under to take anything.

The concentration of homeless families in particular estates could itself cause social problems. A new brick-built, low-rise, high-density estate in south London became a socially disturbed ghetto within two years of first being occupied because most of the one-bedroom flats were let to teenage, 'homeless' mothers and their babies in a concerted drive to reduce the numbers in bed and breakfast accommodation. Homelessness became a funnel down which the most needy were pushed.

The GLC's survey (Parker and Dugmore, 1976) analysed the problem of discriminatory lettings to homeless families before the Labour government introduced legislation in 1977 to ensure that councils gave priority to homeless families. It concluded that: 'The most significant social variables associated with variations in the quality of accommodation are homelessness and colour' (Parker and Dugmore, 1976, p. 31). Within the GLC's four main priority groups for rehousing ('decant', homeless, special groups, general needs), homeless families consistently fared worst, although they enjoyed high priority for access. About 45 per cent of them were allocated to prewar flats (the least popular housing type) compared with 8 per cent of rehoused (decanted) households. The GLC also found that homeless families were offered old flats 2.8 times more frequently than they were offered a more popular home.

The GLC (Parker and Dugmore, 1976, p. 30) was able to show that homeless families were younger, more often with a female head, more often non-white, and twice as likely to be unemployed as the rest of the population. The wider problems made poor offers even more likely.

Housing (Homeless Persons) Act 1977

The 1977 Housing (Homeless Persons) Act broke new ground in lettings policies. It imposed on local authority housing departments the duty to find rehousing for homeless families and families threatened with homelessness, homeless pregnant women, and other 'vulnerable' persons threatened with homelessness.

Many local authorities argue that the 1977 Act 'opened the floodgates' to 'problem' families and made certain that more needy households would be increasingly concentrated on the least popular estates. In fact, local authorities were already supposed to give priority to such applicants. However, the rapid shrinkage of the private rented sector and the expansion in the overall number of households[1] made an increase in threatened homelessness inevitable. By the same token, the vast and rapid expansion of public housing made councils the obvious providers of shelter for those without a secure roof.

Future homelessness became much more probable because most councils adhered to unnecessary allocation restrictions long after the acute shortage of housing had disappeared. Most councils implicitly regarded homeless families as inferior to other tenants, and therefore ineligible for the better housing. The ghettoization of homeless families, given their obvious vulnerability by virtue of their need, in turn made the stigmatization of homelessness more inevitable.

Certain estates and housing areas that were already seriously rundown became so stigmatized and socially explosive because of the high concentrations of vulnerable homeless families that demolition sometimes came to be regarded as the only solution. One estate in Islington, Blythe Mansions, used primarily for homeless families as a deliberate policy, was demolished in 1978, because the stigma attaching to the estate became so intense. The estate was structurally sound. The stigma derived from homelessness and the associated poverty, numbers of children, the incidence of one-parent families, and the disproportionate concentration of racial minorities among homeless families (Power, 1977). As vacancies become hard to fill on the worst estates through 'normal' channels of selection, the homeless category grew and took up the slack.

The Housing (Homeless Persons) Act of 1977 should have been a pathfinder in opening up socially owned housing to those who really needed it. Because of the tight allocation system and its inevitable sifting, the Act was turned into a management albatross rightly forcing councils to expand greatly their provision for vulnerable groups while doing nothing to ensure the equitable access for poor tenants to good council homes. The business of sitting in judgement over who got what became even more entrenched. The Act was not the *cause* of the problem. It heightened the problem because councils were still not prepared to follow a policy of dispersal or to abandon their more general approach of sifting allocations in favour of a less judgemental and more straightforward system (Shenton, 1980).

For vulnerable families who had been homeless, deprivation and poor housing conditions continued to be linked within the council sector. The 1977 Act did nothing to ensure equal access to good accommodation in the light of the now statutory obligation on local authorities to rehouse the homeless. Therefore segregation, if anything, became more intense after 1977 and homeless families have been increasingly blamed for the continuing decline in conditions on many of the poorest estates. Homeless families rarely enjoyed automatic access to the best estates, although Lambeth has experimented successfully with ensuring proportional access for homeless and minority families to all types of property. In most areas, they are rigidly designated as eligible only for the worst.

The restrictive allocations system has made the most desperate households resort increasingly to the homelessness legislation while councils are faced with unprecedented growth in emergency rehousing. Each family that is forced through the route of homelessness into inadequate council accommodation becomes a potentially alienated and debilitated household. The long-term effects of homelessness as an access route to empty council dwellings has not yet been carefully assessed. But the social cost is already visible for 'a large proportion of Council housing displays that type of neglect which suggests lack of pride rather than lack of money' (Reade, 1982, p. 36).

Opening Up Lettings

In 1977, the Department of the Environment, while conducting the Housing Policy Review, published a consultation paper (DOE, 1977a) on allocation and access to council housing, advocating a much looser approach to allocation. The abolition of residential qualifications and publication of allocation methods were recommended anew as a way of opening up the system. There was a refreshing recognition of the need to widen the social make-up of the public sector as it increasingly became the only alternative to owner-occupation, and in the face of reduced demand from slum clearance and redevelopment areas. Cullingworth some years previously had asked councils to provide housing for local professionals as well as for less affluent, more needy households. But whereas Cullingworth, with the same basic recommendations, had stressed need, the government was now stressing a broad social mix. There was growing awareness of the need for communities to have a cross-section of interests, ages and classes. Councils like the GLC began to introduce open-access, first-come, first-served policies, though these only ever applied to difficult-to-let estates.

The Scottish Housing Advisory Committee in 1980 went even further in attempting to broaden the public view of allocations: 'Insensitive allocations and transfers contribute to the creation of difficult-to-let estates and [allocations] have an important role in improving conditions too' (1980, p. 89). The Committee recommended that date-order allocations should be adopted as the method of distributing the most popular dwellings, thereby abolishing grading and merit as the determinants for the best property. It did not address the problems of urgent cases still being concentrated where demand was slackest.

However, the Committee envisaged compensatory allocation measures on difficult-to-let estates. It proposed that unpopular dwellings should be taken outside the normal lettings system and special lettings devices should be adopted. This included reducing the number of socially disadvantaged people on these estates, reducing high child densities, and filling vacancies with tenants who did not add problems. A reversal of the standard lettings and transfers procedures would be involved, and an aggressive approach to recruitment of more socially ambitious households was implied, in order to fill the large number of vacant and 'unlettable' dwellings on difficult-to-let estates. However, ideas voiced in advisory reports simply marked progress in thinking among those not hewing at the coal face. Lettings procedures barely changed, and the more vulnerable households were not generally able to gain access to more popular housing, any more than the worst estates were to become more socially mixed.

Housing Act 1980 and the Right to Buy

The 1980 Act was intended to tackle the thorny problem of allocation procedures by legislation, but fell short of the conventional wisdom by failing to abolish residential qualifications for council housing. It did, however, make it legally binding on councils to publish their allocation systems. The government hoped that a general leaven of ownership on large estates would combat some of the social problems resulting from the sifting of allocations. So far, however, it appears that the right to buy is achieving the exact opposite effect. The more attractive and popular council houses, primarily in suburban and rural authorities and on smaller estates, have sold well. But many tenants, on the unpopular estates with large concentrations of poverty and unemployment, could not afford to buy, even on the very favourable terms of the Act. The large flatted estates in the predominantly Labour-run big cities were not only unpopular, but were also inaccessible for owner-occupation to low-income occupants by virtue of service charges, high rates charges over and above mortgage repayments, and social breakdown. The additional discounts for flats are unlikely to have a significant effect on sales of flats for these reasons. The major deterrent is likely to be the difficulty in reselling to a new owner. Therefore the social polarization that originated in the councils' own allocation systems has been exacerbated by the right to buy.

In addition, the right to buy has reduced the supply of better property needed for a flexible transfer system, as the 700,000 dwellings sold so far are concentrated largely on more popular estates and involve very few flats – only one out of every twenty-five dwellings (DOE figures, 1986). The result is a drop in transfers, a decline in the average quality of the council stock and a sense of bitterness among those who feel forced to stay within it with fewer opportunities for transferring up the ladder. However, this dissatisfaction is generating pressure to improve the more run-down estates.

The tenants most likely to move out of council accommodation and buy in the private sector, rather than buy their existing council dwelling, are those living in *undesirable* council property that they do not wish to buy. Therefore as a result of the general spread of owner-occupation, vacancies will be even further concentrated in the least popular estates rather than in the more popular dwellings. In sum, transfers can no longer be used as a central plank of allocation policy and as a safety valve for unpopular estates.

The wider processes, as we have discussed, have created a growing disparity between owner-occupiers and tenants (DOE, 1977b, Part 1, p. 97), as owner-occupation has become financially and socially the most advantageous tenure. Many council tenants say they would prefer to be owner-occupiers, but only one-fifth would want to buy their existing council home (Building Societies Association Report, 1983; General Household Survey, 1983). Most tenants did not *choose* to be council tenants but felt pushed into it by bad housing conditions, demolition or lack of alternatives (DOE, 1973).

Not only does this sense of lack of choice determine the unpopularity of much council housing; it also disguises major differences in the economic and social well-being of residents in the public and the private sectors. Council tenants are substantially poorer on average (Hamnett, 1983), more often unskilled, and with poorer educational qualifications than owner-occupiers (Census data, 1971–81, and General Household Survey, 1981). A much higher proportion are claimants of supplementary benefit or are unemployed (Donnison and Ungerson, 1982, p. 237). Two-thirds of separated families dependent on means-tested benefits are housed within the public sector (DOE, 1977b, Part 1; General Household Survey, 1981). Racial minorities are also increasingly, and in the case of residents of Caribbean origin, disproportionately concentrated in council accommodation (Rose, 1969, p. 134; Parker and Dugmore, 1976, p. 11; Labour Force Survey, 1981).

The council sector itself is shrinking in absolute numbers, but is expected to remain at over 4 million homes for a long way into the future and comprises 25 per cent of the total housing stock, a very sizeable chunk of the housing market. Therefore its increasing undesirability and poverty pose bigger problems than ever before, coupled as they are with the demoralization that these trends are causing both among occupants and housing staff within local authorities.

It is not clear whether council policies have directly created the social stigma that accompanies the least popular estates, housing the most vulnerable and disadvantaged people, or whether the fact that some estates have proved intrinsically unpopular has led to policies which accommodate the social reality of a hierarchy of applicants. It appears that some otherwise attractive and well-situated estates have been stigmatized exclusively by the way they have been allocated, and that adjacent and similar estates or blocks sometimes differ dramatically from each other in standards and general popularity, seemingly because of their social make-up.

There is no overriding determinism, and so many elements come into play that we may never be able fully to answer why or how the present situation emerged. However, the estates, which were conceived of as the solution to established slums, have too often themselves inherited the same title.

Conclusion

Need seemed a sensible criterion of access to council housing in the face of housing shortages and slum conditions, and yet it has been much harder to translate into fair allocation practice than it should be.

The City University Housing Research team (Legg, 1981, pp. 74–85) suggested that the very size and complexity of housing department systems led to a many-faceted, interlocking hierarchy of decisions where events and individuals were totally lost in computers and paper work. It has proved hard to open up, as Cullingworth and others have proposed, a system that was so big.

Allocation systems are still largely the invisible arm of housing management and local political structures. Having examined the inequities of present allocation systems and their serious consequences for the poorest members of our society and the worst estates, it becomes tempting to argue that local political masters should not control directly the allocation of homes for their electors. The room for trade-offs and pressure is too great. The poor under such a system would be always vulnerable, and the more dynamic members of the electorate able to manoeuvre political power to their own housing advantage.

In the areas of the country where there is now a surplus of council housing, local authorities are advertising property, diversifying their intake of tenants and relaxing all criteria of access. In areas of shortage and need, this is harder to do, and some overriding priority must be given to the homeless. Even so, more open access and faster re-letting of empty property on more relaxed criteria could *reduce* the incidence of homelessness and broaden the social base of many estates.

Note to Chapter 5

1 The population increased by one-tenth in the thirty years after the war, but households increased by one-quarter (Donnison and Ungerson, 1982, pp. 21–3).

PART TWO

A Survey of New Housing Problems

Chapter Six

The Worst Estates

What would once have seemed incredible is that this abandonment of [council] housing is going on in big, old cities – the places where housing stress seemed worst and scarcity insurmountable ... Similar things can be seen in Tower Hamlets, Lambeth, Hackney and other parts of Inner London.

(Donnison, *New Society*, 14 June 1979, p. 635)

In 1974, the government officially recognized the problem of unpopular postwar council housing for the first time. Based on a survey of all local authorities (DOE, 1974), the government estimated that over half the problem estates were in metropolitan areas; three-quarters were flats; and over half of the difficult-to-let estates were less than ten years old. The main causes of unpopularity were given as design, vandalism and social stigma. Tower blocks comprised a small proportion of the problem.

Local authorities listed the reasons which their housing managers considered 'very important' in causing the unpopularity of estates (Table 6.1). The most frequently cited reason nationally for unpopularity was design, followed closely by vandalism with which it was associated. The third major cause was social stigma. Social stigma is often generated by the operation of the lettings system, which in turn is influenced by unpopular design, vandalism and wider social problems. Design, vandalism and social stigma were so far ahead of all other reasons as to be considered the major causes of unpopularity. Many of the subsidiary reasons, such as external appearance and unsuitable environment, the next most common causes, were strongly linked to the three central reasons.

The reason given least frequently for unpopularity was the internal appearance of the dwelling. This would be partly because many of the dwellings were modern with good amenities. It would also bear out the general impression that applicants and residents care more about the overall 'feel' of an estate and its social and physical aspect than the

Table 6.1 Reasons Held by Housing Managers to be Very Important in Unpopularity

Reasons	No. of times cited
Design of dwellings	109
Vandalism	104
Social stigma attaching to estate	94
External appearance	68
Unsuitable environment	66
High-rise dwellings*	49
Lack of local facilities	35
Too far from the main centre	32
Inadequacy of public transport	26
Internal appearance	21

*The definition of high-rise, according to CIPFA, is five storeys or more.
Source: DOE, 1974.

particular amenities of a home. High-rise blocks as a major factor in unpopularity ranked fairly low. So did the inconvenience or general lack of facilities of an estate, although there were estates where this was considered the overriding problem.

The survey was of limited use, partly because 'no reliable overall picture exists of the form in which the post-war housing stock has been built', the paucity of information being one of the most significant findings of the survey (ibid.). Because of the lack of detailed information, the government from 1978 onwards asked all local authorities to inform it annually of dwellings that are difficult to let (known as the Housing Investment Programme (HIP) returns). Based on these returns, the Department of the Environment estimated that in 1983 there were over 300,000 council dwellings classed by local authorities as difficult to let. Figure 6.1 shows the uneven distribution of difficult-to-let dwellings.

The vast majority of difficult-to-let estates were found in the cities, with 247,000, out of the total of over 300,000, in London and the metropolitan authorities. The proportion of difficult-to-let dwellings in each area of the country paralleled almost exactly the size of the local authority total stock. The bigger *number* of the council-owned dwellings, the greater the *proportion* of unpopular dwellings. This tied the scale of unpopular council housing to the *size* of landlord and indicated a management cause as part of the problem.

The Department of the Environment's report 'An investigation of difficult-to-let housing', mounted in 1976 (Burbidge *et al.*, Vols 1–3, 1981) provided the first published account of the problem. It talked of

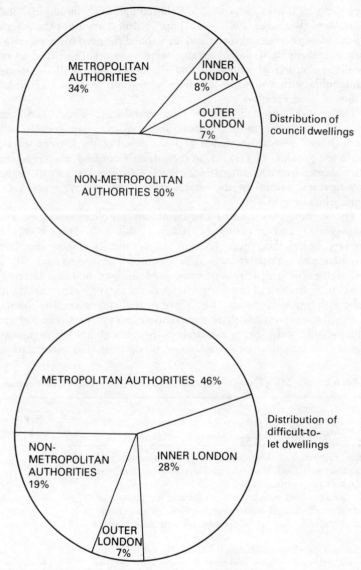

Figure 6.1 Distribution of council stock and difficult-to-let stock by area

Source: HIP Returns, 1983.

'appalling bleakness', 'squalor', 'unrelieved ugliness', 'monotony' and 'harshness' (Burbidge, 1981, Vol. 1, pp. 13–16). It spelt out the design failure of large modern estates and underlined the need for compensatory management if flatted estates were to work. The decline of localized housing management and the concentration of desperate households within unpopular estates were both identified as direct causes of disintegration.

The report suggested that only by introducing a wide range of remedies, including more personal and sensitive management and maintenance, physical remedies and a reversal of the lettings spiral, could the problem be tackled. In the estates examined, the problems often seemed overwhelming and the level of distress was a shock to the investigators. Several of the estates in the survey have since been demolished or sold.

The investigators ranked the dominant problems under social, management and environment issues (Table 6.2). Design was a primary issue: the 'preoccupation with slum clearance and fast production of alternative housing led to unsuitable designs for families and well-publicised defects of some industrialised building systems' (ibid., p. 3). Sixteen of the thirty estates in the survey were industrially built with 'massive concrete facades of overwhelming severity' (ibid., p. 3). All the estates bar three were dense blocks of flats. The intense communality 'made heavy demands on people's ability to live amicably at close quarters with neighbours' (ibid., p. 4). The investigation

Table 6.2 The Main Problems on Case Study Estates in Order of Frequency

Problems identified	No. of estates out of 30
Social factors, including concentrations of families with problems, high child density and 'divided community or lack of community spirit'	23
Management and maintenance problems, including vandalism, insufficient management, repairs or caretaking, and physical neglect due to insufficient maintenance funds	18
Estate surroundings, including lack of play facilities, impersonal public spaces, and lack of community facilities	18
The vast size, physical separateness, and labelling of the estates	14
Dwellings shortcomings, primarily condensation or water penetration, and outdated fittings	9

Source: Burbidge *et al.*, 1981, Vol. 1, p. 4.

found that many estates suffered from damp and water penetration, lift failure, and defective heating systems. 'Lifts were often of inferior quality and too few for the volume of traffic. No authority visited had yet coped with defective lifts' (ibid., p. 15).

Following the investigation it was recognized by the government in the face of overwhelming problems on the worst estates, that the administration, political structure and policies governing local authority housing and 'the frequent failure to recognise the full extent of this role' (ibid., p. 35) caused general problems in the public stock that backed up into the worst estates, where the system finally failed altogether to hold things together within bounds. 'The resulting attitudes of staff often seemed to be those of embattled gatekeepers, rather than an accessible client-oriented service' (ibid., p. 8).

A direct result of the combination of communal design and inadequate management was the decayed and dirty environment of most survey estates: 'At first glance what most of the case study estates needed was a thorough clean-up, not as a once and for all exercise, *but as a prelude* to continuous care and attention' (ibid., p. 13). It is hard to imagine an official investigation of any other public service that would be forced either to specify 'dirt' as a key finding, or to recommend continuous cleaning as a critical solution. Florence Nightingale's criticism of conditions in the Crimean hospitals was possibly the last comparable indictment of a government-sponsored and funded service.

The difficult-to-let investigation proposed that to cope with the major repairs problems of the estates, 'Maintenance should be a personal and responsive service' (ibid., p. 14). Housing management was recognized as the missing link: 'The frequent failure to recognise the full extent of the role [of housing management] has probably played a large part in precipitating or accelerating the downward spiral in status and acceptability of many estates' (ibid., p. 35). The report concluded that demolition, perhaps the most obvious solution to the most undesirable dwellings, should not be considered before other options had been tried, although the investigators were so depressed by some of the more modernistic estates as to consider that they had only a limited life: 'The long-term future ... seems bleak' (ibid., Vol. 2, p. 31).

The evidence of the investigation was damning, cautiously worded as it was, and it highlighted beyond doubt both the magnitude of the design failure of some modern estates and the total inadequacy of some housing management and maintenance organizations. Most importantly, it stressed the social disarray and ghetto-like communities that were generated through a lettings system that pushed the most desperate households to the worst estates, and it exposed officially for the first time a crude over-supply of council dwellings in some areas of the country, particularly Tyneside (ibid., Vols 2, 3).

The ringing phrases of the report came hard upon the euphoria of the mass housing boom:

> Both the dank asphalt galleries and workhouse stairs of the old blocks and the bleak entrances of some of the new ones were dirty and cheerless. Many entrances were dark, tortuous, mean, unsupervised and inviting misuse and petty crime. Refuse hoppers and chambers were frequently sited close to entrance halls and staircase landings, and their litter and smells contributed to the squalor ... As a result of economy, 'streets in the sky' could be very narrow, and were frequently littered, puddled and fouled by the huge dogs kept by tenants for protection against intruders.
>
> (ibid., Vol. 1, pp. 4–5)

The combination of problems of design with problems of management and maintenance found in the difficult-to-let investigation led the government to change the emphasis of public housing policy. Greater attention was paid to how estates were run and to how the least popular estates could be rescued. The focus on difficulties in letting property served to underline a basic gap in management organization. The full-time estate office and the involvement of residents in their own destiny had become accepted within the Department of the Environment as the base-line for making any serious inroads into the problem of difficult-to-let estates. The local office was also the only avenue of direct contact with tenants on management issues and the only way of organizing an effective day-to-day landlord service within local authorities with a large stock of council dwellings. Most other attempted solutions, including re-design, major improvements and social and community initiatives, had failed on their own to reverse the fortunes of badly stigmatized estates without rehousing the existing community.

In March 1979 the Department of the Environment set up the Priority Estates Project to run three pilot schemes in Hackney, Bolton and Lambeth, experimenting in a radically new form of locally based housing management with the direct involvement of residents. In 1983 the Priority Estates Project was extended to Wales. Over a period of five years seventy-two local authorities in England and Wales which had sought advice on problem estates or were taking the initiative in doing something about them were visited by the author. Through this work, the author came into contact with most local authorities in the country with a serious problem of unpopular housing. The following account of twenty local housing initiatives on run-down estates is based on the author's own work for the Priority Estates Project.

PEP: Survey Method

In 1982 a national survey was conducted for the Priority Estates Project of all local authorities that had established a full-time estate management office on stigmatized estates. The aim of the survey was to find out how local offices were organzied and what, if any, success they were having.

When the survey was initiated, it was not known that the earliest estate offices in the country would be located exclusively on difficult-to-let estates. This turned out to be the case. Later, the more ambitious local authorities, which had already marked up some success with a local office on their worst estates, became keen to decentralize their housing management further and set up offices on a wider scale to serve many or all of their estates, including more popular areas. Walsall, Lambeth, Islington and Newcastle-upon-Tyne were at the forefront of this effort to spread local management beyond problem offices.

By January 1982, the cut-off date for inclusion in the survey, nineteen local authorities had opened forty-five full-time local management offices, staffed with full-time workers, on unpopular estates. Only the first office to be opened was selected from each local authority, with the exception of the GLC. Two of the GLC's local initiatives were included because they were based in different boroughs and as a result used very different approaches. The total number of estates included in the survey was therefore twenty. (For a full examination of the method of selection and collection of data, see Power, 1984.)

The following chapters examine in detail the problems leading to the local initiatives. The main sources of information were interviews with the staff who initiated the projects and the council reports that formed the basis of the political decision to make a major departure from previous housing management practice. A questionnaire, covering the decline of the estates, the improvements, the management changes, and the performance records of each office, was completed in each of the nineteen local authorities with the help of the housing department and locally based staff.

The initial survey was written up in brief form for the Priority Estates Project in order to demonstrate to councillors, housing department staff and estate workers that local management was effective (Power, 1984).

The detailed findings of the 1982 survey provide the most accurate record to date of the decline of a representative cross-section of the most problematic council housing. Based on findings of the earlier DOE Survey and HIP returns, the estates included in the 1982 local

Table 6.3 Local Authorities and Estate initiative in Survey

Local authority	Estate	No. of units	Type of estate/ date built	Starting date of initiative
Brent	Chalkhill	1,849	modern 1964–70	1970
Bolton	Willows	473	cottage 1930s	1980
Gateshead	Springwell	1,000	cottage 1940s–1950s	1980
Greenwich	Ferrier	1,898	modern 1971–4	1980
Hackney	Wenlock Barn	698	walk-up 1950s	1979
Hammersmith and Fulham	Edward Woods	812	modern 1970	1979
Haringey	Broadwater Farm	1,063	modern 1970	1981
Islington	Mayville	559	walk-up 1949	1978
GLC/Lambeth	Tulse Hill	882	walk-up 1930s	1980
Lambeth	Stockwell Park	1,500	modern 1972	1979
Leicester	Braunstone North	1,975	cottage 1930s	1981
GLC/Lewisham	Honor Oak	1,350	walk-up 1930s	1979
Lewisham	Milton Court	1,114	modern 1969	1978
Liverpool	Chatsworth	1,930	mixed postwar	1979
Newcastle-upon-Tyne	Cowgate	1,000	cottage 1920s–30s	1978
Rochdale	Ashfield Valley	1,014	modern 1960s–70s	1981
Stockton-on-Tees	Ragworth and adjacent estates	393+ 800	cottage 1940s	1981
Tameside	The Brushes	312	cottage 1930s	1981
Walsall	Goscote	350	cottage 1930s	1982
Wandsworth	Henry Prince	272	walk-up 1930s	1981

Source: Information collected during 1982 survey.

management survey appeared to be broadly representative of the range of problems.

It must be emphasized that the often shocking conditions described in the following pages prevailed before the projects began, and bear no relation to current conditions in the local authorities concerned or on the project estates.

The Twenty Estates

According to the 1983 difficult-to-let returns to the Department of the Environment, the nineteen local authorities included in the survey of twenty estates contained 13 per cent of all English council housing, but 37 per cent of all difficult-to-let dwellings. The projects were set up in areas where the problem of unpopular estates existed on a large scale and not just on the particular estates in the survey. One in six dwellings in these local authorities was difficult-to-let, compared with the national average of one in twenty. Figure 6.2 shows the location of the estates.

Two-thirds of the estates comprised flats and the remainder were prewar, unmodernized cottage estates on the edge of urban areas. The average size of estate was over 1,000 dwellings. The estates were spread across the country in Greater London, the Midlands, Greater Manchester, Merseyside, Tyneside and the north-east (Figure 6.2). Of the nineteen local authorities in the survey, eleven were in Greater London and seven in metropolitan areas. The offices were found within most areas of the country with concentrations of difficult-to-let estates.

The problems faced by all the estate communities were oppressively varied and all-encompassing. Table 6.4 summarizes the nature and extent of the main problems. Snapshot descriptions of a cross-section of the estates in the survey will give some idea of the range and extent of the problems, and the causes of residents' despair.

A large prewar cottage estate on Tyneside was built on the edge of the city before the war. The estate was isolated, with poor shopping facilities. The 900 dwellings were terraced cottages, with 110 flats added since the war. At the time of the survey, the male unemployment rate was 60 per cent. Decline accelerated from 1974, when transfers were made easier, because of the large supply of newer dwellings elsewhere. As the number of empty dwellings rose, so did vandalism. By 1978, there were about 100 vandalized empty homes (one in nine dwellings). Many gardens had been abandoned as fencing had decayed or 'disappeared'. The backlog of repairs awaiting action ran into thousands.

Figure 6.2 Location of twenty estate-based management projects.

Source: Power, 1984, p. 5.

1 Inner city slum: Upper Ground Place, Southwark, 1923 (London County Council).

2 Local estate office: London County Council estate office, Pleasance Road, Roehampton, 1926 (London County Council).

3   Slum clearance (Shelter).

4   Slum clearance site: St Ann's Estate, Stepney, London,
1961 (London County Council).

5   Industrialized
building in progress:
GLC Savona Estate,
London, early 1970s
(Greater London
Council).

6   Honor Oak
Estate, Lewisham,
built in the 1930s.

7   St Cuthbert's
Village Estate,
Gateshead, built
1969–71.

8   Penrhys Estate, Rhondda – vandalism, litter and dogs, 1984.

9   Stockwell Park Estate, Lambeth – entrance corridor, 1982.

10   Wenlock Barn Estate, Hackney – before improvement, 1979.

11 Goscote Estate, Walsall – before improvement, 1982.

12 Goscote Estate, Walsall – after improvement, 1982.

13 Honor Oak Estate, Lewisham – environmental improvements, 1982.

14   Maisonette block in Knowsley
before improvement.

15   Maisonette block in Knowsley after 'lopping off'
improvements.

16   Broadwater Farm Estate, Haringey – neighbourhood
housing office, 1985.

17   Cloverhall Tenant Cooperative, Rochdale – Tenant
Selection Committee, 1985 (Paul Herrmann).

18   Cottage estate in the North West in the 1970s (Richard Olivier, Save the Children Fund).

19   Tulse Hill Estate, Lambeth – playgroup 1980 (Jane Bown).

20   Penrhys Estate, Rhondda – mothers and children (Photo Valley Workshop).

Table 6.4 Characteristics which Led to the Establishment of Estate-Based Management

Characteristic	No. of estates out of 20
Neglected, rubbish-strewn environment	20
Poor repairs and maintenance	19
High levels of crime and vandalism	19
Higher than local authority average of unemployed and tenants on welfare benefits	16
Higher than local authority average of one-parent families	16
Higher than local authority average tenancy turnover	16
Higher than local authority average rent arrears	16
Higher than local authority average child density	15
Hard to let	15
Little previous community involvement	14
Higher than local authority average of lettings to homeless	14
Higher than local authority average level of empty property	14
Unmodernized dwellings	11
Isolated position with few shopping/social facilities	11
Structural repair problems	10
Ethnic minorities disproportionately allocated to unpopular estates	9
Particularly unsuitable design*	7
Continuing stigma of first allocations from slum clearance area	5

*Unsuitable design: walkways with bridges linking blocks, underground garages, etc.
Source: Local Housing Management, Anne Power, Department of Environment 1984.

A deck-access estate in Greater Manchester was built outside the city, next to the abandoned Manchester Ship Canal. The twenty-six slab blocks, comprising 1,014 units, named from A to Z (Appleby to Zennor), were linked with open decks and bridges. The early blocks at the top of the alphabet let fairly easily. But by the time the housing department reached Zennor at the tail of the alphabet, willing applicants had dried up. Half of the offers were turned down. It was held that single male migrants from Donegal docked in Liverpool and headed straight for the estate having heard about the empty new flats.

The estate had unlettable one-bedroom flats on staircase landings of every block. These were bricked in. The Council spent £250,000 repairing the exposed and leaking decks, but the water still came in in places. There were constant lift breakdowns and the entry phones that were later installed in the least popular blocks to try and curb crime and fear of crime did not work from the outset because they were wrongly wired. In 1982 there were 270 empty dwellings on the estate and the council was reluctantly considering disposing of parts of it. Many people argued that it should be demolished.

A system-built, modern concrete complex estate in inner London, comprising 1,000 dwellings, was one of the early low-rise, high-density estates, a hoped-for answer to the 'tower-block blues' and to the desire of inner-city dwellers to stay put. Practically the entire ground area was a vast cavernous, unused car park, and the estate was on stilts above. The overground walkways linked all dwellings, providing several miles of bleak, concrete corridors. Mugging and break-ins were common in 1982 when the survey was carried out. The level of squatting, following on the large number of empty dwellings (sixty-three in 1979), caused such social disarray that the tenants' association began to let flats direct, bypassing completely the council housing department. During the riots in 1981, the estate temporarily became a no-go area as youths used the underground garages and walkways as 'safe' areas and police were temporarily stopped from coming on to the estate. The estate was used as the location for the film *Black Joy*, a mixed celebration of reggae, crime, dope and urban rebellion. When the police set up a special beat-policing experiment there, in 1979, reported crime went up by 185 per cent.

A prewar balcony-block estate in South London was built by the LCC on spare railway and allotment land in the early 1930s to rehouse dockland families from slum-clearance areas. Because it was designated to help the most needy, the new population was selected on the basis of poverty, illness and handicap from the existing slums. The flats, 1,100 of them in twenty-seven barrack-like blocks, were built to a minimal standard, so that rents would be low enough for the poor families they were being built for. The result was an ill-suited location, high density, a total lack of communal facilities, strife-prone communal bathrooms, tiny bedrooms and so on. The other result was an almost uniformly impoverished population, which estate officers, social workers, community workers and teachers were later to try and change. There was no church. From the very outset people had an overriding desire to leave the estate.

Before the Second World War, a pacifist support unit set up a special project to try and help the new and unsettled community (Burbidge *et al.*, 1981, Vol. 3, p. 17). The task was constantly undermined by the people's hatred of the estate: 'Because life in Tenement Town is so unsatisfactory, the families with higher standards of living, instead of playing their part in raising the general level, only lived for the day when they could escape to more congenial surroundings' (White, 1946). As early as 1937, about one-third of the tenants left each year.

Over the years many attempts were made to upgrade the estate, some with, some without the tenants. In 1976, when the difficult-to-let survey was conducted, the GLC was undertaking an ill-thought-out, piecemeal improvement programme with some blocks being emptied of tenants to the envy of the remaining residents, while other blocks received a limited set of improvements with the residents remaining in occupation, and yet others were left for later programmes. Eight years later, some courtyards had been improved but others were as barren and bleak as ever.

In 1981, a survey of three blocks revealed that 43 per cent of households belonged to ethnic minorities; half the families had only one parent; 70 per cent were in rent arrears. The estate, without local management or repairs, without major reinvestment, security, resident caretaking or a lead from within the demoralized community, could not rise above its original designation – 'a slum rehousing estate' – carrying all the scornful and pitying type-casting that went with a somewhat meanly executed plan. The environmental works softened the contours of the estate somewhat, but the long bleak blocks still looked more like a prison than home.

The estates in the survey were all difficult places to run and on the whole unpleasant places to live in. Many of the awful consequences of management failure and social decline were undreamt of. The local authorities, towards the end of the 1970s, finally accepted that the wrong system of management was being applied, leading them to examine problems in depth, and set up alternative structures in the hope of mitigating some of the disastrous conditions found on our original survey visits before the estate offices were opened.

The Basic Problems

It is hard to separate out physical from social and organizational factors, since each element interlocks with the other. However, we will first consider the physical aspects of the twenty estates and the extent to which their design contributed to their unpopularity. There were three main types of estates: 'cottage' estates of houses with gardens, built mainly between the wars, with some dwellings added in the early postwar period; 'balcony/walk-up estates' comprising blocks of flats built in the 1930s and the 1950s usually up to four storeys; 'modern concrete-complex' estates built since the 1960s in large units, usually linked together with 'modern' architectural features such as decks, high-rise blocks, underground garages and futuristic layouts.

131

Design

The twenty estates represented an even spread between the main three design types of council estate, with seven cottage estates, six balcony/walk-up estates, and seven modern concrete complex estates (Figure 6.3).

The design problems of the twenty estates could be summarized under several headings. The size and scale of most of the estates, the isolation from the surrounding community, the omnipresent communal areas, the abandoned, unguarded territory such as allotments, gardens and garages, made the estates look and feel neglected, decayed and poor. On the thirteen flatted estates, oppressive, ugly blocks and communal internal areas created a sense of anonymity and fear that depressed and repelled residents. In the case of the modern estates especially, which shared all the disadvantages of older flatted estates, problems were compounded by industrialized construction of gigantic proportions. Table 6.5 shows the severity of design problems, particularly on flatted estates, and more especially on modern ones. The

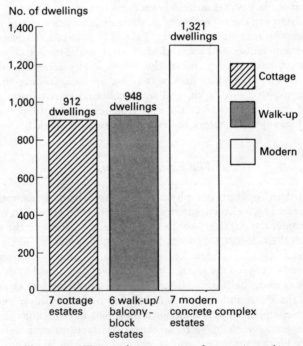

Figure 6.3 Type and average size of estates in study.

Source: Power, 1984, p. 9.

Table 6.5 Design Problems on Twenty Estates, Leading to Their Unpopularity and Decline

Problem	Cottage	Balcony	Modern	Total
Over 200 dwellings	7	6	7	20
Abandoned land	7	6	7	20
Unmaintained, communal areas	7	6	7	20
Dark, unsupervised areas	2	6	7	15
Damaged communal entrances	0	6	7	13
Open balconies and decks	0	6	7	13
Unprotected stairwells and entrances	0	6	7	13
Unpopular location	7	2	4	13
Noise problems caused or enhanced by design	2	4	4	10
Unused garages	0	3	6	9
Vulnerable lifts	0	3	6	9
Industrialized building methods	1	1	6	8
Few or no community facilities	4	2	1	7
Damp and condensation	1	1	4	6
Poorly guarded or abused community facilities	3	2	1	6
Failed improvements				
entry telephones	0	1	4	5
house modernization	1	2	0	3
environmental improvements	1	1	1	3
Total Design Problems	43	64	86	193
Average no. of problems per estate	6	10	12	9

Source: Power, 1984, pp. 8–14.

problems arose roughly in order of complexity of design and construction and it can be seen from the table that the modern flatted estates suffered from twice as many design problems as cottage estates.

Some problems on flatted estates were quite intractable, capable of amelioration only if backed by intensive management. On cottage estates, size, communality and neglect took their toll, too, but it was much easier to see how these problems could be rectified through well-

organized management, sensitive modernization and proper supervision of all communal areas.

Generally the environmental decay was so severe that the estates
were readily identifiable by residents and visitors as unpopular and
hard to let.

Size of Estates
The estates in the survey averaged 1,010 dwellings, which is way above
the size of community with which a majority of people can readily
identify. The smallest estates had 272 dwellings, the largest 1,898.
Figure 6.4 shows the range of sizes of the estates in the survey. The
modern estates were the biggest and fourteen of the estates had over
800 dwellings.

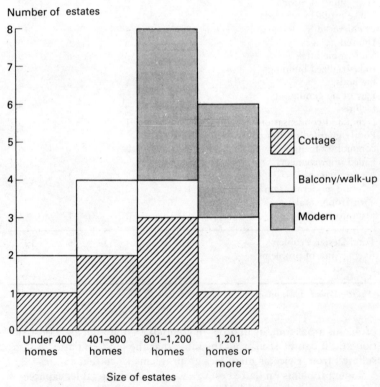

Figure 6.4 Different sizes of estates in survey.

Source: Power, 1984, p. 10.

The problems created on the survey estates by virtue of their size seemed to be anonymity; a lack of identification of tenants with their estate; a sense of isolation; loss of social control; increased vandalism and crime through difficulties of detection; loss of management control; a desire to leave; and a general dislike of the environment. It was hard for workers or residents to articulate the reasons for size creating such a sense of dismay. However, it was such a constantly recurring theme, echoing many other writings on the subject (Burbidge, 1981, p. 5; Dunleavy, 1981, p. 27; Legg, 1981), that it dominated people's sense of dissatisfaction. We concluded that it was a major cause of social and management decline.

Although we know that the large estates in the survey posed management difficulties and tended to be unpopular with tenants, we do not know the size of problem estates on the whole, nor how they compare with council estates in general. The estates in the difficult-to-let investigation averaged over 600 dwellings, although these estates were selected because local authorities had taken some initiative in improving them. The fact that the average for our survey was 1,000 dwellings might illustrate not the typical size of problem estates, but the extreme end of the problem, which councils had a strong incentive to tackle. Large estates tended to provide a greater incentive to opening a local management office because they were a convenient size patch for a team – unlike smaller problem estates. There were, however, many unpopular estates substantially bigger than 1,000, including three in this survey of over 1,800. It appears that problem estates rarely number less than 200 dwellings and more usually have over 500.

The Estate Concept

On most of the survey estates it was difficult for residents to identify with their community. It was also difficult for council staff to identify with the estate because of the sense of uniformity, anonymity and alienation. The visual character of the estates was such that they were separate from the surrounding area. An unnatural boundary was created, by the estates' physical definition, by their size and by the stigma attached to them. The larger the estate, the more stark this definition was likely to be. Not only was the estate physically separate and identifiable; there was an unusually strong but invariably inarticulated community of interest within each estate, above all because of the common landlord.

But the poorest estates often seemed to residents more like a collection of failures from somewhere else than a community of interest. Their size and separation helped set in train a circular decline, as their unpopularity invited low-income, vulnerable residents who also disliked the estate for the same reasons and who found it hard to identify with their neighbours because of the overpowering anonymity. Their failure to identify with their community in turn enhanced the estate's problems. People with intense social and economic problems often did not want to identify with others in the same boat.

The estates therefore housed an increasingly reluctant population; creating a double problem of separateness and inner discord. For this reason unpopular estates have often been likened to prisons or ghettos (Dunleavy, 1981, p. 221).

Chapter Seven

The Design of Unpopular Estates

... Suitable, hygienic dwellings for the poorer classes at a substantially lower rent than that charged for accommodation of the normal type.   (White, 1946)

The Cottage Estates

It was surprising that one-third of the estates in the survey consisted of houses and gardens. For Londoners and residents of flats, it seems unthinkable that cottage estates should be difficult to let or hard to manage. However, the cottage estates were not located in the major cities of London, Birmingham, Manchester and Liverpool, but in areas where flatted estates are much rarer and the cottage style predominates. In fact, the 'cottage' stock was seriously underrepresented among the problem estates since over two-thirds of the national stock has been built as houses and gardens, and the proportion outside London, Birmingham, Manchester and Liverpool would be over 75 per cent. This bears out the overall impression that flats are overwhelmingly more unpopular than houses. Nonetheless, age, size, and social stigmatization resulting mainly from lettings policies and poor management caused some cottage estates to be unpopular, and set in train the familiar cycle of decay, neglect and finally abandonment of dwellings and facilities that would signal the social extremes to which poor cottage estates could sink. Low general demand in many areas of the country and antiquated amenities in kitchens, bathrooms and heating appliances would also have an impact on the lettability of a cottage estate, as would location and the original image of the estate.

Cottage estates were unpopular because they were built with a communal uniformity, a mean stamp on them, and 'estate atmos-

137

phere' that residents rejected. All the cottage estates in the survey were built away from the town centres, and residents disliked feeling cut off from relatives, friends and services. Life seemed to be happening somewhere else. Three of the cottage estates in the survey had always been stigmatized because they rehoused *en bloc* residents of a prewar slum clearance area. Six of the seven cottage estates were completely unmodernized at the outset of the local management initiative, and all were at least forty years old. This fact dominated tenants' dissatisfaction and the difficulties in letting empty dwellings, which in turn led to rehousing of last resort or 'dumping'. The subsequent stigma gathered its own momentum and unless radical management and community initiatives were undertaken, modernization itself could fail to reverse the declining fortunes of these estates. On one of the seven estates in the Midlands, earlier improvements were simply stripped out by thieves making an illegal living from selling council central heating systems on the black market (Seabrook, 1984, pp. 49–50). Other cottage estates not in the survey had experienced the failure of modernization in the mid-1970s through lack of management back-up and inability to move a family in faster than the vandals could get to the dwelling (ibid., p. 42). Therefore modernization, while a prerequisite for restoring run-down property to lettability, was not alone the answer to an estate's problems.

The interior design of the houses on cottage estates was often problematic, especially because of very small kitchens. As basic dwellings, they offered workable and generally acceptable, if cramped, homes that in most cases simply needed repair and updating, although the layout, location and dwelling design of cottage estates contributed to their management problems (Daunton, 1984, p. 32).

The other design problem of cottage estates was that on the one hand they were built in the prewar period when there was little acknowledgement of the need for community facilities, such as a community hall, a children's playground or a football pitch; on the other hand, they were built with verges and stretches of grass which required constant maintenance and litter-picking, back alleys (or runnels) that were badly lit and unkempt; and odd corners of land that had simply not been built on. No one any longer knew why these abandoned areas were there. Often they were simply at the end of a terrace of houses, not big enough to build on, but too big for someone's garden. Estate roads, by contrast, were usually narrow, designed for an era when no ordinary people owned cars. Grass verges on all the estates were used for car-parking. The result in winter was deeply rutted, muddy verges that the council pointed to as proof that they could do little to improve the estates in the face of such irresponsible tenants' action. On at least one estate, residents had knocked down the walls of their front gardens in order to park their cars outside their living rooms. Fear of car theft was a real element in this.

In no case had an estate office or a repairs base been developed while the estate was being built or in the forty or more years that had since elapsed. Shops were purpose-built, but because of their relatively pristine conditions, rents and rates were high, and shops had difficulty getting established. Because shopkeepers were on the whole not willing to live as tenants on the premises on a poor estate, shops were often unguarded, frequently broken into and heavily vandalized. Many shops were boarded up or abandoned.

On no cottage estate had a community centre been built with the estate, though community facilities were added in later years. Belatedly, playgrounds of sorts had been added in several cases. Overall, on the cottage estates, the public landlord was over-generous, if not positively casual, in the use of the land, while giving very little coherent thought either to its future use or maintenance, or looking at all carefully at the social needs of the uprooted residents.

Many of the cottage estates were not architect-designed, and very little planning skill was brought to bear either. Most local authorities did not employ architects at the time these estates were built (Dunleavy, 1981, p. 12). It was considered sufficient to put up rows of adequate houses of standard design and leave spaces between, very much as the nineteenth-century industrialists had built the inner-city terraces, only with more generous space.

Cottage estates, with their houses and gardens, were far more enclosed and controlled than the flatted estates. But on the seven cottage estates in our survey, many front gardens had become abandoned rubbish heaps. In fact on two estates, the council had communalized front gardens, turning them into open-plan grass verges because private gardens were so neglected. Needless to say, communalized front gardens were not properly maintained either. Back gardens were an even bigger problem and on most estates, over the forty years of the estates' life, fences disappeared and many back gardens became communal tips and shortcuts. 'Defensible space' did not automatically operate in a very poor, demoralized community; residents could simply give up all attempts at guarding or caring for their own property in the face of landlord neglect.

On one cottage estate in the north, environmental improvements costing £250,000 were carried out without any local management or tenant involvement, and were destroyed completely over the following two years. Many other estates not in the survey made similar attempts either at environmental improvements, communalizing abandoned private gardens, reinstating tumbledown garden fences, planting out courtyards, enclosing entrances, providing garages, or removing dry-ing areas. They failed where they were not coupled with tenant involvement and intensive management, except where the existing population was moved out and the estate was effectively rebuilt.

The overall effect of the widespread abandonment, neglect, and rubbish dumping on public open space and in private gardens was to generate an atmosphere of depression and abandonment that deterred self-respecting people from considering moving to the estate and forced more ambitious tenants to leave. They rejected the low standing of such a neglected estate.

In spite of the general atmosphere of decay, many individual gardens were enclosed and well cared for, albeit often with home-made fencing. Many tenants made endless use of the areas attached to their houses, whether or not the fencing was still standing. Intrinsi-cally, the cottage estates in the survey were adequately, if unimagina-tively, built and laid out, and it was relatively easy to conceive of making them perfectly acceptable. The same could not be said of the thirteen flatted estates. Unsightly and wasteful as the derelict areas were on the cottage estates, they could not be compared with the ubiquitous squalor of almost every square foot of territory on the flatted estates. Flat-dwellers did not have outdoor space to make use of, only space that was abused.

The Flatted Estates

The thirteen flatted estates in the survey were all oppressively built at high density, with a mean finish. They were larger, on the whole, than the cottage estates and this increased the dense atmosphere. The greatest impact was created by the closeness of the blocks. Many of the flatted estates were built at over 200 bed-spaces to the acre and some up to 400. All the survey estates were in this sense extremely oppressive, whereas the cottage estates with about sixty bed-spaces to the acre seemed open and airy by comparison. Alice Coleman argues that density is not a factor in problem estates, citing the much greater density of old city streets as evidence (Coleman, 1985, p. 156). However, high density was associated with the size of blocks and scale of estates and had a serious impact on the environment of the flatted estates we visited (Jacobs, 1962, Ch. 9).

Communal Space, Dogs and Children
It was the intense communality of the flatted estates, where your children, your dog, your rubbish and your milk were shared because

you could not keep them to yourselves, that people seemed to hate most of all.

Dogs illustrated the problem well. They were a menace on all estates and were somehow associated with communal space. Many people with dogs tended to treat the open areas as a private house resident treats his or her garden. They would open the door and simply put the dog out. It is hard to appreciate how great a loss of control the dog problem represented on the estates we visited. The one feature that seemed to explain it, other than a cussed fecklessness among dog-owning residents, was the lack of private space and the extensive communal areas. However, it was also a function of weak, negligent management and illustrated the need to enforce communal rules strictly. Dogs had been explicitly forbidden in most tenancy agreements but the rule was simply ignored. Dogs were ubiquitous. In one tower block in Liverpool, that was one-third empty, stray dogs lived inside the building and wandered in and out of the lifts with the legal occupants, moving between floors and waiting for lifts just as the two-legged occupants did.

It is not possible to link dogs directly with design, but they did somehow epitomize the problem. Dogs were acquired primarily for security and companionship, as a result of the fears generated by flat-living; but secondarily, as a compensation for cramped estate-living where a dog represented freedom and outdoor space. Unfortunately, only brutally rigid management enforcement could contain the dog problem and this was missing from all of the survey estates.

Many children became equally communal, put outside the front doors to play. Again, this was often taken to be simple fecklessness on the part of uncaring parents, but it was more an acknowledgement of the fact that children through the ages have spent most of their time out of doors, when not in school or asleep. In a minimally designed flat, the imperative to escape to the outdoors is stronger than ever, and can only be repressed at serious cost to the children's development and the mother's nerves. But the communal design of flatted estates militated against the kind of play that was compatible with adult needs, the safety of the children and the survival of communal facilities.

Children and dogs, therefore, came to be viewed as uncontrollable threats, proof of the slum character of the estates, and also a source of much direct damage. Our impression was that this resulted more from the design of the estates and the living patterns they generated than from the nature of the poeple, although as always the one fed the other. Both problems seemed substantially more severe on the flatted estates than on the cottage estates.

Responsibility for the communal areas of flatted estates

The major distinguishing feature of the flatted estates, apart from the block structure and their height, was the ubiquitous no man's land of common parts. A flat opens out on to a string of common areas that are neither clearly public, nor clearly private (Newman, 1972, p. 32; Coleman, 1985, p. 74), and therefore belong neither to an individual tenant nor to the community of tenants as a body. They actually belong to the landlord, and therefore must be cared for by the landlord, as the philanthropic trusts have accepted over the last century or so. Local authorities have not taken this blanket responsibility seriously and in almost every case have assumed that at least some of the responsibility belongs to tenants as individuals or as some kind of undefined collective body (Legg, 1981, pp. 17, 51). Tenants have not on the whole taken on this responsibility. Tenants' collective responsibility for common areas that they do not own, but that are part of their estate, has not been defined in law and could not be enforced if it was, unless tenants collectively became the legal landlord, as happens in the rare cases where they form a co-operative. In all other cases, the landlord is entirely, solely and exclusively responsible for communal areas, a responsibility that was not executed with any diligence on the twenty estates.

The absurdly high densities within blocks was compensated for by *too much* unused or abused open space. The design of flats dictated communal entrances, stairwells, rubbish collection areas and so on within each block. In addition, design fantasies created frightening dark areas. The general lack of security and the major problems of policing caused by such design features as underground car parks, multi-storey car parks remote from dwellings, overhead pedestrian walkways, linking bridges, long open decks and enclosed corridors, under-used, sometimes abandoned shopping precincts, unguarded, communal drying rooms and rubbish stores within blocks, all helped generate fear of crime and invited noise, vandalism and graffiti. Often a communalistic design fantasy turned into an ugly and abused eyesore.

Communal parts of blocks

The communal parts of the buildings themselves posed the most difficult problem. These areas were constantly damaged, dirty, or simply badly designed and unable to stand up to the wear and tear of so many users. They required constant maintenance and supervision, not just because of greater use and abuse, but because they relied more on vulnerable externals such as lighting and working hinges and locks, without which they became dangerous and even unusable. Rubbish stores and collecting points sometimes became unusable because doors were broken off and not replaced. As a result, the rubbish store would be abused and council rubbish collectors would refuse to collect from it. Drying rooms, garages and store sheds were widely abandoned because doors were ripped off and not replaced. Balconies and stairwells were sometimes unlit for weeks because light fittings were broken and bulbs constantly stolen.[1]

In many local authorities we visited, attempts at keeping doors on their hinges and lights working had quite simply been abandoned. On several estates no stairwell window had glass in it and no door, either to rubbish areas or to entrances, was in working order.

Unguarded lifts and communal entrances

There were lifts on at least some blocks of all the more modern flatted estates. Lifts were a constant attraction to abuse, providing a challenge to ingenuity and daring. Boys would ride on the roofs of lifts, try to open doors between floors and even try to trap unsuspecting people in them. Lifts would often be vandalized and in tower blocks on at least three of the project estates in the survey they broke down continually. On two of the estates, in tower blocks seventeen and twenty-three storeys high, lifts were out of commission more often than they were working. In one case, new lifts had to be installed. On both estates, elderly people and very young children lived in the tower blocks and were dependent on lifts to reach their homes.

Lift breakdown was associated with cheap installation, ineffective maintenance and the lack of door controls or resident porter/caretakers; but it was also a function of the numbers of children using and abusing the lifts and the challenge they represented to youth as a communal collecting point and a technological adventure. Because of their anonymous, unguarded nature, lifts never represented among the young a vital service they needed to protect, rather a source of fun or an object of their scorn – a way of getting even with an environment with which they did not identify.

Lifts were a frequent source of fear; people were afraid to travel in them alone for fear of attack; and, even more commonly, people were ashamed of their visitors using the lifts because of the smell of urine. It is unclear whether lifts were abused in this way through the need for a toilet because of the distance of dwellings from the ground, or as a symbol of the lack of esteem in which the community, the estate, and especially its common parts were held. People do not deface what they respect as belonging to others or what they know is guarded or overlooked. An unguarded lift, because it is enclosed, partly private and partly public, a source of fear and a symbol of precarious dependence on others, appeared to bring out the very worst of the aggressive desire to abuse. It was extremely rare to enter a clean-smelling, undefaced lift.

No local authority we visited guarded lifts from the time they were first installed. On six of the thirteen estates, attempts were made, after initial damage, at installing entry telephones in flats where there was lift access. But without resident custodians all these attempts failed and the telephones themselves became the targets of even greater vandalism (Bright, *et al.*, 1986). Entry telephones in lift access blocks were the only changes to communal areas attempted prior to local management.

Communal entrances and lifts were probably more menacing than the other areas because they were the residents' only means of access to their home or from their home to the outside world. The ease with which they could be damaged made residents feel vulnerable and therefore incited bullying behaviour as weak spots always do. For this reason, without tight control, the failure to improve security to entrances was to be expected.

Decks and bridges

Decks and bridges were integral to the blocks and therefore provided a direct link to people's homes. They were a special feature of the modern estates, along with the underground or freestanding, multi-storey car parks. All but one of the modern concrete complex estates in the survey had linking bridges between already large blocks. The idea, as we know, was to provide 'streets in the sky'. Their effect was to break down even further any sense of neighbourliness or identity within a block, each of which could contain over a hundred dwellings. In physical terms they were extremely ugly, combining the worst features of main-road subways and overhead bridges. Instead of providing an arterial link within a community, they seemed to provide a strangulating line of access and escape for strangers. The police argued forcibly that they created a muggers' paradise, giving constant cover and escape routes. One estate was described by the housing manager as a 'giant climbing frame'. Crime was alleged to be a bigger problem on these estates than anywhere else, although the lack of accurate figures made it hard to establish the exact truth of this claim. The police in any event found them the hardest to protect; caretakers the hardest to maintain; and residents, the most frightening. Many estates were not policed at all until recently because 'estates roads' and communal parts of buildings, including balconies and decks, were classed as private council property. There was no obligation on the police to patrol them. This in itself was an incredible anomaly, and may have contributed to a major build-up of crime and fear on the most vulnerable estates (Hough and Mayhew, 1983). By the very anonymity and inter-connectedness that they created between 3,000 or more residents, no stranger could be challenged, no outsider detected. Everywhere was made to belong to everyone. And yet unlike streets, they were not public nor guarded by everyone's eyes. They were often partially hidden and infrequently used. Their exposed and public character disguised an unnerving atmosphere of abandon and secrecy.

The open decks along the blocks past people's front doors created another major problem, with the noise they generated. They were almost always directly above someone else's bedroom. There was the noise of constant coming and going; and they were also ideal for skateboarding, roller skating and even cycling. They were the first play area beyond the front door and they were fun because they were long and flat and were linked to the next deck and the next. There was no easy way that a tenant on one deck could detect the children on another deck making a noise. There was no direct connection between one deck and the next, even though they were all linked.

Decks were in many cases a wind trap, with driving rain in bad weather causing surface puddling. Decks were not originally built as roofs or as roads, and yet they needed to function as both. In practice they neither kept out the weather in many cases, nor bore the continual traffic successfully.

Garages

There has been a disastrous multiplication of free-standing rows of unguarded garages. There was demand for very few of them because of their vulnerability. They provided ready rubbish dumps, refuges for tramps and other social outcasts, cover for glue-sniffing, drug abuse, and more innocent teenage pranks (Burbidge (ed.), 1981, pp. 49, 61). On older estates in the survey, abandoned garages have been demolished by the council, having been half destroyed by vandals, simply because they could not be protected. Even worse were the communal underground garages that formed dungeon-like cellars under vast blocks on four estates in the survey. On one estate, because of bitter experience elsewhere, the underground garages were blocked up and made unusable before the estate was ever let. Multi-storey car parks, separate from the blocks, were actually scheduled for demolition in one case. The expensive and useless provision was derided as planning folly.

Industrial Building Systems

Seven of the thirteen flatted estates and part of one cottage estate were system-built with concrete slabs. All of the modern estates and all the tower blocks were system-built. As a design method, it was not only ugly and unpopular with residents; it carried with it the liability of

145

size, since it was not worth using the machinery and the large-scale building operation involved unless it handled a big contract. Its main drawback turned out to be its failure to weatherproof, the most basic requirement of a dwelling. In some cases, flat roofs, external rooms and exposed decks actually leaked, flooding rainwater into dwellings. More commonly, the concrete slab components of the blocks and houses formed cold bridges into the dwellings causing intense damp, condensation and mould formation. This was common to all the system-built estates. Tenants were often told that cooking, washing, running hot baths and drying clothes in their homes were the *cause* of damp problems. Of course, domestic activities also generated moisture but the building failure was not accepted except in the most extreme cases.

The problems of cold bridges were intensified on several of the estates by projecting, overhanging bedrooms, sometimes exposed to the wind and weather on five out of six sides of the room. On one estate, the problem of cold and damp due to outhanging bedrooms was so severe that the projecting bedrooms were simply bricked up. The inadequate insulation was made worse on all the modern estates by the exposed nature of *all* the sites and by the creation of wind tunnels and the even greater cooling effect that resulted. It is not by chance that the estates were located on exposed sites. Their scale and their late arrival on the housing scene determined that on the whole only the most unfavoured sites were still available. Several estates, including two in Sheffield and one in the Rhondda, not in the survey, were so exposed and windy that elderly people found it hard to walk upright through the estate in bad weather. The design of the estates enhanced the force and the impact of the wind, particularly on the deck access estates in Sheffield where able-bodied adults sometimes had difficulty rounding corners on the exposed decks.

Attempts had been made at rectifying the design disaster of cold, damp and exposure. These varied from sticking polystyrene tiles on inside walls to re-lining decks and, in one case, glazing parts of the overhead walkways. The solutions were almost as costly as the original industrial building system. The only satisfactory solution appeared to be to build a second 'skin' round the dwelling to provide normal protection from the elements. It seemed the ultimate irony to propose building a completely new outer skin to an uninsulated, damp, cold, 'modern' house. It was being seriously considered on one estate not in the survey.

Tower Blocks

Five of the system-built estates included some tower blocks, two on walk-up estates and three on modern estates. All the tower blocks were system-built. However, they were on the whole less problematic than the tower blocks which had balconies, corridors and decks. An enclosed building with only one or two entrances and generally only four flats accessible on each floor posed fewer problems than the open balcony or the interlinking, open walkway and corridor blocks. The tower blocks rarely had flats with more than two bedrooms, whereas the vast majority of other council dwellings comprised family accommodation with three bedrooms or more. As a result, child densities in tower blocks were usually lower than in other parts of the estates, although three London authorities with great lettings difficulties had rehoused many previously homeless, one-parent families in tower blocks in the survey estates. Many of these families suffered severe distress. Tower blocks were far from problem-free but they posed less of a threat than their reputation would have suggested.

Abandoned, Unused Areas

There were areas on the flatted estates that were dark and unfrequented. Bulky rubbish that would not fit in normal containers or the chutes provided – old fridges; abandoned beds; settees, and burnt-out or abandoned vehicles – would be deposited on open spaces.

All these half-hidden, unguarded and often totally unseen areas invited dismantling and rebuilding of cars, recycling of council heating radiators, light fittings, and more random scrap. More menacingly, they also sometimes harboured drug-abuse and glue-sniffing.

Sometimes the derelict areas were totally deserted and invited nothing other than the fear that abandoned, dark and unclaimed territory can inspire. But the occasional violent crime or mysterious disaster generated a general sense of horror towards the abandoned areas. A large area of overgrown allotments along the edge of an inner London estate was widely hated and feared by residents and staff because a dead baby had been found hidden in the undergrowth in the late 1970s. The identity of the baby was never discovered. The very desolation and lack of users, legal or illegal, put a jinx on these areas.

Need for Management Back-Up

The design of flatted estates required the provision of resident custodial staff, caretakers, porters, janitors, or continental-style concierges. Many communally built estates of houses and gardens required an estate warden or caretaker too. Without a resident caretaker, it was impossible to maintain such areas in functioning order. In some of the local authorities where the projects were located, resident caretakers were no longer employed prior to the local management initiative, and in others they never had been. On some estates resident caretakers had been withdrawn after vicious attacks on them personally, or vandal damage to their flats and intimidation of their families. Isolated incidents, which changes in working practices could perhaps have overcome, were allowed to generate a level of fear among staff that caused the collapse of a vital ingredient in the management of communal blocks of flats. On one estate, only the most defeated of caretakers would stay. Even then they would only work in pairs, and only three of the eight posts were filled.

Community Facilities on Estates

Community facilities, wherever they existed, tended to be beset with major difficulties, and yet it has been a criticism of estate design that in so many cases large communities were rehoused into dwellings without the proper provision of community facilities. On a large pre-war flatted estate in Lewisham, the failure of the community was blamed on the lack of community halls or play areas in the dense blocks (White, 1946). On other estates, the opposite was true, with a number of community facilities being built in an attempt to restore the estate, some of which generated intense and continuing problems, and none of which restored the popularity of the estate (Burbidge, *et al.*, 1981, Vol. 3).

Laundry facilities and drying rooms epitomized the contradiction between needed communal provision and communal abuse. On every balcony on a GLC estate in Lambeth in 1979, there was an abandoned, smashed, glass-strewn, windowless, doorless drying room. On a Welsh estate the council agreed to brick up drying areas at the end of corridors as a concession to tenants' desires to improve their cramped but appallingly misused environment. Yet on modern estates without laundries it was a major plank of tenant protest that there were no communal drying facilities. There simply was not room in the small flats for drying clothes. The result was quite typical of communal provision. If a facility was not there, it was often considered a major cause of estate problems. If it was there, it became a major focus of estate destruction.

It may be asked *why* large estates should not work like a village, separated as they are, and usually large enough to support their own facilities. Indeed many a modern planner conceived of estates in exactly that light, encompassing schools, launderettes and hairdressers, shops, community centre and even a pub and a church. Of course, many estates had none of these things and that was a major source of complaint, making it very difficult for tenants to get together. Fourteen of the survey estates had few facilities; a few had some facilities that worked reasonably. However, it was common on the problem estates in the survey with reasonable facilities to find the shops boarded up and the community centre or play areas a source of friction and factionalism, if not violence; and most facilities were expensive, dirty and vulnerable to break-ins.

Shops and community centres often resembled fortresses. Desperately needed play areas were often ransacked and abandoned. Where well used, they were often too near dwellings for comfort and a frequent source of tension between youngsters and elderly people. On one estate, there was a totally derelict play area on the edge of dense, ugly, deck-access blocks. The local authority could not restore it, badly needed as it was, because of the volume of complaints it had generated from residents. But neither could it summon the courage to remove it because of the rampant youthful vandalism that it believed would be grossly exacerbated by such an act.

Communal facilities and communal areas did not run themselves. Unfortunately, because of the design of estates, and the social alienation, they needed to be run and guarded by the landlord or by community organizations acting on the landlord's behalf. This happened on only one of the estates in the survey prior to local management. On the other estates, because of inadequate mechanisms for maintaining and supervising facilities, they were invariably ruined.

Youth Gatherings

Communal facilities and communal areas posed special problems in relation to youth. These areas attracted vandal damage and youthful congregation. Youth always found the unguarded corner to hang around on. A bench, a lamp-post, a fire-gate or an entrance way, a bridge or a shop-front, all on different estates, provided a physical focus for the social instincts of youth. It was then only a matter of time before the bench was dismantled, the gate off its hinge, the entrance chipped with gang names or sprayed with verbal abuse, or the light fitting torn out. The energy of youth attacked the unguarded areas with surprising venom. In winter, on modern estates with communal heating systems, boys would collect around the heating vents from the main boiler because of the warmth they provided. These youthful collecting points not only generated physical damage to the particular area of congregation. They also generated genuine fear among smaller children and older people. The fear was born of isolated incidents of unusual horror, which somehow spread a threatening reputation to any so-called gang of young people, who in most cases caused little damage, but simply identified themselves through their numbers and noise and physical dominance as a group to be feared.

The most horrifying example of youthful abuse was on a large, old balcony estate in inner London. There a group of about ten youths hid themselves in the toilets of the community centre until the thirty or so old-age pensioners of the estate had come in for their lunch club. They then locked the exit doors, guarded them, held all the old people up with knives and took their purses. The youths escaped with their paltry haul of less than £50, leaving a terrorized group of elderly residents, a defeated staff, and a paralysed community centre. An example of a more common problem was a northern estate where benches, newly installed on the steep hills to help elderly residents on their way home from shopping, were used nightly by gangs of youths as a collecting point. Older residents, after several hysterical meetings, got the new benches removed. In fact on many estates, benches were removed as part of tenant-led 'improvements', to prevent youth from congregating, and it was the strangest proof of an estate's disintegration that social facilities needed by everyone had to be withdrawn to pacify irate tenants and contain the explosive energy of youth. The design of the estates provided many vulnerable targets for the youth gangs that have always existed in poor areas. The remote council landlord highlighted the general inability to hold behaviour within bounds.

The lack of imaginative provision for youth was a noticeable failure on the survey estates. Local schools were often opened as youth centres in the evenings. Club halls were also often made over to estate youth clubs. Adventure playgrounds existed on several estates, though only one was well-run with permanent leaders who could control the older youth. The leaders were residents, themselves only slightly older than the youths themselves. Yet on every estate threatening gangs appeared and reappeared. They were often much tamer than their appearance or reputation. But in a crowd they were certainly capable of menacing, if not actually harming, others. It was rare to hear of attempts by tenants to reach these young people, and police were frequently called in by residents to disperse them. Confrontation always seemed part of the sport, but an estate could rarely take the strain. Unemployment was inevitably exacerbating the problems of youth. There was no obvious outlet for the most energetic and creative period of life.

Note to Chapter 7

1 Alice Coleman's research indicates that the more dwellings share a communal entrance, stairs, corridors, the greater the level of dirt, vandalism and other abuse (Coleman, 1985, pp. 34, 38, 39).

Chapter Eight

The Management of Unpopular Estates: Allocations and Empty Property

> One of the evils of much that is done for the poor springs from the want of delicacy felt and courtesy shown and that we cannot beneficially help in any spirit different to that in which we help those who are better off.
>
> (Hill, 1883, p. 42)

Important management issues followed on from the design of the estates, their inherent unpopularity and seeming unmanageability. The problem of letting empty dwellings was the most basic indicator of unpopularity. The maintenance of communal areas was another. The support for and survival of communal facilities was another. The level of neglect, damage and even total destruction to these areas spoke volumes about the scale of the management tasks of the public landlord, reflecting conditions before the local authorities opened an estate office.

Lettings Control

Although lettings are one of the key elements in housing management, the allocation of coucil housing has always been a politically sensitive activity over which extremely tight control has been retained. In fact, in many local authorities, elected members still intervene personally in favour of individual constituents and also create pressure against such changes as relaxing the residence requirements for access to council housing or making a wider range of offers to homeless families, or monitoring lettings to racial minorities in an attempt to identify discrimination.

In several local authorities in the survey, only one housing officer or one tightly organized and secretive section of the housing department, actually called a 'lettings cell' in one local authority, knew the workings of the whole lettings system, in order to 'ensure fairness' and to prevent housing managers, prey to pushy tenants or hard-luck stories, from being able to influence decisions.

This closed and centralized approach to lettings created enormous delays in the system. On no estate before local management was there a swift, locally run re-let system. Even the GLC's so-called 'instant lettings' took up to three months to clear the queue of ready applicants each time it formed in response to advertisements.

Thus, for primarily political reasons, one of the key ingredients of day-to-day housing management had been kept out of the hands of local housing managers. Before estate-based offices opened, none of the estate officers in our twenty estates did more than handle some of the mechanics of the lettings procedure, such as showing applicants a property or signing them up as tenants after an offer had been accepted. Nor did they have *any* responsibility for finding suitable and willing tenants, ensuring that there was a waiting list to fill any dwelling the moment it came empty, or controlling transfers. This separation of the lettings function from other parts of housing management made housing management itself 'toothless'. Estate officers were often bitter that applicants from the centre refused offers on their estate. They were frustrated at their inability to tackle empty dwellings. Because they had no say in lettings, it became easier for housing officers to blame the tenants for the estate not working well, especially in the face of severe social problems. Management of the estate was clearly and firmly out of their hands and in the hands of the central bureaucracy and political machine, often anxious to be fair but unable to deliver.

Lettings Problems

It is hard to establish to what extent the twenty estates became hard to let through the way they were designed and run, and to what extent it was the result of lettings policies as such. Very few local authorities were prepared to admit that they had a 'dumping' policy. But in practice, they all used their problem estates to rehouse the most economically and socially vulnerable households. Exact figures were not obtained for all twenty estates and we relied heavily on the evidence of council staff for our overall findings, but it was clear that fifteen of the twenty were hard to let within the normal council allocations system. As a direct result, these estates housed disproportionate numbers of vulnerable one-parent and homeless families, unemployed people, households headed by a member of an ethnic minority, and disproportionate numbers of children. Further evidence of lettings problems and unpopularity lay in the high turnover of tenants on the estates, the high incidence of empty dwellings and the high rent arrears (Table 6.3). Only two estates did not have lettings difficulties.

Lettings policies at the centre, as exercised in relation to the twenty estates we examined, produced socially isolated communities at the bottom of the public housing ladder, although it would probably be more accurate to suggest that the social disadvantages of the worst estates were a result of lettings policies towards more popular estates where a system of queuing and selection worked to the advantage of better-off tenants.

One-Parent Families

The numbers of one-parent families were known for eleven of the twenty estates. On average, 17 per cent of households were one-parent families, compared with 4 per cent nationally. On some estates, half of all the families with children had only one parent. Residents themselves were conscious of the social stress this caused, often mentioning the numbers of one-parent families as proof of how unstable the community was.

One-parent families were less likely to have economic choice, and were more prone to allied problems such as homelessness. They were also more vulnerable to sickness and family crisis. They were far more likely to be in financial difficulties, especially over rent payments, than two-parent households (Duncan and Kirby, 1984, p. 41). The tenants' common diagnosis of their community as a 'dump' had a crude grounding in reality (Shenton, 1976, p. 25; Reynolds, 1986, p. 25).

The disproportionate numbers of one-parent families on estates where people on the whole did not want to live was as much a reflection of their own housing need and lack of choice, as the relative ease with which the council could fit them into estates with a high turnover. It can be argued that existing tenants pressing for transfers off the unpopular estates should not be given that right, thereby ensuring a supply of empty dwellings for more desperate households on the better estates. This would bottle up the more ambitious tenants on the estates that needed drastic improvements, so ensuring a lot of drive to bring them about; it would help prevent ghettoization and it would ensure a better chance for poorer households. In practice, however, though all the local authorities we visited paid lip service to helping the needy and opposed grading of tenants and 'dumping', they took the line of least resistance, adopted progressive transfer policies for 'good' tenants (that is tenants with no arrears and tenants whose house was in a good state of redecoration for re-letting), and let the vacated dwellings on the twenty survey estates to the vulnerable families, who had very little resilience or choice. The survey estate in Newcastle traced its latest decline to the period in the mid-1970s, when transfers became easier and many of the established tenants left for a 'better' area, while the vacated unmodernized dwellings could not attract more ambitious and choosy tenants. The difficult-to-let investigation expresses the problem clearly: 'If liberalising transfers affects only the better off or "good" tenants then it will reinforce polarisation between estates and exacerbate problems . . . eventually producing a transit camp atmosphere' (Burbidge *et al.*, 1981, Vol. 1, p. 12).

One indicator of the extent of upwardly mobile transfers was that the turnover of tenants on sixteen of the twenty estates was higher than the local authority average. It would not have been possible in almost all cases to transfer to a worse estate within the local authority since these were the very bottom of the pile. Therefore it must be assumed that the vast majority of transfers were to better estates.

Child Density

Fifteen of the estates had higher than the local authority average of child densities. A major cause of this was the predominance of three-bedroom dwellings on most estates, but many of the large families were seriously overcrowded (London Borough of Lambeth, 1984). Although exact figures were only available for nine estates, Table 8.1 shows that the proportion of children under 16 on these estates ranged

Table 8.1   Proportion of Children Under Sixteen on Nine Survey Estates

Estate	Proportion under 16
Springwell	31
Braunstone North	38
Cowgate	31
Ragworth	45
Chalkhill	40
Broadwater Farm	27
Stockwell Park	34
Tulse Hill	23
Edward Wood	30
Average for all survey estates	33
National average	22

Source: 1981 Census.

from 23 per cent to 45 per cent, higher than the national average of 22 per cent (1981 Census). Large families have often been concentrated on the poorer estates.

Although it has been demonstrated that a high density of children causes problems such as noise and vandalism, this should not itself increase an estate's unpopularity since many suburban owner-occupied estates must have similar child ratios. It is a function of the weak social controls and the large amounts of unfilled time through truancy and unemployment among the youth, coupled with unsuitable design, high-density building and the intense communality but poor community spirit of most estates that children seemed to cause so much trouble (Wilson, 1978, pp. 52–5).

Children inevitably created noise, instinctively congregated in groups and had an irrepressible exuberance that displayed itself in daring and damage, depending on how much they could get away with. The behaviour of children was not only determined in large measure by what adults allowed them to do. It was also a function of estate living as such, for both adults and children. The estate, as a separated but unintegrated community, as a vast uncontrolled but boring no man's land, the estate as an environment often hostile to family living and to children's love of the outdoors and thirst for adventure, caused the loss of confidence by adults in their own community of children. Children became both the perpetrators and the victims. Nothing could represent more vividly the failure of public housing than the use of numbers of children as an actual measure of unpopularity. Maybe it is a symptom of our ageing society, and a reflection of our loss of a sense of the future, that makes us connect children so glibly to a more general social malaise, and blame them directly for problems on unpopular estates.

Ironically, on the most unpopular estates in areas of very low demand, such as Merseyside and Greater Manchester, few families were moving on to the estates in the survey, and existing families were as far as possible being moved off the flatted estates in these areas. They were largely replaced by young, single people, and the absence of family life was felt to generate even more instability and transience. This would indicate that the root problem was neither the children nor the young, single people but the overall management structure, which was totally inadequate to cope with the problems of running a large, poorly designed estate.

Homelessness
Fourteen of the estates housed disproportionate numbers of homeless families. On several estates, especially in London, the bulk of all lettings, up to 90 per cent in one case, were to previously homeless

families. Homeless families were not only disproportionately made up of one-parent families, but they were often black. In four boroughs, the majority of homeless families rehoused on the estates in the survey were black. There is evidence that racial discrimination plays a part in this process, as has been experienced on some of the estates in our survey. The exact overlap between race, homelessness, and lone parenthood was not known for the survey estates but the three categories of housing disadvantage overlapped and sifted applicants to the bottom of the lettings pile (Parker and Dugmore, 1976). The poorest estates, such as we visited, became a lettings net to catch those rejected by the system.

By establishing strict criteria of need, of which homelessness is the most acute and most irrefutable, and by running a dual system where good estates are for those in less acute need who can wait, or those who 'deserve' better as a result of their tenancy record, and where bad estates are difficult to let and can therefore be used readily for those whose need forces them to accept whatever is offered, certain estates became earmarked as suitable for the poor and the homeless.

Families had to go through the fight, the pain and the stigma of homelessness because they could not hold their family home together without abdicating self-reliance and declaring themselves homeless. They could not find their own home through normal channels and were forced into declared homelessness by severely restrictive allocation policies. In this, strict allocation appeared to replicate on the survey estates what private renting had produced: dense, crowded, poorly serviced and segregated areas of low-income housing.

Allocation through homelessness to the unpopular estates was a kind of slavery, a way of breaking a family's will to independence. One of the major effects was a kind of truculent resentment of the local authority, 'the master', and angry resignation to the stigma and the dependence that went with it. Desperate homeless families being rehoused by the GLC on their worst estates had little sense of gratitude or relief. This was one of the biggest factors in demoralizing and even angering estate staff. Not only did homeless families resent their landlord, but the landlord's representatives on the ground, the estate officers or housing managers, often resented homeless families for either grudgingly accepting or refusing offers on their estate. In London, where homelessness was a dominant avenue of access, it was considered the main problem and was constantly thrown up by housing officials and local politicians as a major reason for the failure to keep up standards of management on problematic estates. As an explanation it was patently absurd. Ironically, the stigma that was attached to homelessness was the very reason that councils were unable to treat homeless applicants like any others, but sometimes restricted offers to them either specifically to unpopular estates or to 'one offer only' or both. In London, two estates in our survey were designated hard to let and were reserved at crisis periods for the homeless families on the grounds that their needs were so great that they must be given priority over all other lettings. At various times they were allowed one offer only. In other words, lettings policies ensured that homelessness became the hallmark of unpopular estates. 'Dumping' was barely disguised.

The fact that homeless families were often relegated to the worst council properties created the impression that homelessness in itself was some kind of social offence. Such a suggestion would be nonsensical. It was simply a rationing system to force the poor and the vulnerable into the dwellings that no one else would choose to live in. The large estates were built with a dream of mass housing but they became minority housing. They would work for the rich but they rehoused almost exclusively the poor. They were meant to end slums, but they became in less than a generation tighter and more closed social ghettos than ever the back-to-backs were.

Racial Discrimination

Ghetto is a dangerously loaded word. None of the estates in the survey were total ghettos, though most of them housed, almost entirely, households from the lowest-income backgrounds, or increasingly unsupported, dependent households. This was much more true outside London than in London, however. Racially none of the estates were true ghettos such as exist in the United States public housing projects (Power, 1979, p. 62). However, in the nine estates of the survey located in areas with a high concentration of ethnic minorities, the estates housed disproportionate numbers of minority households. On the seven estates for which there were specific figures, the average number of households headed by a member of an ethnic minority was over 40 per cent. Yet the average for surrounding areas was 27 per cent. Therefore the gap between a representative proportion and the actual concentrations was considerable. On some estates half or more of the population belonged to racial minorities. The rehousing bias did not represent the housing choice of ethnic minorities, but a further mark of its unpopularity and decline.[1] In fact, very often minority households exercised no housing choice at all since they were coming across the rehousing system for the first time, were often in very great need and were vulnerable outsiders to the council housing market.

The incidence of homelessness and single parenthood was higher among non-white families seeking access to council accommodation than among white families (Parker and Dugmore, 1976, p. 23), and access to the least popular estates was most often linked with these three factors. On one survey estate in south-west London, before 1982 about 90 per cent of lettings were to homeless families, of whom 60 per cent were black. However, the relationship between homelessness and race did not account for the whole concentration of ethnic minorities on unpopular estates (ibid., p. 30). What seemed to happen was that, through homelessness, non-white families would get the most disfavoured and restricted offers. Within that narrow range, they would be concentrated on the very worst estates or the estates where there were already many non-white families.

The concentration of minority households was often taken as a proof of stigma, referred to frequently by estate staff as both a cause and a clear sign of the estate's decline. However, among residents, racial issues were rarely raised as evidence of decline.

Unemployment

Specific unemployment rates were known for ten of the twenty survey estates (1981 Census). The average number of males of working age seeking employment but unemployed on these estates was 57 per cent. Estates in Merseyside, Greater Manchester, and Tyneside were found where over 70 per cent of households had no breadwinner. Even on the London estates, where rates were much lower, unemployment was a rapidly growing problem, especially among the young, and was more than double the national average. For example, at Tulse Hill, Brixton, 40 per cent of all working-age adults were unemployed (1981 Census).

These unemployment figures showed a most serious position which is likely to have deteriorated significantly since 1981. It is hard to define at exactly what point a community breaks under social and economic dependence. But if more than half the population is not economically self-supporting, the consequent poverty and marginality of that community makes it extremely vulnerable. The consequences of such a state of affairs were experienced in the United States in widespread communal violence, rioting and looting, a pale shadow of which was seen in this country in 1981 and 1985. Many of the riots in the United States began in public housing estate ghettos (Kerner Commission, 1969, p. 68). The youth problems which were commonplace on the survey estates, coupled with the unemployment levels here described, made a Molotov cocktail which seriously alarmed local authorities.

Empty Property

The corollary of lettings problems was empty property. The number of empty properties on the estates was the clearest and crudest indicator both of the unpopularity of the estates and the cumbersome

Table 8.2 Void Properties on Twenty Estates (Excluding Voids in Capital Programmes)

Type of estate	Project starting date	Number of voids at start of project	Voids as % of total dwellings on estate
Cottage, north-west England	1979	7	1.5
Cottage, north of England	Feb. 1980	19	1.9
Cottage, Midlands	Feb. 1979	50	2.5
Cottage, north of England	1979	41	4.1
Cottage, north of England	July 1981	21	5.3
Cottage, Midlands	Jan. 1982	100	35.0
Cottage, north-west England	Jan. 1981	9	2.9
Walk-up, London	Apr. 1980	15	2.2
Walk-up, London	1978	*c.* 100	18.0
Walk-up, London	Mar. 1980	68	7.7
Walk-up, London		unknown	
Mainly walk-up, north-west England	Feb. 1980	79	4.1
Walk-up, London	July 1981	43	16.0
Modern, London	1980	8	0.5
Modern, London	1970	unknown	
Modern, London	1980	10*	1.2
Modern, London	Aug. 1981	34	3.2
Modern, London	Aug. 1979	62	6.2
Modern, London	July 1978	123	11.0
Modern, north-west England	Feb. 1981	140	13.8

Cottage average – 34
Walk-up average – 61
Modern average – 61

*Average
Source: Power, 1984, p. 19.

lettings policies. Only three of the twenty estates had a tenancy turnover and number of empty dwellings comparable with the rest of the local authority stock. But even these three estates had lettings problems in that they were unpopular with higher priority applicants and were difficult to let except to the most desperate households. A high turnover of tenants was common to sixteen of the estates, creating a constant supply of empty property.

At the outset of the special projects on eighteen of the twenty estates there was a total of over 900 empty dwellings (5 per cent of the total) with an average of fifty on each estate. However, there were wide fluctuations between estates that seemed as much a reflection of lettings incompetence or management diligence as of housing demand. Thus several London estates in areas of serious homelessness had more than 100 empty dwellings. Conversely, several northern estates in areas of low demand had relatively few empty dwellings. According to the 1981 Census, the 'voids' level in inner London was double the rate for outer London or for England as a whole. Voids on the survey estates within London varied greatly too, ranging from less than 1 per cent to 18 per cent (Table 8.2).

Repairs, control of empty property and rent collection were integrally connected with the smooth function of lettings, but were run totally separately. Therefore lettings departments took responsibility *only* for selecting tenants. They did not take responsibility for any of its consequences.

Empty dwellings forged a whole chain of problems that fed into the main arteries of estate life. They were a poor advertisement for the estates. It became hard to recruit caretakers to the estates with empty dwellings. Applicants for housing would be more likely to refuse an offer on a balcony or street with several other boarded-up properties. On some estates the local authority had all but abandoned attempts at letting property. In Liverpool, there were a number of estates where certain blocks were simply not offered by lettings staff to applicants.

Loss of Rent

The result of empty properties was the direct loss of rent and rates income to the council. The remote management structures and the global accounting systems put little emphasis on maximizing income as a way of paying for management and maintenance, on the strength of which dwellings would be kept occupied as a very high priority.

However, a strong incentive now lies in the substantial rent and rates income that each occupied dwelling generates since the big rent rises of the Conservative era (1979 onwards). We calculated that ten occupied dwellings paid the salary of one estate worker (Power, 1984, p. 21). On that basis, on average each of the twenty estates could in theory have generated enough income to pay for five additional estate workers if they were fully occupied. Several of the local authorities we visited, which had not established local management, claimed that they had no way of paying for local management and maintenance. Income from rent and rates was often earmarked to repay debt charges and to provide general council services, such as housing advice, homelessness admissions, members' inquiries and complaints. The idea had not taken root that management and maintenance were directly linked to rent incomes, even though such a high proportion of rent income now comes from housing benefit. Nor did local authorities generally recognize their primary housing duty as providing efficient landlord services. Town hall based functions were often more highly paid and valued than front-line jobs such as estate officers or caretakers. It was the vandalism and the cost of continually re-repairing damaged empty property rather than the loss of rent that forced remedial action upon the local authorities.

Vandalism

Empty dwellings on all but one of the estates in the survey were invariably heavily vandalized, usually within a few days of them becoming empty. Where the dwelling was modernized or was being modernized, everything of value would be stripped out. Most local authorities were convinced that it was the work of experienced thieves, although it was still commonly classed as vandalism. In one case, it was suggested that the building contractor actually being paid to do the repair work was also responsible for stealing the heating systems and other fittings. On only one estate was any kind of effective guarding instituted, and it was a continuous battle on all the others to outwit the vandals. On one estate, impregnable steel shuttering at the windows inspired vandalizing youth to climb on the roof, take the tiles off and force a way in. Only a human guard proved really effective and in eighteen out of twenty estates this was not contemplated because of the cost. Yet each vandalized property cost anything between £700 and £8,000 to restore. The cost of a full-time night-guard plus relief would be in the region of £12,000 a year, so any estate with twenty empty dwellings a year would have spent less on a guard than on repair to vandal-damage.

On the twenty estates, neighbours did not see fit to guard the empty property next door, in spite of their direct interest in seeing it occupied rather than destroyed. There were a number of reasons for this. If the police were called, it was claimed they often took two hours to come. In some cases, it was held, they never came. There was a genuine fear almost everywhere of reprisals. The process of alienation had bitten so deep that people often felt there was nothing to be gained by trying anyway. It was a lost cause. This latter view was based on long experience of nothing working. There was no sense of ownership or control on the part of landlord or tenant. Councils in every case blamed residents for failing to stop vandalism to empty property that did not even belong to them. Councils, by some strange misinterpretation of the meaning of a socially responsible landlord, assumed that the estate as a collective entity belonged to the collective residents who happened to live there, rather than to the council.

On the survey estate in Newcastle, it became cheaper to remove all the fittings, including the central heating system, when a house became empty and reinstate them later when an occupant was ready to move

161

in, because otherwise each time a house became vacant about £2,000 was lost through theft and vandalism. Similar experiences could be cited for most of the twenty estates.

As well as theft-oriented or purposeful vandalism, aimless vandalism occurred. Breaking things has always given a curious satisfaction, like crunching a Coca-Cola can underfoot. Occupied property was very rarely vandalized on any of the estates. In fact, it was almost unheard of except for broken windows. Even vandalism to occupied garages was much less common than to unoccupied garages. Most of the vandalism to empty properties on the poor estates should therefore have been stoppable, if the above analysis is correct, by simply occupying or providing guards for all property. The same logic should apply to open spaces and all other communal or unoccupied areas, as well as to dwellings. Occupation and use have proved the most useful deterrents to vandalism.

Squatting

Squatting is a further consequence of empty property. It has one element in common with vandalism: it is a cause and effect of lawlessness on the poorer estates. There is an almost irrefutable logic to the argument that needy people have a right to occupy empty property that would otherwise be vandalized. Squatting took place at some point on ten of the twenty estates, but only five estates, all in London, housed squatters on any scale. The fact that the problem was concentrated in London was mainly a result of the loss of private-rented accommodation and the demolition of most old, decayed areas where people on the edge of the economy and the law previously tucked themselves away. There was real housing need among squatting groups, found cheek by jowl with empty council property, on a large scale in some boroughs. The empty property represented lack of management rather than lack of need. The boroughs that came down hard on squatters tended to keep their property occupied and avoid the problem. The inner London boroughs, with serious management problems, tended to attract squatters into their many empty council dwellings. Ironically these were often areas of great social need and a high incidence of homelessness. The inefficient lettings system with large numbers of empty dwellings seemed to be coupled with widespread squatting. It was tempting to conclude that the highly centralized lettings system to some extent generated both squatting and homelessness.

It was the experience of residents and housing managers up and down the country that squatting sometimes brought with it many forms of social abuse including drugs, noise, all-night parties, large numbers of extra occupants, and disregard of neighbourhood conventions. Conflict with bona fide tenants has been common among squatting groups in the inner London boroughs, and the complete lack of sympathy meted out to squatters by estate residents was not necessarily, as is often suggested by liberal outside observers, a sign of bigotry and intolerance on the part of more traditional residents. Rather it was a function of the extreme difficulties of estate-living, where one group, whose members were in any case prepared to run the gauntlet of the law and were not afraid of the police or the courts, did not accept that noise and other anti-social behaviour was the business of those directly affected by it. Associated as squatting has often become with an anarchistic and individualistic view of society, it was likely, leaving aside the more extreme forms of social abuse, that squatters would not accommodate easily to a densely built-up and often dissatisfied community where individual behaviour is magnified and impact on others maximized.

Transient Occupiers

On some estates unused buildings encouraged unsettled, transient occupiers, the casualties from society's safety net. It seemed fair that they should fit in where they could and it was perhaps inevitable that they would find a niche in the least desirable estates. However, their presence threatened even further the many tentative balances within the community.

Increasingly, travellers and gypsies were moving in and out of the least popular peripheral estates as camp sites were drying up around the northern parts of the country, and even in one case in inner London and another in central Birmingham. Illegal transient occupants caused a staggering amount of grief and dismay on three estates we visited, partly because of the noise of numerous dogs and children, but mainly because of their trade in refuse, their lorries and caravans and their asphalting equipment (now part of many travellers' trade), parked on the open areas of estates.

Squatting and transient occupation seemed inevitable where empty property on a wide scale existed alongside housing need. They created resentment where they were coupled with failure to generate or back up strong social controls aimed at restricting behaviour to acceptable levels of noise and nuisance. Illegal occupation was not the only source of social abuse, but on several estates it was a major element in a general environment of disarray.

Conclusion

Lettings officers were hand-picked and trained to have as little sense of identity with individual applicants as possible in order to detach them from the highly pressured and stressful situations of both the customers for council housing and the receiving communities. Estate workers therefore exercised very little control or influence over lettings.

The combined impact of centralized, segregating letting policies and large numbers of empty and vandalized dwellings was endlessly depressing to residents and estate workers.

Note to Chapter 8

1   This may no longer be true of some Asian-dominated estates in the Spitalfields area of Tower Hamlets.

Chapter Nine

Repairs, Rents, Cleansing and Caretaking

> Overriding concern with numbers of dwellings built appears to have diverted attention from the need for increased housing management and maintenance to keep step with numbers and to cope with new sophisticated designs.
>
> (Burbidge *et al.*, 1981, Vol. 1, p. 3)

Repairs were central to the estate officers' direct relations with tenants, but almost always totally removed from his or her influence or jurisdiction. In all cases in the survey bar one, repairs were handled by a separate department. Therefore even the chief housing officer was unable to exact the necessary repairs service since its delivery was not under his or her control. Without direct control over or responsibility for day-to-day repairs, an estate manager could not satisfy tenants' needs (Burbidge *et al.*, 1981, Vol. 1, p. 8), since at least 60 per cent of tenants' requests related to repairs (Parliamentary Commission for Administration, 1983). The more remote and inefficient the repairs service, the higher that percentage was likely to be. In addition, the basic fabric of a house must be kept in good working order if it is not to become a slum.

Yet the repairs departments are not directly responsible in most local authorities for keeping houses in good order. This is the Housing Department's responsibility. The repairs departments are expected to respond as best they can to housing officers' requests for work. The endless inter-departmental squabbles that arise from that relationship, the so-called 'client-role' – lost job tickets, incorrectly ordered jobs, access problems, incomplete work, trade demarcations and other bureaucratic confusions – serve only to eat up resources and alienate tenants. In the end neither department took responsibility for the repairs. In the local authorities we visited, complaints from senior officers in the repairs departments about the incompetence and inefficiency of housing management and the irresponsibility and destructiveness of tenants were endless. Similarly, housing officers' tales of badly done work, long delays, and lost job tickets were almost continuous. On all but one of the estates in the survey, prior to local management, the repairs service was inefficient, and in some cases, delinquent, with patently dishonest practices at work. In three cases this resulted in investigations and legal action.

In Hackney, the manual unions calculated that only 33 per cent of their time was spent on actual repairs (Federation of Hackney Tenants' Associations, 1982, p. 2); the rest went on travel, paper work, waiting for materials and so on. Men were often tied to bonus systems that allowed almost no flexibility. In one direct labour organization, job times were calculated down to tenths of a second. In most local authorities, job times, on which bonuses were based, encouraged shoddy work and made some jobs much more desirable than others. Maximum bonus for the week could sometimes be earned by Tuesday. In one case the men earned a better bonus if they sat doing nothing than if they worked – they simply ensured that jobs were left undone through 'no access'. In another local authority where there were bonus penalties for no access, the records for genuinely abortive jobs calls through no access were simply destroyed. All record of the job ever having been reported was thereby lost.

Trade demarcations also attempted to lay down to the last nail and splinter of wood whose job was what, so a carpenter or plumber, if both were needed for a job, could both get their bonuses. Often one tradesman would finish his part of the job and collect his bonus, but the rest of the job would be left undone, either because the complicated system of a job being complete for one trade but requiring re-ordering for another broke down, or because the bonus for finishing off a job might not be good enough.

On flatted estates, workers would fight over who got ground floor jobs; materials would be dropped over balconies instead of the more laborious method of carrying them downstairs. Where glass panes were being replaced, it was common to hammer out the glass and leave it lying on the tarmac or grass below. Many a grass-cutting machine was damaged in this way. Spare materials were left lying around, as this was easier than carrying them back to the van or the depot. When a tenant of a GLC estate complained about a cast-iron drainpipe that had been left outside her door by the repairsmen for weeks, the foreman said: 'That's odd, it should have been pinched by now. We never take left-overs away.'

Tenants' views of this type of service ranged from scorn to anger. Estate officers, unaware that it should be a normal part of their job to *run* a repairs service, either accepted with cynicism or despair the hopelessness of trying to get things done better, or added their anger and frustration to the tenants'. In our survey, no repairs service worked to the satisfaction of housing managers prior to local management. It was the major cause of the physical decline of property.

We had no way of judging whether the repairs service to better estates was better, but it is very probable that this would be the case. There would be more political impetus, more pressure from the community, and a better housing stock to work with. Repairsmen also preferred to work on better estates, like everyone else.

Because there was no commitment within the local authorities either to base repairs locally or to integrate them firmly with estate management, the estates in the survey ranged from dilapidated and decayed to positively dangerous. The recent stock condition survey (DOE, 1985) lends weight to this contention. The long-term prognosis for many of the estates was as a consequence fatal, and in many people's minds poor council housing was like poor quality furniture. It wore out quickly, was not worth repairing and should be junked rather than restored.

Rents, Arrears and Legal Sanctions

With little or no say in lettings and little or no control over repairs, local estate officers often seemed like the emperor with no clothes, parading authority but commanding very little. There were numerous partial tasks that accrued to the local housing officer, from checking empty property, to inspecting the dwelling of a tenant wanting a transfer. City University counted over thirty designated jobs for housing managers in one of the survey authorities (Legg, 1981, p. 74). The one area they were invariably held responsible for was rent arrears which took up a major chunk of a housing officer's time (ibid., pp. 76–81, 92). However, on most estates, the estate officer's control over actual rent collection was minimal since only three of the local authorities in our survey still used door-to-door collection. All three projects were on cottage estates outside or on the edge of the big cities, and in two of the three, door-to-door collection was only carried out on the better and 'safer' parts of the estate. Only where door-to-door collection applied to all tenants did it really work since, given the choice, irregular payers often opted out of the door-to-door system in favour of other methods (Duncan and Kirby, 1984, p. 26). Rent collections provided an umbilical link between the households and the landlord, and served to pick up repairs orders and complaints, as well as endless other queries and problems. Arrears were lower on the three estates, but were still much higher on two of the three estates than for the rest of the local authority stock. Door-to-door collection overcame many of the hurdles to rent payment, even where there were economic and social problems. This was partly because of the personal contact, the pressure and the mutual sense of responsibility it created. Most important, it gave shape and identity to the landlord and it placed the initiative for achieving the goal of rent payment firmly in the hands of the housing officer.

On the remaining seventeen estates, tenants either paid at a rent office, a rent van or the district office, or they paid by giro (Table 9.1). Department of Environment research showed that nationally giro payment was the most arrears-prone system (ibid., p. 26). Rent arrears on the twenty problem estates were held by the local authorities to be much higher than in the rest of the local authority with only one exception. On thirteen of the fourteen estates where arrears information was complete, the unpopular project estates had on average double the arrears of their local authority as a whole.

The average arrears level across *all* households on nineteen of the twenty estates was over £50 per household (Table 9.2), whereas only *one council tenant in twenty* was found in the DOE report to have arrears of over £50 (ibid., p. 20). The extremely high levels of arrears were not surprising given the levels of unemployment, the incidence of one-parent families, the previous experience of homelessness, and the large proportion of children. All these factors influenced levels of arrears (ibid., pp. 41, 42, 45). Arrears were worse in the big cities, and almost certainly related directly to the nature of the stock, the proportion of flats, the social deprivation, the size of landlord, and the housing management structures. The proportion of elderly tenants in arrears was extremely small everywhere (ibid., p. 41). It was felt that elderly people had reached a settled point in their life and had become, with hard experience, better managers. Elderly people were less susceptible to fluctuating incomes. It is also possible that older people

Table 9.1 Methods of Rent Payment

	Number of estates*
Rent collected door to door	3
At estate office	6
Fortnightly rent van	1
At district office or area rent office	12
Giro	9

*Some estates had more than one method of rent payment, therefore total exceeds twenty.

Source: Power, 1984, p. 23.

Table 9.2 Rent Collection Method, Type of Estate and Arrears

Estate	Main method of rent collection	Average gross rent 1982–3	Average debt per household for *all* households 1982–3
Cottage, north-west England	door-to-door; rent office	£14–50	£14–49
Cottage, North	giro	£19	£63
Cottage, Midlands	estate office; district office	£22	£95
Cottage, north of England	rent office	£22	£160
Cottage, north of England	estate office; door-to-door	£19	£76
Cottage, north-west England	district office	£20	£81
Cottage, Midlands	estate office; door-to-door	£22	£170
Walk-up, London	giro; rent office	£25	£98
Walk-up, London	fortnightly rent van; district office	£25	£54
Walk-up, London	giro	£25	£186
Walk-up, London	estate office	£25	£218
Walk-up, north-west England	giro; district office	£30*	£230
Walk-up, London	giro; district rent offices	£21	NA
Modern, London	estate office; district office	£39*	£50
Modern, London	giro	£30	£128
Modern, London	giro	£33*	£188
Modern, London	giro; district rent office	£39*	£253
Modern, London	district office	£26	£235
Modern, north-west England	estate office, district office	£22	£114
Modern, London	district office; giro	£40*	£368

*includes district heating charge.
Source: Power, 1984, p. 70.

were more 'grateful' to the landlord and had better rent-paying habits, born in the years of chronic shortage and more ruthless evictions. Pensioners are in real terms no longer as poor as the poorest families, particularly large families, one-parent families, and families with no wage-earner. The demands and needs of children are often very hard for poor families to meet (Piachaud, 1979).

According to the Department of Environment study, the most significant group of households in serious arrears was one-parent families, one-quarter of whom were seriously behind with their rent (over £50) (Duncan and Kirby, 1984). On the estates in the survey, and on problem estates in general, the proportion of one-parent families was extremely high. This would help account for very high arrears in the survey estates.

The actual cost of operating the rent accounts under the mechanical system was high and, under the giro system, usually higher than the labour-intensive door-to-door system (Audit Commission, 1984, p. 32). Of course, added to the actual cost was the cost in greatly increased arrears. Staff jobs had been cut on the ground, but banking services, giro charges, computer systems within the local authority and the multiplication of paper procedures that went with the increasing remoteness had all added to costs while reducing efficiency.

City University research (Legg, 1981, pp. 90–1) showed that even after the abolition of door-to-door rent collection and the computer-ization of rent accounting, over 50 per cent of housing managers' and estate officers' time was spent on checking and chasing arrears (mainly checking). Because of the increases in arrears,[1] this had inevitably been an expanding and increasingly burdensome part of the estate officer's role, even though some local authorities had given up door-to-door collection in the hope of releasing management time for more productive work (LCC, Minutes of Housing Committee, 28 Sept. 1960).

Table 9.3 Pattern of Arrears

		Average arrears in weeks
Location	Out of London	5
	In London	7
Type of estate	Cottage	4.4
	Flatted	6
Collection method	Door-to-door	4
	Office	6
	Giro	6

Source: Power, 1984, pp. 23–5.

Table 9.3 shows the number of weeks in arrears owed on average by each household according to different types and location of estates in the survey. Weeks in arrears were the clearest measure because they took account of differences in rent levels in different boroughs. However, average arrears problems did not reflect household differences and other factors influencing arrears levels (Duncan and Kirby, 1984, pp. 41–6). Flatted estates, location in London, and impersonal rent collection were all shown to be related to high arrears. The incidence of one-parent families was greater in London and this may also have affected arrears levels.

The exhaustive Department of the Environment rent arrears survey (ibid., pp. 97–9) found that management, as well as social factors, were closely related to arrears (see Figure 9.1). Figure 9.2 illustrates clearly the relationship nationally between method of collection and serious arrears. Only 6 per cent of serious arrears cases were part of the door-to-door system, while 42 per cent of all tenants paid their rent that way. Over 80 per cent of tenants paying a rent collector had no arrears, but only 65 per cent of tenants paying by giro had no arrears. By contrast, 6 per cent of tenants in serious arrears paid a collector whereas 94 per cent of tenants with serious arrears paid either at an office or through some purely impersonal method (Figure 9.3). However, because of the threat of attack on rent collectors it appeared highly unlikely that door-to-door collection would be reintroduced in major cities.

The Audit Commission report on local authorities' rent arrears in 1984 drew similar conclusions from its close look at the London boroughs. Arrears were up to 50 per cent higher in poorly managed

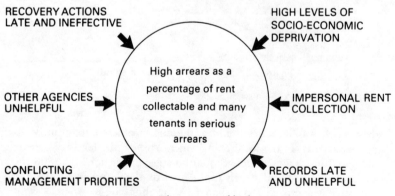

Figure 9.1 The pattern of high arrears

Source: Duncan and Kirby, 1984

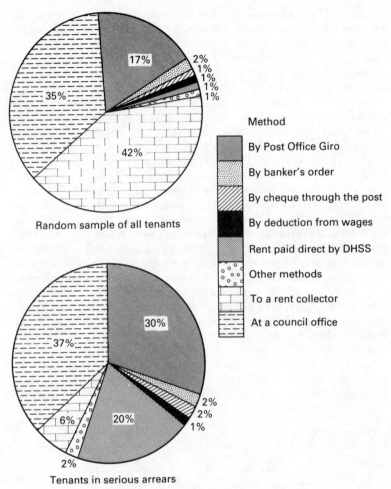

Figure 9.2 Usual rent payment method

Source: Duncan and Kirby, 1984, p. 26.

areas with similar social and economic problems than in well-managed areas. In the local management survey, the levels of arrears fluctuated more widely between authorities and regions than did the levels of poverty and deprivation. Five of the London estates had arrears that averaged more than £200 per household, whereas eight estates (seven of which were outside London) carried an average debt per household of less than £100. The range from £14 average debt on

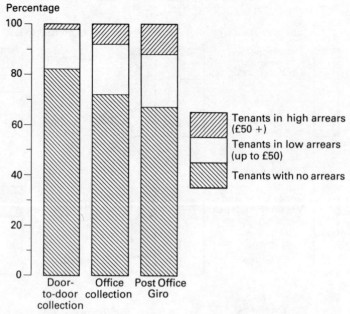

Figure 9.3 Percentage of tenants in arrears for each major payment method

Source: Duncan and Kirby, 1984, p. 27.

the lowest estate (north) to £368 on the highest (London) clearly related to management methods and wider factors as well as family circumstances, and rent levels, given the lower unemployment rates on the London estates than in the north. Average rents outside London were £19 a week and in London £30 a week. Arrears varied between authorities by a factor of twenty-five. A major factor was the style of the local authority landlord. Figure 9.4 illustrates the range of interlocking problems affecting arrears levels, in relation to more general problems on difficult-to-let estates. The most significant finding illustrated is the growing use of eviction as a tool of arrears control in authorities with impersonal rent collection methods.

For the estate officer, as with virtually all other aspects of his or her job, rents had become a thankless, remote, seemingly endless task of harassment and paper chasing. He or she no longer actually did the job in most cases but had to try to make the Post Office or the computer do it instead. In one of the local authorities in the survey, there were forty-three possible stages in the rent arrears procedure (Legg, 1981, pp. 76–81), only a handful of which would be personally

173

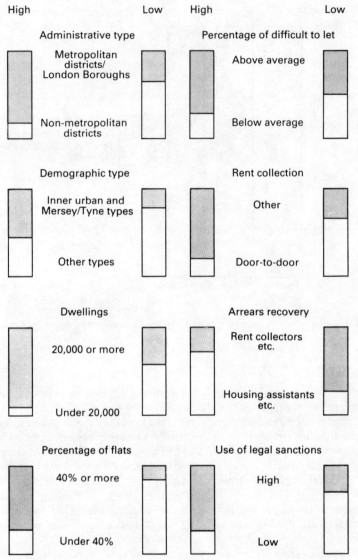

Figure 9.4 Key characteristics of high and low arrears authorities

Source: Duncan and Kirby, 1984, p. 97.

performed by the estate officer. It is hard to retain a sense of control or standards of efficiency over so many transactions.

It was ironic that local authorities with high arrears more frequently resorted to legal sanctions, primarily eviction. In many cases, this was ineffective in recovering arrears because the process was slow and rarely backed up with personal contact, and the action was often initiated after the rent debt had already reached an almost irretrievable level.

The central problem with the removal of door-to-door collection was that the threat of eviction became the commonest sanction. Previously, personal contact exercised a strong pull on the tenant, avoiding a direct legal threat. Because eviction was the culmination of a complex legal procedure, long drawn-out steps had to be taken. Court proceedings were not only extremely costly and time-consuming, they were intensely alienating to the tenant and in many cases were simply ignored. In Lambeth, only a minority of tenants showed up in court for the final possession proceedings. Living on the council's very worst estates, they were often resigned to the prospect of being evicted by the council and taken in again as homeless. Sometimes they were ignorant of the court process altogether. From the point of view of the estate officer, the initiation of court proceedings was often a purely mechanical operation. Senior officers rather than estate officers actually went to court and, in most cases, an eviction had to be authorized by the housing committee itself. Therefore the estate officer had very little involvement in the court proceedings or any sense of the ultimate consequences for the family. Eviction, as a central tool of rent collection, was generating a growing pool of disaffected, indebted households who were almost past being afraid of it.

Most directors of housing we spoke to cited the difficulty in obtaining an eviction, and the statutory obligation to rehouse homeless families after they had been evicted, as major causes of arrears. They felt they had no sanctions that worked. We came across no case where families with children were evicted purely for rent arrears and refused rehousing on the grounds that they were intentionally homeless. But the fact that eviction is used much more rarely where there is door-to-door collection underlines the need not for tougher sanctions, but for a more personal and direct approach.

In our view, the fact that rehousing after eviction removed the harshest edge from court sanctions against arrears was not a cause of increasing arrears. Rather the constant resort to ineffectual rent retrieval methods, the remote collection method and the bureaucratic, de-personalized follow-up, including the threat of eviction, were the major causes of higher arrears. The problems of eviction, with the disaffection and transience they bred, simply highlighted the need for a very different approach – with speedy, personal follow-up to prevent the brutalization and further transience of the most vulnerable households who no longer felt responsible for their debts because the system was so far removed.

There was a chain-effect between housing a poor population with many one-parent families, adopting arrears-prone methods of collection and debt recovery, preventing transfers of arrears cases but facilitating transfers of other households, thus enhancing the incidence of disadvantaged households (frequently one-parent families), and arrears cases. The impact on the households who did pay and on estate staff was both to accelerate flight and to encourage greater delinquency among those remaining. It was alarmingly common to be told by tenants: 'They don't pay their rent, so why should I?' People's alienation from their surroundings and their awareness that they were receiving a bad service, made them much less willing to pay their rent (Legg, 1981, pp. 76–81; Power, 1984, p. 24). Withholding rent was one of the few weapons tenants felt they had. The fact that arrears in the end led to eviction, even poorer (if possible) rehousing offers and subsequent reduced motivation to pay rent completed the cycle that led directly to 'sink' estates. For where else could 'bad tenants' be evicted to?

Cleansing and Caretaking

Parks Department and Care of Open Space

On a majority of estates in the survey, the parks department, quite separately from housing, repairs and maintenance, or cleansing, was responsible for maintaining communal gardens, grass verges, lawns and flower beds. Most estates had open planted areas. An absurd situation commonly arose whereby the parks department was not responsible for removing litter from grass and flower beds though it *was* responsible for cutting, hoeing and weeding. Lawn mowers commonly shredded litter while they cut the grass. Decorative shrubberies and rose-beds, where they survived, were often packed with litter between the bushes. Only on the philanthropic housing trust estates, among all those we visited, was this problem resolved by uniting within one job, under the estate manager, the warden/cleaner/porter who was also responsible for any planted areas.

It was an administrative nonsense that housing departments were actually paying out from their meagre management budgets substantial amounts to parks departments for a job that could more easily be done by resident staff within the housing department. It was also ironic that the generous planning of open space to provide often large green areas on some of the most depressing and deprived estates should be so poorly maintained. Parks departments were prepared to mow up the litter along with the grass because they were working on housing territory and *not* a park or a 'public' grass verge; therefore they did not feel responsible for the quality of job they did. Most parks departments do an excellent job *except* on estates; it is extremely rare even in the most depressed cities to see a dirty, unkempt park.

Refuse and Cleansing Service

On all estates, street cleaning and refuse disposal were dealt with by other departments. It would have been quite possible to deduce on some estates that no rates were being paid and residents were not entitled to a refuse service. On one estate, where there were large numbers of families with over three children, the very large families were entitled to a second dustbin. The dustmen simply threw the additional bins into the automated dustcarts after they were issued to the families and the housing department felt powerless to do anything. The director said that if he took any action, all the men would be out on strike and there would be no refuse service at all. It turned out on investigation that no one had discussed with the men the extra dustbin emptying involved. Industrial relations within the local authority were notoriously bad. Elsewhere, shopkeepers in a row of shops that backed on to a very large estate simply put out and piled up their refuse all week at the back of the shops, on the tarmac courtyard of the estate, on to which the front doors of the blocks of flats opened. The Chinese take-away put out piles of chewed spare-ribs. From there they were spread by dogs around the flats. The rates and valuers' department was in charge of shop rentals. It took eighteen months for the three departments – housing, rates and cleansing – to agree on the siting and structure of a refuse store for the shops. There had never been one before.

On another estate the paladins (large moveable dustbins) were too small to take all the refuse from the chutes. Previous daily collections were reduced to twice weekly collections. The dustmen were paid a 'spillage bonus' because of the overflow of rubbish, on which basis caretakers would not sweep up on refuse days. The dustmen did not clear up either, since no one checked on them. In addition they refused to empty overfull paladins because it was extremely difficult and dirty work to pull them out of the normally blocked rubbish chutes. So for the following week, tenants had to put rubbish in plastic bags outside the overflowing refuse area. Dogs tore open the bags and scattered the rubbish. The men the following week had even stronger grounds for refusing to remove the rubbish or empty the bins since the whole area around the chute was blocked. Rubbish sometimes went over the balcony as a gesture of defiant alienation and aggression.

A farcical refuse problem arose on an estate where no dustbins were provided and where there were large concrete litter bins dotted around the estate. Tenants put their black plastic rubbish bags in these bins in an attempt to dispose of refuse tidily, so the bins were constantly overflowing. The response of the cleansing department was to remove the litter bins altogether. They pointed to the resulting filth on the estate as proof that tenants were the cause of the problem.

The kind of cowboy refuse services described here were prevalent in various fragments on fourteen of the estates in the survey, and all twenty estates were dirty, although the cleansing department was not responsible for keeping estate areas clean, only for organized refuse collection and some of the estate roads. We found only one housing department in the country (not among the nineteen local authorities in the survey) where an adequate cleansing service operated on large, poor estates. Only where there was strong housing management and a well-organized manual caretaking service to supplement refuse collection did the cleansing system work at all adequately. It was useless to leave the whole responsibility to a separate department.

The way the estates were built greatly enhanced the refuse problems. House by house, in streets, it has been possible to expand refuse capacity. But in blocks of flats, refuse storage areas and rubbish chutes, if they were big enough thirty to fifty years ago, often no longer are. It is costly and difficult to expand them and their inherent problems remain: easy to block with bulky rubbish, accessible to dogs if protective doors are not maintained, subject to fires and other vandalism because they are unguarded targets.

Refuse stores in basements of blocks were equally unworkable. Bags would burst as refuse men tried to clear them. They would then refuse to move the spilt rubbish and the area would degenerate. Dogs would get in, communal keys would get lost, doors would finally get broken. Caretakers would give up on a losing battle to keep them clean.

There was a continuous flow of surplus rubbish on all the estates, but especially on the dense, flatted estates and no effective system for staying ahead of it. Without more capacity to hold the rubbish, the estates could not be kept clean, and they were not.

Caretaking

It was of overriding importance to have resident caretaking in the management of flatted estates. Cleaning of communal areas, maintenance of balcony and staircase lighting, emergencies in lifts, a contact point for calls to the police, and evening patrols were all vital roles for a resident caretaker. Without a resident caretaker, it became extremely difficult to deal with emergencies such as flooding, which could affect flats several floors below.

There were thirteen flatted estates in our survey. Eleven of these had resident caretakers prior to local management, but on several there were only resident caretakers in the tower blocks, and on two, less than half the designated caretaking posts were filled. Housing directors often said that it was no longer possible to recruit resident caretakers to such estates, in spite of offering rent-free accommodation and secure, long-term employment.

Parts of most estates comprising maisonettes and flats in large blocks from four to eight storeys were without resident caretakers. One estate had an unpopular mobile caretaking service where gangs of men would move in and out of large numbers of estates, somewhat similar to Panda-car policing. No one knew who they were, when they were to come, or how long they might stay. Caretakers' unions sometimes pressed hard for a conversion to the mobile system as a way out of the growing unpopularity of the resident posts and the fear of attack. On one survey estate, caretakers were only prepared to work in pairs, after attacks on staff. Union leaders argued fiercely that with proper organization the mobile system would work as well as, or even better than the resident system. But tenants felt that it threw the baby out with the bathwater, making the caretaking role unpopular and ineffectual. That is exactly what happened on one estate in the survey, where resident jobs were converted to mobile jobs and were finally withdrawn altogether.

On no estate were caretakers answerable to estate officers, or even integrated with them in a team approach to the estate as the only other estate-based housing employees. On two of the estates, dedicated caretakers were holding together the basic housing management against almost impossible odds. On most estates, caretakers felt unsupported and unsupervised, vulnerable to physical abuse and attack, unappreciated by tenants, and carrying out hopeless and undignified tasks that were no sooner done than they would be undone. The trend was definitely away from caretaking as a resident, manual job. And yet without it, it was impossible to see how the flatted estates could be managed at all. A most essential job had been undervalued. Resident caretaking was the last line to the landlord and it had almost seized up.

Social Services Responsibility

One major department that should have been closely involved on the twenty estates was the social services department. In practice, however, although many or the majority of social work clients live on council estates, it was rare to encounter a social worker in the course

179

of housing management work on the twenty estates. There is a historic adversary relationship between housing workers and social workers, because housing workers have to try and keep the lid on social problems for the sake of good management and the majority population of an estate. They are frequently forced to argue either for the removal of a household causing nuisance on an estate or for the transfer of a 'good' tenant away from a 'bad' one. They are also expected to take proceedings against tenants for rent arrears and eventually go to court 'against' the family for possession of their home. Social workers, on the other hand, have a duty to support the families with housing problems and also to argue for the housing rights of the most needy and sometimes the most disturbed families.

An ex-social services director, who became housing director in a northern authority, summed up the conflict of roles: 'Why should I worry about rent arrears? It's more important for the kids to have shoes for school.' He resigned as housing director three years later. A good housing officer is supposed to run a tight ship in tune with the vast majority of 'respectable, rent-paying, quiet, clean and orderly households' (Macey and Baker, 1982, p. 304). A good social worker is supposed to understand the multiple problems of people who cannot cope and to help them without judging or pressuring them. Therefore the housing officer is likely to see the social worker as soft, starry-eyed and even a do-gooder, while the social worker will often see the housing officer as hard-bitten, judgemental, bigoted, unjust and superior, or simply tough.

Social services departments were often pouring in disproportionate resources to an unco-ordinated and seemingly fruitless effort. As an illustration, on a northern cottage estate there were at one time eight social workers and community workers and not a single full-time housing worker. The social problems of that estate continued to mount out of all proportion to its size or physical characteristics, and the very enlightened and constructive social services department appeared powerless to change it. This estate was not included in our survey because there was still no local housing management and it was still in a relentless state of decline.

Given the incidence of homelessness, single-parenthood, unemployment and the lack of skilled wage-earners, it was not surprising that unpopular estates had disproportionate recourse to the social services. The number of social services referrals on a London estate in the survey was six times higher than for the surrounding areas (Burbidge *et al.*, 1981, Vol. 3). The social needs of unpopular estates were out of all proportion to the size of the population they housed.

A disturbing finding of the survey was that in no case had there been any formal liaison between housing and the social services departments in operation, prior to local housing management. It does not mean that in most cases relations were bad. This was the exception. But generally, as with cleansing, repairs and parks, each department held the other responsible for the shortcomings of divided responsibility. In the case of social services, it was hard to see a way of combining the best interests of both departments within the present framework.

Socially Disturbed Households

It was not commonly recognized either by housing or social services departments that anti-social behaviour could not be adequately contained on large, unpopular estates, particularly of flats. Unneighbourly households are in a tiny minority (CHAC, 1969, p. 2), and while their access to council housing is important, special social and housing provision must be made to support them and constrain their impact. Otherwise, there is no community within which such households can be contained and various institutions, prisons, children's homes and mental hospitals take over. Sadly, on many poor estates, both housing management and social services support are so weak that such families may drive out more normal, coping families and end up in a ransacked, half empty, crazed slum, which tenants can only think of demolishing as the way out. Blocks in Salford, Islington and Liverpool reached this state.[2] None of these communities survived.

This could happen on a much bigger scale unless the resources of social services departments are somehow brought to bear on local housing management. The need for housing officers and caretakers to respond to social needs was becoming constantly more pressing. Elderly people and small children were particularly vulnerable and easy to keep an eye on, yet this was rarely done. As one London housing director put it, 'We're here to run estates, not look after people'. Housing management is about both, although estates must of course be run properly if they are to be of any use.

Enforcement of Tenancy Conditions

Each tenant makes a legally binding agreement with the landlord, giving him the right to enjoy the peace and security of his home, and the duty to help his neighbours enjoy the same, as well as to protect the landlord's property and use it only as a home.

But estate officers and caretakers in the survey authorities universally felt that they had lost their previous authority and status, and that it was pointless even attempting to control noise, dog abuse, rubbish nuisance, disputes, or even, on some estates, illegal occupancy, all of which could constitute legally prosecutable offences. These abuses disrupted the lives of many or most residents to varying degrees on all the estates.

The only management tools invoked to resolve the social conflicts generated by abuse were transfers away from the problem for the discontented tenant who appeared to be the injured party, commonly known as a 'management transfer', or eviction for those in arrears. Eviction was almost never used on other management grounds. The result was virtual anarchy on some estates and very little respect for tenancy conditions among some tenants on all the estates. Because of the social disarray that resulted, council employees often despised and disregarded the communities they were employed to serve. The communities themselves felt quite unable to enforce standards of behaviour on their neighbours. There was fear of victimization, a feeling that you should mind your own business and a sense of not belonging. It was hard to collaborate with neighbours who were often seen as part of the problem. Prior to opening the estate office on an inner London estate, the commonest complaint was the abuse of neighbours (summary of findings from tenant consultations, June to September 1980, Power, PEP, 1980). With careful investigation and questioning, the extreme transgressors were narrowed down to eight households on an estate of over 900 flats. Yet many tenants lived in fear of burglary, mugging, squatting, dogs and drugs. There had indeed been several violent and vicious attacks and the world beyond the front door was felt to be dangerous as a result.

Notes to Chapter 9

1 Arrears increased by 35 per cent in the nineteen local authorities between 1979 and 1982.
2 Ordsall Flats, Salford; Myrtle Gardens, Liverpool; Blythe Mansions, Islington; none of which were in our survey because no attempt was made to tackle the problems through housing management. Ordsall Flats and Myrtle Gardens were emptied of tenants and sold to private developers; Blythe Mansions were demolished.

PART THREE

Changing the Landlord Tradition: Findings of the Survey

Chapter Ten

Local Offices on Unpopular Estates

Genius is one per cent inspiration and ninety-nine per cent perspiration.

(Thomas A. Edison, 1896)

Where an estate had declined through neglect, poverty and lack of coherent management, a local base was needed from which essential services, contact with residents and supervision of work could be organized. Other attempts had been made on many of the estates, primarily costly physical improvements or adaptations, but also sometimes initiatives involving social services, community provision and changes in lettings policies. The fortunes of problem estates were not to be reversed by these piecemeal attacks on a multi-sided problem that constantly reappeared in a new shape.

A few authorities had operated part-time surgeries without allocating full-time staff with responsibility for day-to-day management to an estate. These provided some kind of link but did not change the central management structure or tackle the problems where they arose. They were most often a simple reporting service. They too failed to reverse the overall conditions of run-down estates.

We were convinced by every visit we made that only a meticulous, detailed, day-by-day approach to all aspects of running an estate – rents, repairs, lettings, caretaking and cleaning, welfare and communal law enforcement – would win back the confidence and self-respect of the residents, thereby providing a basis for rebuilding a sound housing investment and a workable housing community.

A Change of Direction: Going Local

In March 1979, only three councils throughout the whole of England had full-time, estate-based management offices (Figure 10.1). In the following three years, the idea gained ground and by January 1982 nineteen councils operated forty-five projects (Power, 1984, pp. 60–2). The nineteen local authorities represented only a tiny minority of the 403 local authorities in England and Wales. By June 1984, the number actually running full-time estate offices had risen to nearer thirty local authorities, but it was still a trifling effort compared with the scale of the problem, although the thirty local authorities involved covered more than a dozen critical London authorities and several other major cities.

Local Offices
The effect of the local offices on the life of the estates in the survey was immediate and extensive. Once tenancy records were moved from the town hall or district to the estate, all contact between the landlord and

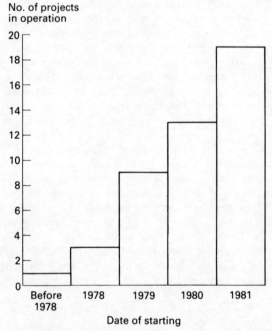

Figure 10.1   Starting dates of estate-based management offices

Source: Power, 1984, p. 15.

tenant was filtered through the local office. This did away with the dual system, based on tenants having to go to a district or central office for what they wanted and, separately, an estate officer having to visit tenants for what the landlord wanted, both sides frequently bypassing the other, and the information and action being constantly disjointed. Many things had been left unreported or unattended by virtue of previous experience of fruitless journeys and abortive visits (Legg, 1981, pp. 67, 72).

The most immediate impact of the local offices was to open the floodgates to tenants' requests and complaints. All full-time offices reported extensive and continuous use. Some did not record carefully how many users came to the office. However, on average one-fifth of residents called at a local office each week (Power, 1984). There were wide fluctuations in the number of callers, depending on three factors: hours of opening; amount of local responsibility; and willingness of staff to give advice and support on welfare and financial matters as well as on housing. The most used office was in Walsall, with 360 callers a week, where all functions were devolved to the neighbourhood management office, and where the office was open all day. In the Rhondda, South Wales (not in the survey), about seventy callers a day was the average over two years on an estate of 1,000 dwellings. We never went to an estate office open to tenants where there was no tenant in the office over some matter. In only one office, where the officer was on his own, did we encounter the strained, beleaguered attitude to tenants so common in large housing departments.

Half the offices were open all day, every day, and these were the offices that did best in controlling empty dwellings. As a result, vandalism was reduced and the general level of management of the estate was raised more quickly. Only one project was opened to the public less than four days a week and we concluded that three days' opening was the minimum for the office to work. The longer opening hours were usually coupled with a greater degree of local responsibility and a greater degree of contact between tenants and staff. This in turn generated confidence, kept information up-to-date, helped prevent damage, and encouraged people to stay on the estate and to bring others to live there. Many local authorities and estate teams argued against opening all day every day on the grounds that it did not allow enough time for 'the work to be done'. However, as long as problems could be dealt with locally as they arose, the constant contact with tenants over all management problems actually ensured that the work was done.

The estate offices were widely regarded as exceptions to the rule in the central system, able to cut through red tape and get things done. Devolution of responsibility to the local offices was far from automatic and in fact apart from chasing rent arrears, ordering repairs, and tenants' advice and liaison, there was no area of management responsibility that was totally passed down to the local office. This was wasteful of time and effort, frustrating to tenants and staff, and illogical in organizational terms. It did not, however, do away with the value of direct contact through the local office, and it did encourage better performance on almost all fronts. This was achieved by endless chasing and pressure, which would have become unnecessary with a fully autonomous local organization.

Local Management Responsibility
There were nine vital areas of day-to-day management that needed to be covered on any estate by the local office:

(1) Responsibility for letting empty flats, organizing transfers within the estate and controlling empty property.
(2) Responsibility for arrears prevention and recovery, and rent collection where feasible, with rent information being provided weekly to enable immediate action.
(3) A locally based repairs team to cover small-scale, day-to-day repairs.
(4) Local supervision of all estate workers including caretakers, cleaners and gardeners.
(5) A co-ordinated local team approach to include all employees, manual and office-based.
(6) Local input from staff and residents into any physical improvements, major repairs, and so on.
(7) Regular monitoring of performance in management and maintenance.
(8) Close liaison with residents on all issues affecting the running of the estate.
(9) Local responsibility for a day-to-day budget.

Table 10.1 shows the number of projects exercising local control over each of the nine key management areas. No projects covered more than six of the nine areas of responsibility; most had responsibility for fewer than half the vital elements (Table 10.2). No local authority at the time of our survey had established a management and maintenance budget for an estate or an area. The projects on cottage estates had control over more functions and had on the whole been more successful in improving conditions. It is of course an easier task than on an estate with dense blocks of flats. Modern concrete complex estates had the fewest locally based responsibilities and correspondingly the least success in improving conditions.

Table 10.1 Areas of Management Responsibility under the Control of the Projects

Responsibility	No. of projects out of 20
Reasonably adequate project control of rent arrears recovery	16
Formal liaison with residents on issues affecting the running of the estate	15
Input by management staff into improvement programme(s)	13
Local lettings	9
Estate-based repairs	8
Co-ordinated team approach	7
Regular monitoring	7
Local supervision of caretakers	3
Local responsibility for a day-to-day budget	0

Source: Power, 1984, p. 36.

Table 10.2 Local Responsibility for Nine Management Functions

No. of functions controlled locally	No. of projects	Type of project
7 to 9	0	
4 to 6	9	4 cottage 4 walk-up blocks 1 modern complex
1 to 3	11	3 cottage 3 walk-up blocks 5 modern complex

Source: Power, 1984, p. 36.

Local Base, Central Systems

To base the estate managers in a local office was the first easy step that all had taken. To break up every aspect of estate management into locally run, multi-skill units was much more difficult. It would be essential to establish clear decentralization of management functions if a local authority wanted to develop estate-based offices on a wider scale. Otherwise a number of decentralized offices could create tremendous confusion through constantly having to refer back to the centre and chase basic services.

The obvious way forward seemed to be the voguish borough-wide decentralization of services. Yet many authorities felt they did not have sufficiently trained and motivated staff to implement intensive management across the board with local responsibility for all key management areas. Many certainly did not have a system that readily lent itself to local autonomy. And the complexities of extricating services, staff and budgets from functional entities at the centre were often overwhelming. In practice, the decentralizing local authorities rarely relinquished central control over budgets, staff performance, lettings or repairs. They rarely organized at estate level either.

In Walsall, Lambeth and Hackney, neighbourhood offices were planned to cover about 1,500–2,500 homes. The units often fitted awkwardly with estate boundaries and were too large if they were geographically spread or covered several large estates. The problems of decentralization for all these authorities were immense, because of the scale of reorganization and because many of the basic management services were still tied to central systems. No authority was contemplating across-the-board estate-level management. Based on our survey, we would argue that estate-based management works better than area-based management. Up to 1,000 dwellings is a workable size. Larger units may need to be divided.

Only tenant management co-operatives had succeeded in extricating from the town hall system a management entity with its own staff, funds and organization, and with local tenants' control (DOE, 1982, p. 49). But most tenants were reluctant to assume such wide responsibility, especially on estates with multiple problems like the estates in the survey. On none of the twenty estates had tenants established a management organization under their own control.[1] Most estate offices were set up with unclear boundaries and a lack of designated authority. Nonetheless, the local offices had a relatively free hand whenever they *could* get hold of the right bit of the system.

Gains

The evidence of improvements on the survey estates under the impact of local offices was drawn from a number of sources: statistical information from the monitoring of management performance and from progress reports submitted to council committees and senior officers; surveys of tenants (Priority Estates Project, 1979, 1983); interviews with project staff and housing department officials; evidence of changed conditions over the period 1979–82. Factual evidence was used as far as possible but the assessments of staff and of tenants were included. To the extent that these assessments were favourable, they reflected, at the least, increased confidence and improved morale. It is unlikely given the previous levels of demoralization and apathy that they reflected nothing more (Power, 1984, pp. 60–82).

The improvements that seemed most important were:

(1) Better general environment, usually remarkably cleaner.
(2) Improved repairs service.
(3) Greater security and less vandalism.
(4) Rent arrears reducing or rising more slowly than the local authority average.
(5) No longer hard to let.
(6) Fewer empty dwellings.
(7) Increased tenant involvement.
(8) Successful physical improvements.
(9) Co-operative local efforts in management and maintenance.
(10) Improved caretaking.

No project was improving in all areas but all were improving in some.

Table 10.3 lists the fifteen principal changes brought about in the twenty projects in order of spread of success. The cottage and walk-up block estates were improving on nine counts, but the modern concrete complex estates were improving on only six (Figure 10.2). The more serious difficulties of the projects on modern concrete complex estates in bringing about improvement were predictable. The physical and

Table 10.3 Changes in the Projects Leading to Increased Popularity of Estates

Change	No. of estates out of 20 bringing about change
Environment improving	19
Increased tenant involvement	18
Major repairs/environmental improvements	18
Improved repairs service	15
Less vandalism and insecurity	15
Co-ordinated approach	14
Fewer empty dwellings	13
Improved caretaking	12
No longer hard to let	11
Lower tenancy turnover	10
Lower child densities	10
Fewer one-parent family allocations	9
Fewer homeless allocations	9
Improvements to homes	9
Rent arrears reducing, or rising more slowly than local authority average	8

Source: Power, 1984, p. 33.

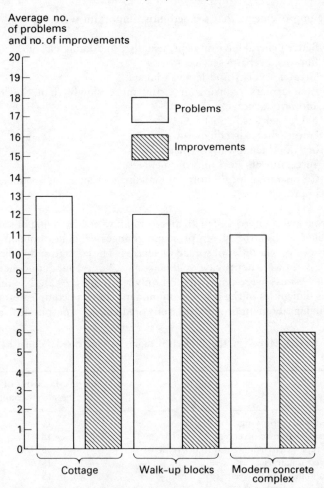

Average no.
of problems
and no. of improvements

Problems

Improvements

Cottage   Walk-up blocks   Modern concrete
complex

Figure 10.2   The number of problems and improvements on different types of estate.
Source: Power, 1984, p. 34.

security problems of large, interlocking communal blocks were immense. The rehousing, often over a short time-span, of a new and unsettled community of several thousand people was a factor which could not quickly be resolved. They had had less time to settle and establish links. The somewhat smaller-scale, more old-fashioned estates were often more run-down but more settled and easier to improve.

Improving on the previous situation was less difficult than many believe, once a local team was given the go-ahead, since the estates were starting from a very low base. The difficulty was in making improvements stick and integrating the various parts of the operation at the local end so that a viable local management unit could become accepted as part of the local authority structure. This happened in the half-dozen authorities that had extended local management beyond the initial experiments.

The two most difficult areas to reverse were rent arrears and social deprivation among incoming tenants. Without generating the full rent income, long-term management and maintenance could only be funded with great difficulty. Without reversing the intense social deprivation, too many of the better-off tenants would go on wanting to leave. Some way of making a more mixed, economically and socially viable community still had to be found. All projects were still so dependent on the central system working in their favour and so circumscribed in their local powers, that it was often difficult to make the next major leap from the initial improvements to sound, long-term management (see Chapter 11).

Staff Organization

In all but two of the survey estates, the number of management staff to properties increased with the local management office – in many cases substantially. Table 10.4 illustrates what happened on the ground.

Many other workers besides estate officers formed part of the local teams. Clerical and administrative staff were found in ten projects. They often performed a wide range of functions, far beyond a purely desk-bound role. In many cases they acted as receptionists and had constant contact with the public. The number of manual workers to properties increased in most projects whereas the number of administrative staff was smaller than in a large centralized bureaucracy.

Table 10.4 Average Staff Input Increases with Local Management

Type of estate	Ratio of estate officers to properties across local authority	Ratio of estate officers to properties within local office
Cottage	1 to 915	1 to 454
Walk-up	1 to 855	1 to 586
Deck/modern	1 to 646	1 to 429

Source: Power, 1984, p. 60.

Repairs workers, cleaners, caretakers and wardens, plus management staff, added up to a sizeable workforce, usually about twenty to a thousand dwellings, or one employee to fifty dwellings. This was about the same ratio as the housing associations and philanthropic trusts employed and, on the whole, it was adequate. It was interesting that in the nineteen local authorities, the average staffing levels across the borough were also one employee to approximately fifty dwellings, including maintenance and caretaking staff, the difference being that many jobs were based in the town hall or district office with layers of vertical supervision and paper-chasing operations. The ground-level staff was often minimal. In the local management offices, the output changed noticeably because jobs were closer to the ground where paper operations could be cut and where results were quick to show.

Team Leaders
All the projects had co-ordinators or senior officers in charge. Twelve project leaders were on senior grades within the local authority structure and eight were on assistant grades (Table 10.5). The poorer management performance on modern estates (Table 10.2) to some extent reflected the lower grading of co-ordinators and their more limited responsibility for management functions.

Local management offered a very different career structure, whereby ambitious young employees or capable and experienced housing managers were choosing to leave the mainstream hierarchy of the housing department for a job with direct responsibility, some seniority and less chance of decisions being made elsewhere.

Table 10.5 Seniority of Project Leaders

Grade in order of seniority	No. of project leaders on grade	Type of estate
Principal Officers (PO1)	2	1 walk-up block 1 modern concrete complex
Senior Officer (SO1/2)	10	4 cottage 4 walk-up block 2 modern concrete complex
Administrative and Professional (AP4/5)	8	3 cottage 1 walk-up block 4 modern concrete complex

Source: Power, 1984, p. 39.

The Cost of Local Management

Thirteen projects were funded entirely from local authority Housing Revenue Accounts, the statutory local purse which all local authorities must set up to pay in rents and subsidies, and to pay out debt charges and management and maintenance costs. The remaining seven projects were funded by a combination of government and local authority support. Three of the offices in our survey were set up by the Priority Estates Project and the local authorities with some government help. In every other case, the local authority had taken the initiative in organizing estate-based management, although in the case of Liverpool, the three Intensive Management Projects were the product of the inner area studies sponsored by the Department of the Environment and were funded by Inner City Partnership. The two Tyneside projects were also funded by Partnership, but were firmly rooted within the local authorities. Ragworth, Stockton-on-Tees, was Urban Aid-funded (Table 10.6).

The Priority Estates Project w. s funded directly by the Department of the Environment. Urban Aid was a form of central government aid to urban areas with central government contributing 75% and local government 25% of the funds. Inner City Partnership funds were distributed on the same basis to specially designated inner city areas with severe problems. The aim of both Urban Aid and Inner City Partnership funds was the regeneration of deprived areas through the funding of new initiatives, both statutory and voluntary. The funds could not be used to finance existing projects.

While most local authorities would argue that they simply could not afford local management, the authorities in the survey argued that they could not afford to leave the estates without local management any longer. Nonetheless, the financing of housing management and maintenance is somewhat precarious. Drastic government cuts since 1979 seriously reduced the amount of money available for major improvements to estates and modernization of older council property. Government support to local rate funds was also cut. Rent incomes

Table 10.6 Sources of Funding for Local Management Projects

Source of funds	No. of projects
Local Authority Housing Revenue Account	13
Inner City Partnership	3
Priority Estates Project	3
Urban Aid	1

Source: Power, 1984, p. 38.

rose steeply but most of the beleaguered inner London boroughs and Metropolitan authorites still depended on subsidy, though even they were in a better position to pay for local management than before rent rises.

Rate-capping could mean that in the high-spending city authorities, management and maintenance must be paid for entirely out of rent income. The precedents for this are not good. Even Octavia Hill and the 5 per cent philanthropists, committed as they were to 'making housing pay its way', found it very hard to make business ends meet with low-income wage-earners in rented housing at the turn of the century. On the other hand, Housing Benefit has become a major rent subsidy and as rents have risen, so more and more tenants have become eligible for it. It should, if it continues, replace rate subsidies to the Housing Revenue Accounts as the main subsidy to management and maintenance budgets. If Housing Benefit were cut, then the financial artery to housing management would be severed.

The actual cost of providing a local full-time office with permanent staff was lower than most critics would suppose (Table 10.7), although there were wide variations between authorities (see Table 10.8). If 25 per cent were added for central overheads, the cost of the local offices would average £2.12 for flats and £1.39 for houses. Even allowing for central overheads (Audit Commission, 1986, p. 22), local offices should be within most local authorities' budgetary limits. The Audit Commission found that there were no known economies of scale in estate management. Conversely, they found that the greater the number of dwellings per local authority, the higher the unit costs tended to be (Audit Commission, 1986, p. 11).

There was a reluctance in most local authorities to give up central

Table 10.7 Management Costs per Dwelling per Week

Average management and maintenance costs in 17 local authorities	£7.17*
Average spending on management in 17 local authorities (borough-wide)	£2.39
Average actual local management costs of local offices on 13 flatted estates	£1.70†
Average actual local management costs with local office on 7 cottage estates	£1.11†
Average estimated management costs on 20 estates including central overheads	£1.75

*The national average for all local authorites was £5.54.
†These figures do not include district or central costs nor the cost of centralized rent or lettings systems, etc.
Source: CIPFA and local Housing Revenue Account statistics, 1982–3.

costs per dwelling per week

Local authority	Management and maintenance costs: local authority average, 1982–3 [a]	Estimated average local authority costs for management only, 1982–3	Estimated local management costs for twelve local housing projects	
			1982–3	Including central overheads [b]
Greenwich	£7.99	£2.66		
Hackney	NA			
Hammersmith and Fulham	£11.89	£3.96		
Islington	NA			
Lambeth	£9.39	£3.13	£1.80	£2.25
Lewisham	£6.51	£2.17	£0.77	£0.96
Wandsworth	£9.42	£3.14	£2.57	£3.21
Brent	£8.96	£2.99	£1.85	£2.31
Haringey	£8.56	£2.85		
Bolton	£3.95	£1.32	£1.15[c]	£1.43
Rochdale	£5.87	£1.96	£1.58	£1.97
Tameside	£4.73	£1.58	£0.62	£0.77
Liverpool	£5.04	£1.68		
Gateshead	£5.16	£1.72	£1.40[c]	£1.75
Newcastle	£5.62	£1.87	£1.62[c]	£2.02
Walsall	£6.09	£2.03	£1.46	£1.82
Stockton-on-Tees	£4.47	£1.49	£0.40[c]	£0.50
Leicester	£6.06	£2.02		
GLC	£12.31	£4.10	£1.62	£2.02
All local authorities	£5.77[d]	£1.92	£1.41	£1.76

[a] CIPFA, *Housing Revenue Account Statistics*, 1983.
[b] Central overheads for administrative back-up and central services have been added to the local figures at 25%.
[c] Represents actual budgets, all other figures are estimates based on staff costs, running costs, etc.
[d] CIPFA estimated average for 1983–4.
Source: Power, 1984; CIPFA, *Housing Revenue Account Statistics*, 1983.

control, coupled with a desire to keep the functionally divided jobs at the centre. This would not be possible with full decentralization to local estate-based management. It was vital that functions should not be duplicated at local, district and central levels. Local management could only work, in the long run, in the place of central management, for all day-to-day matters.

Most of the local authorities in the survey had not accepted the logic of full local autonomy, even though they appreciated the gains made by the projects and their cost effectiveness.

Savings

It is important to give some idea of the possible benefits of local management. The number of empty dwellings at the outset of the projects was over 900. By 1982 this total had dropped by about 20 per cent, making a total gain in rent and rates income of nearly quarter of a million pounds a year. The saving on vandal damage to these now occupied properties would have been a minimum of £90,000, and savings on boarding up and other security measures, in the region of £36,000. Reduced rent arrears had brought savings in four projects. There the savings were in the region of £100,000. The savings through local repairs could be judged by Lambeth's experience, where the cost of a greatly improved service was half the previous cost, a saving on one estate of about £150,000 (Power, 1984, p. 19). The cost of local repairs on the Cloverhall Estate, Rochdale, was also halved (Bevington, 1986). Other savings included reduced vandalism to garages and lifts. In Liverpool, on one estate in one tower block, the saving was £50,000 in the first year of employing door guards. The savings through the use of vandal-resistant light shades (to protect bulbs) on one estate was £14,400. These partial estimates made an average saving in each project of approximately £39,500, well above the salary costs of additional staff. Assuming that improved performance in management and maintenance continued, the savings would also continue. Certainly the converse was true, that any relaxation in standards or input led to a swift decline in performance and reversal in conditions. This occurred temporarily on at least three estates.

The list of possible and actual savings could be extended. Under local management, the estates were costing less than expected, and the decline and damage were arrested. In sixteen of the nineteen authorities, further local offices have been opened, and paid for out of the Housing Revenue Account. The balance of judgement lay in the continuation of the projects. To our knowledge, all of the local offices survived the severe cut-backs of the last few years.

The Local Office and Resident Caretakers

With constrained budgets, with staff usually recruited from within the existing workforce and with limited direct control over performance, it is important to see how effectively basic tasks were performed in the local offices. Twelve of the thirteen flatted estates had resident caretakers (Table 10.9). They operated on a highly intensive and localized basis. As residents, they were extremely vulnerable to fellow-tenants' criticisms if their efforts were diluted.

Estate-based supervision of caretakers was essential to success. Only three of the local management projects had direct formal control over the standard of caretaking, with caretakers fully absorbed into the local teams. Most caretakers were answerable to supervisors outside the project in the town hall. This often made for difficulties of co-ordination over jobs to be done, relations with tenants and team effort. However, most of the projects had good informal liaison with caretakers. Any wider decentralization would need to incorporate caretakers, cleaners and other estate-based staff within the local team structures. Where this was done, standards of caretaking were high. (Davey, 1986; Sutton Housing Trust, undated).

On eight estates, caretakers patrolled the communal areas. This helped keep a finger on the pulse. Where there was a serious threat of intimidation, caretakers patrolled in pairs. Caretakers also provided a vital link for emergencies. They played an important preventive role.

Caretaking standards had improved on all twelve of the project estates with a resident service. This was usually achieved with existing staff. The caretakers' role was highly visible. Therefore, caretakers often enjoyed recognition and praise on survey estates, especially for cleaning, an otherwise thankless task that was noticed by visitors and residents alike. On some estates caretakers did minor repairs, helped in cases of flooding or other disasters, and also got involved in community activities. This broader and more flexible role enhanced their status. The changes in environmental conditions brought about

Table 10.9   Ratio of Caretakers to Properties

Ratio	No. of projects
1 caretaker for up to 150 properties	7
1 caretaker for 151–250 properties	3
1 caretaker for 350 properties	2
Total	12

Source: Power, 1984, p. 26.

through good caretaking were highlighted in the tenants' surveys (PEP Household Surveys 1979 to 1983).

There were only two non-resident caretakers out of a total of eighty-three caretakers in the twelve projects. The consensus was that caretakers should be resident on the estate they served.

Resident caretaking was a manual job. Cleaning common areas, tackling emergency floods and replacing lights were three examples of their role. Some authorities and union representatives seem to think manual work is only good for someone else, and that caretakers would gain status by becoming office-based. This undermines the value of the essential manual jobs on which our whole society depends. Uniforms were re-introduced on several estates, at the caretakers' request, to ensure easy recognition, to deter vandalism and to enhance the caretakers' sense of identity. Training for caretakers was being introduced. Caretaking is a complex job, based on a manual function with a major human component. It is one of the few truly traditional jobs to survive and be indispensable and irreplaceable. Without caretakers, the flatted estates were not viable.

Local Repairs

Repairs were the most difficult and costly problem to sort out. Because they were not normally run by the housing department, they were rarely integrated into the local management structure. However, with one exception, all repairs ordering was done through the estate office. This had the great advantage that tenants could at least pin down the person they had reported their repairs to, and estate officers could make instant reference to repairs records and could chase them by telephone with the tenant in attendance.

In fifteen of the twenty estates the repairs service was reported to be improving. Because proper monitoring of repairs was almost non-existent, it was extremely difficult to extract more than impressionistic information in most authorities, either about the central repairs system or the impact of the local office. However, we gleaned uniform evidence to show that only where there was a local repairs team based on the estate, working in concert with the local office, were staff and residents satisfied with the service provided.

There was a vast difference between the repairs service offered by an estate-based team on eight estates and that offered by a district or centrally based system on the remaining twelve (Figure 10.3). A majority of the district-based repairs services had improved somewhat in the project estates as a result of on-the-spot staff, quick reporting, better liaison with tenants through the estate office, better relations

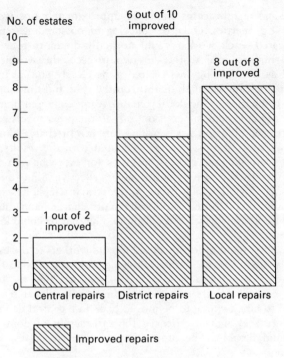

Figure 10.3 Improvements in repairs

Source: Power, 1984, p. 18.

between local housing staff and repairs workers and fewer access problems. However, the district and central service was still cumbersome, inflexible, slow and difficult to control, causing many headaches and disagreements. Only where the local project could bend and adapt the system on a local basis and integrate repairs into local management did repairs give satisfaction.

There was almost overnight improvement with a well-supervised local repairs team on eight estates. Given how critical staff and residents were in general of repairs, we have no reason to doubt the validity of the local support for estate-based repairs teams.

The backlog of jobs had been cleared in four projects. The number of jobs completed by each worker had increased significantly in four projects. Costs were halved in one team (Power, 1984, pp. 67–8). Travelling time and paperwork had been reduced by virtue of on-the-spot liaison The experience of the local repairs teams is borne out by recent research in Scotland (Stanforth *et al.*, 1986, pp. 5, 81).

The local repairs teams employed approximately one worker for every 100 properties. Once the backlog of outstanding repairs had been cleared, each worker could normally do more preventive or planned maintenance work. On two projects the workforce was reduced as the backlog was cleared. One clearly vital element in a good repairs team was high-quality, on-the-spot, full-time supervision and co-ordination. One local repairs team collapsed temporarily because of inadequate supervision, but all the other teams seemed to have attracted able and hardworking foremen or charge-hands.

Tenants and estate staff were delighted with the results. Repairs workers were no longer the scapegoats for everyone's frustrations. Liaison was usually friendly, informal and effective. Many unexpected benefits accrued. On one estate where entry telephones had been continually out of order, the local repairs charge-hand did a daily round with a screwdriver and oilcan, finding that he could keep them functioning.

The commitment of locally based repairs workers to the estate was often a major element in their agreeing to work outside the tight, defensive and sometimes absurd demarcations that so beset the average council repairs system. The men in the local teams were reported to be unwilling to be moved back to a central depot system when once they had experienced the satisfaction of doing the job locally and flexibly. The praise they received from residents was unstinting.

In spite of the success, no local repairs team was regarded as safe from the axe and several were under constant threat. Technical Services Departments were almost unanimous in their resistance to local teams and their reluctance to set them up. Sensing that direct labour organizations were in for an increasingly thin time, they were jealous of what power they had and guarded it zealously. They were centralist in their organizational approach, believing firmly in economies of scale, investment in expensive hardware, and centralized stores. These organizations were often unsuited to the small-scale, labour-intensive, messy nature of most day-to-day repairs.

Most survey estates were large enough to carry a local direct labour team of five to ten repairs workers. In two estate projects, small building firms ran a highly effective local repairs service, both on estates of 200–400 dwellings. Carpentry and plumbing were the basic trades required locally, covering a majority of day-to-day repairs. Most maintenance requests were for small jobs, although it was important to localize the control and repair of empty property and emergencies. It was possible to have viable local teams for small and frequent jobs, keeping larger, more complex and more specialist jobs within the bigger central organization. In some places a local team was unviable except over a large area because tradesmen would only agree to be supervised by a foreman from their own trade. This meant doubling the size of the team and was obviously unworkable on a smaller scale. In Liverpool, the local repairs team was large because of trade by trade supervision. In spite of that, the team was 57 per cent more productive than the central Direct Labour Organization (DLO) (Power, 1984, p. 68).

Generally, it seemed likely that higher productivity, savings on travel and central administration, a reduction in paper operations, an improvement in access to tenants, a high level of tenant satisfaction and a high standard of maintenance by virtue of eliminating the backlog of repairs would make local teams cost-effective and possibly more economical than the centrally run services. An unusually frank borough treasurer asserted that it would be impossible not to save with a local team, given the costs and inefficiency of the centre. According to more recent information, it costs around £5.50 a week per dwelling to run an estate-based, day-to-day repairs service (Welsh Office, 1985), although full-scale maintenance would cost more (Audit Commission Report, 1986). It is now generally recognized that without localized repairs, estate-based management offices are unlikely to be effective.

Major Improvements on the Estates

Modernization of outdated interiors to dwellings and environmental works to surroundings were going on on eighteen of the twenty estates. On thirteen of the estates, local staff and residents had some influence over what happened. Table 10.10 shows a breakdown of areas of work and how the work was funded.

The most extensive improvements were to the estate surroundings. Almost all estates were being upgraded by landscaping, repainting, planting, and provision of play areas. But there was a growing tendency for tenants' priorities, such as lighting and strong doors, to take precedence over elaborate landscaping. This was not to say that tenants did not appreciate greenery. On many estates they were actively involved in planting. But they set the highest premium on security and other basic items and wanted them first. Tenants on two large balcony estates persuaded the GLC to postpone landscaping in favour of improved lighting and refuse disposal (Power, 1982, p. 12).

Entry telephones or secure doors were essential for communal blocks and were being installed on ten of the thirteen flatted estates, but were a dismal failure on half the estates, even after the local office was involved. This was for a variety of reasons. Often they were

Table 10.10 Capital Improvements

Type of improvement	Number of estates	Source of funding (% of total cost of work)	
Exterior of blocks and dwellings and work to the environment	18	67%	HIP
		33%	Urban Aid/Inner City Partnership
Inside homes	11	100%	HIP
Entry telephones	9	100%	HIP
Community facilities	8	67%	HIP
		33%	Urban Aid/Inner City Partnership
No improvements	2		

Source: Power, 1984, p. 17.

installed *prior* to resident consultation and in several cases prior to the opening of a local office. In one case, they were wrongly wired up and had never worked over a three-year period. In some cases, poor, vandal-prone doors and breakable glass were used. In one case, the glass was never put in. And in some areas where social pressures were too severe, entry telephones could only be made to work with full-time door-porters acting as security guards. After numerous failures, this was tried successfully in Liverpool. Human back-up to physical remedies was often needed. Entry telephones only worked where other areas of management, particularly tenant involvement, caretaking, lettings and maintenance, were operating properly. Long-term maintenance contracts were essential (Stanforth *et al*, 1986; Bright *et al*, 1986).

The enclosure of public open space to provide private front and back gardens or patios, whether for flats or houses, was probably the easiest, most radical and most successful of the small-scale environmental innovations, totally transforming the physical aspect and social atmosphere of many of the estates.

Most estates more than thirty years old were being modernized. There were two innovative and exciting experiments in modernization. One was the tenants' grants scheme whereby tenants themselves became responsible for hiring a builder to modernize their kitchen, bathroom and heating system, with professional advice from the council and a range of choices open to the tenants. The results saved money, accelerated the programme, involved the tenants directly and attained a higher standard of workmanship, although this experiment had its organizational problems too. The other was the GLC's ambitious rolling programme of package conversions on its prewar flatted estates, which included the two GLC estates in our survey (Shankland Cox, 1977). The GLC hired contractors to rip out and replace complete kitchens and bathrooms and install full central heating over a five-day period. The work was carried out only if the tenant agreed. Special arrangements were made with neighbours for emergency water supply and cooking and no one was without services overnight. The modernization, basic as it was, cost half of the normal internal modernizations and caused minimal disruption. The GLC package scheme was cheaper, faster and more efficient than any other modernization scheme we encountered. Tenants widely supported it.

Because of the pressure on their stock and the expense, eight out of eleven councils were no longer rehousing families, but were carrying out modernization around the family or at most, temporarily rehousing them for the worst few weeks. The biggest frustrations were the unkept promises of council staff and the unrealistic timetables of builders.

The most radical major innovation was 'lopping off' the top one or two storeys of four- and five-storey blocks of maisonettes and flats. While costing at least £8,000 per dwelling (1984 prices), it produced an attractive row of houses from an unlettable block of flats in areas where there was a crude housing surplus, such as Merseyside, greater Manchester and Tyneside. It avoided the scarred sites and upheaval of total demolition. It invariably restored confidence in a devastated estate. The 'lopped' houses were very popular.

Often relatively minor improvements which were not very expensive made an important difference to the overall conditions. Cavity wall insulation on a cottage estate (Leicester), gas fires in the living room with a back boiler to heat the water (Stockton), anti-graffiti paint in hallways and on staircases (Rochdale), laminated glass in windows in vulnerable public areas and vandal-proof light covers on exposed balconies (GLC), strong, solid front doors on crime-prone corridors (Haringey and Brent) had an immeasurable effect on the quality of life. Each improvement might cost £50 to £250 per dwelling, the type of investment that could be replicated many times over. The improvements listed above were a direct result of tenants' pleadings. The needs and requirements of the tenants were often far more immediate and basic than the council had previously contemplated. The involvement of architects, surveyors and building contractors at the wrong level and on the wrong scale had often distorted the progress of maintenance and continual renovation into a kind of new-build approach to old dwellings. The innovations in local management enhanced the tenants' ability to ask for and oversee sensible and modest improvements, which were so much more likely to fulfil the object of the exercise.

All the estates in the survey needed substantial sums spent on them on a continuing basis, either by virtue of their age or their design or both. However, we concluded that large-scale building contracts on dense, fully occupied estates were cumbersome, disruptive, costly and wasteful. It seemed more logical to disaggregate the work needed, organize small-block or area-based contracts and generally do sections of the work on an incremental basis. Then it became easier to pick up mistakes. The amounts of money, the penalties and any faulty plans became more manageable and rectifiable. This incremental approach, with resident involvement in decision-making, was increasingly being adopted as funds became more scarce and previous blunders more apparent.

Project staff attempted to achieve a co-ordinated capital programme by liaising with council architects, surveyors and engineers, building contractors and sub-contractors (often several firms), private consultant architects, the tenants affected by the work, the central lettings department where rehousing was required, finance department for payment of contracts, legal department for checking contracts and pursuing any breaches, and sometimes the direct labour organization for repairs *while* the major works got under way.

A problem in all the projects was the way spending was affected by sudden cuts. Capital spending was the puppet of central and local government financial problems and this militated against rolling programmes of planned maintenance, incremental improvements or clear local co-ordination.

The real need in the projects was for a competent repairs team able to take on bigger and more regular maintenance, such as roof overhaul, plumbing replacements, and cyclical repainting, thereby reducing the need for disruptive, unwieldy and often wasteful crash programmes when an estate had reached a serious point of decay. There was no reason why the maintenance programme should not include continual upgrading of the inside of dwellings and of communal areas. This approach was being tried on one estate. In the long run, long-term continuous maintenance would be cheaper and more intelligible to residents than slow decay followed by major capital works.

Local Lettings

Nine estates ran lettings from the local office but on sixteen of the survey estates, there were changes in lettings policy after the local office opened, in an attempt to reverse the social distress of the estates. In one or two cases, homeless families were no longer offered that estate for a time in an attempt to balance the large numbers of vulnerable households; in others all applicants were carefully screened to prevent households with severe social problems being 'dumped' on the already distressed estate. On the flatted estates, there was an effort to reduce child densities, either by under-letting large dwellings or by restricting access for families to lower floors. In all tower blocks there was a declared policy to move families out, though this was proving increasingly difficult to implement in London because of growing housing pressures and the sale of houses.

All restrictions on lettings policies carried their own liabilities. Under-letting larger dwellings to smaller families and childless households, unless rents were reduced, imposed a big rent and rates burden on a low-earning household. More importantly, heating and furnishing a dwelling that was larger than necessary was a serious problem. Under-letting in many areas was no longer considered a sensible solution unless a tenant particularly wanted a larger dwelling and was able to cover the extra cost. Excluding families from tower blocks was successful, both for the families who moved out and for childless households who moved in, but to extend that policy to upper floors of four-storey flats or maisonettes, as was done in Liverpool and Rochdale, so narrowed demand that there was a surplus in many areas of three-bedroom upper floor dwellings for which the only demand was from single people.

Most of the single applicants in areas of severe economic decline were unskilled, unemployed, transient youngsters who had just left home and who could not yet furnish a large flat, connect gas and electricity and pay for rent and rates. The turnover was very high under such lettings and moonlight flits were common, very often leaving hire purchase and fuel bills as well as rent arrears. The trail of debts enhanced the poor reputation of an estate, leading to the common refusal of shops to grant hire purchase to more stable tenants. Local authorities were reluctant to ask for deposits or guarantors, yet such precautions were the only ways of protecting the stock and the tenants, who were sometimes made miserable by freewheeling youngsters not yet used to the fragile independence they had found. The blocks and dwellings themselves were often totally unsuitable for young single people. A different style of resident management with furnished lettings and a careful maintenance and cleaning service could turn lettings to young single people into a financial and social asset.

Excluding the homeless and other low-income groups from the poor estates proved socially divisive and politically sensitive. It was hard to justify, given the existence of empty dwellings and the patent housing need of some households. A policy that overtly limited the rehousing of homeless families on bad estates made the immediate connection between homelessness and unpopular estates, often seeming to blame homeless families for poor conditions. Making a wider range of offers to homeless families in areas of high demand was the obvious alternative, but was not a policy that was widely adopted. The only other solution was to open up demand through better management. With intensive management, there was no intrinsic reason why lettings to homeless families should be restricted. The crucial point was to give them as *much* choice as everyone else in other areas than the most stigmatized.

Eleven of the projects still had centrally run lettings systems but seven of these enjoyed special policies in an attempt to prevent social ghettos. In only four of the estates was there no change in lettings policies and virtually no flexibility. There, the management staff had a serious uphill battle to make anything work. Where there was some flexibility, local managers were able to intervene and effect lettings practices if not carry them out themselves. This greatly enhanced the sense of purpose and satisfaction of the local staff and often involved residents in lettings matters too. It also produced more applicants.

On the eleven estates without local lettings, the total number of empty homes had increased fractionally from 496 at the outset, to 522 in 1982. On one highly unpopular modern concrete complex estate, without local lettings or an estate-based waiting list, empty flats increased by 150 to 29 per cent of all dwellings. The increase happened in spite of special lettings policies and some flexibility. By reducing the number of lettings to families with children and to disadvantaged groups in an area of low housing demand, the town hall uncovered grave difficulty in finding applicants at all. However, on five of the eleven estates the number of empty dwellings was falling.

A Local Waiting List

Where lettings were handled entirely by the local office, there was much greater success. This happened on nine estates. All but one were able to generate some local demand. Under local lettings, anyone wanting a home and eligible for rehousing could register in the queue at the local office for the dwellings available. The overriding priority was to get the dwellings occupied although allocation through local lettings followed the council's own priority system. This local method of letting worked because it was fast, it enhanced tenants' choice and commitment, and it was even-handed. No one sat in judgement over anyone else.

Local lettings reduced the numbers of empty properties[2] in every case except one (Table 10.11). Relatives, friends and local people were often willing to move on to a local estate that was unpopular with

Table 10.11 Lettings and Empty Dwellings

Type of letting	No. of projects	Voids down	Voids same	Voids up	No information
Central	11	5	1	3	2
Lettings from estate office	9	8	1	0	0

Source: Power, 1984, p. 20.

outsiders, because of their roots in the neighbourhood. The local list included applicants referred from the town hall and people applying direct to the local office. Under local lettings in some authorities, only households registered on the central waiting list were eligible. Rehousing was in these cases based on the council's points system, with homeless families and other urgent cases taking automatic precedence. The difference was that the families were asked to register at the local office, thereby making a commitment to rehousing on the estate.

In some areas, council lettings took place on a first-come, first-served basis at the local office if general demand was low. Dwellings were let literally over the counter. The local waiting list generated applicants if it was open to all-comers, and a large pool of willing applicants was essential if local lettings were to work. Even in areas where through the central or district system there appeared to be few applicants, such as Liverpool, Newcastle and Gateshead, a local office, letting empty dwellings direct, was likely to recruit people who otherwise would not consider living on these estates. The change of psychology was born partly of the impact of local management. More importantly, it overcame the absurd pecking order that commonly passed as tenants' choice whereby, through the central lettings system, applicants were asked to rank on paper their top choices of estates. On that basis, of course, applicants had rarely asked for the estates in our survey.

Impact of the Local Office on Lettings
The number of empty homes in the nine projects with local lettings had dropped from a total of 435 at the outset of the projects to 225 in 1982–3 when we conducted our survey. Figure 10.4 shows the changes that were brought about in the number of empty dwellings where the local offices handled lettings. The average level of empty dwellings on all the survey estates was 8 per cent at the outset of the projects and had fallen to just under 5 per cent at the time of the survey. Only three estates had increasing numbers of empty dwellings. Table 10.12 illustrates progress.

Table 10.12 Numbers of Empty Properties and Change in the Rate of Voids Since the Local Office Opened

Type of estate	No. of voids		Empties as % of total in 1982	% change from start of project
	At start of office	At time of survey		
Cottage, north west England	few	7	1.5	same*
Cottage, north of England	19	15	1.5	−21.0*
Cottage, Midlands	50	30	1.5	−40.0*
Cottage, north of England	41	10	1.0	−76.0*
Cottage, north of England	21	23	6.0	+10.0
Cottage, Midlands	100	44	15.0	−44.0*
Cottage, north-west England	9	5	1.6	−44.0*
Balcony, London	15	22	3.2	+45.0
Balcony, London	c. 100	26	4.7	−74.0
Balcony, London	68	43	4.9	−36.0*
Balcony, London	unknown	22	2.0	NA
Mainly balcony, north-west England	79	37	1.9	−53.0*
Balcony, London	43	17	6.2	−60.0
Modern, London	6–10	6–10	0.5	some
Modern, London	unknown	30	1.6	NA
Modern, London	10	average 6–7	0.8	−33.0
Modern, London	34	27	2.5	−21.0
Modern London	62	34	3.4	−45.0*
Modern, London	123	average 55	4.9	−55.0
Modern, north-west England	140	293	29.0	+109.0

*Estates with local lettings.
Source: Power, 1984, p. 69.

Local lettings brought in extra rent and rates and reduced vandal damage to now occupied property. Savings on repairs to empty property and reduced vandal damage were between £500 and £2,000 per property. Rent and rates income for each occupied property was £1,000 a year.[3] Local control of lettings on difficult-to-let estates was a major contribution to the arrest of decline.

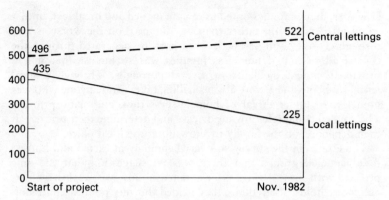

Figure 10.4 Change in the number of empty properties under local and central lettings in all projects from the outset of the projects to the time of the survey

Source: Power, 1984, p. 21.

Note: The projects started at various times. We used figures recorded for each project when it began, regardless of actual dates.

Opposition to Local Lettings

In spite of the obvious advantages of devolving lettings to the local offices, chief housing officers and senior politicians on the whole took unkindly to the idea. The notion that council housing was strictly rationed and that you had to queue for it, prove your overriding need for it, and earn the dwelling and estate you wanted according to council-determined criteria was deeply ingrained in the psyche of officers and politicians. Any freer, more localized and more autonomous lettings system seemed synonymous with 'queue-jumping' and parochial bigotry. There were genuine fears that local lettings might discriminate against minorities. Local lettings were rarely initiated from the centre. Almost always they followed logically upon the local office struggling with the problem of failing to fill empty dwellings while the centre failed to supply sufficient willing applicants. Some local officers took the initiative in going to the centre, identifying names from the central waiting list and contacting eligible applicants direct. By the same token, when once the office was on the estate, tenants would bring in sons and daughters, friends and relatives, needing a home of their own. The idea proved itself through informal initiatives.

In the hard-pressed London boroughs, the constant pressure of homelessness caused central allocations departments to resist local lettings, often bitterly. They wanted (and needed) to commandeer a majority of vacant dwellings for the endless demands of homelessness.

However, many families opted to remain in 'bed and breakfast' until a 'good offer' came up, rather than be 'dumped' on the worst estates through central lettings. The level of hostility generated through the central admission of homeless families was so intense that it had provoked violent incidents in several boroughs. Through a local lettings scheme, there were always willing takers and anyone who was homeless or under threat of homelessness took automatic priority. The council could refer any needy case and determine their priority. It then depended on the family to show up at the local office.

The estates in the survey so overwhelmingly attracted and housed disadvantaged groups that there was no suggestion that the nine projects with local lettings discriminated in any way against vulnerable households. If anything, they helped the very poorest communities regain self-respect by enabling fast lettings and encouraging a full estate, the surest indicator of communal well-being. The three main areas of conflict over local lettings were borough-wide lettings priorities, opportunities for discretion or discrimination, and management priorities of an estate taking precedence over allocation priorities. These objections could be overcome if efficient, properly monitored local allocations procedures were established, linked effectively to a central system.

There is only an argument against the local administration of lettings where there are very few empty dwellings and a high level of need with conflicting demands for available property. It is essential that local lettings be monitored carefully from the centre and that recognized procedures be followed. On popular estates the lettings problems discussed here do not arise, and policies for those estates need to be different.

Transfers

Transfers continued to be facilitated as a way of overcoming tenant dissatisfaction, and on all estates there was still a substantial volume of re-lets, although this was declining as the estates improved. 'Management transfers' where a 'good' tenant was moved off a 'bad' estate because he was being harassed by 'bad' neighbours were counterproductive and were being increasingly replaced by sorting out the problem direct. There were numerous cases, ranging from attacks by dogs to noise nuisance and racial abuse. Whatever the cause, management transfers were the most damaging way out, breaking the resolve of those who remained, including staff, to curb the nuisance. Alternative approaches to abuse are discussed in the following chapter.

212

Because of slack housing demand in many areas, the turnover of tenants continued to be high and it did not seem reasonable to deny people transfers. Yet only when vacancy and transfer rates began to fall did an estate community usually begin to galvanize itself. A lot of management effort was focused on reducing the demand for transfers.

One way of satisfying changing housing needs, while retaining the community, was to organize internal transfers locally. Six of the projects without local lettings were allowed to give priority to internal transfers on the estate. Allowing tenants to transfer to another home within the estate through the estate office was a tremendous boost to the morale of the tenants and workers and had the opposite effect of normal off-estate transfers. Ready internal transfers, as an alternative to transferring off the estate, helped to keep down the number of empty homes on the unpopular estates and held together the tenuous community links which were so vital for a healthy future. Tenants were often willing to stay on the estate if their other housing problems could be solved (Burbidge *et al.*, 1981, Vol. 1, p. 13). It did mean that the 'better' dwellings would be snapped up by existing residents if they became vacant. But vacated dwellings could in turn be brought up to standard and it was less destabilizing than a complete exodus.

Rent Arrears

Fourteen projects had no responsibility at all for rent collection. This was probably a critical weakness in the local management system. All the projects dealt with rent arrears but on four estates there was insufficient control over arrears procedures to allow the local management office to operate efficiently. Arrears information in general was often incomplete, or slow in arriving at the local office. Six estates did not have proper information.

Of all the responsibilities tackled locally, arrears was the most time-absorbing duty of estate officers. Unfortunately, chasing arrears without a localized rent accounting system was prone to mistakes and was difficult to sustain. The existence of the local office and local control did not radically alter the approach to arrears, although there was more emphasis on debt counselling and advice, and relative to the rest of the local authority most of the project estates were holding their own or improving somewhat.

Tenants on the most modern estates often paid the highest rents, and had the highest arrears (Figure 10.5). There was the additional problem that, on five estates, tenants were paying often uneconomic heating charges, based on the 1960s fashion for district heating systems, which had looked like a good buy when they were part of a

No. of projects

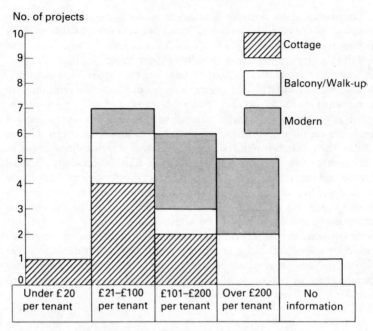

Figure 10.5 Average rent arrears, 1982

Source: Power, 1984, p. 24.

massive building contract but which proved very expensive to run in the post-oil crisis of the 1970s and 1980s. (They also often broke down.) This greatly increased the debt burden on poor households that simply could not afford high weekly heating charges they could not control. This, too, applied most often to the modern estates.

Since the projects began, four projects had reduced their total arrears figure. This was very much the opposite of the national trend (Duncan and Kirby, 1984, p. 5), or the trend within the survey authorities. A further four had more slowly rising arrears than the rest of the local authority. Only two were doing worse than the local authorities as a whole (Table 10.13).

Reducing Arrears
The survey showed that there was no effective method for preventing worsening arrears other than speedy personal intervention or, as a last resort, concerted legal action. The withdrawal of door-to-door collection meant that any approach to tenants over rents automatically implied arrears and debts. The local offices which worked so hard to

Table 10.13 Impact of Estate-Based Management on Arrears

Arrears reducing	4
Arrears increasing more slowly than local authority rate of increase	4
Arrears increasing as much as local authority rate of increase	4
Arrears increasing faster than local authority rate of increase	2
Information not available	6

Source: Power, 1984, p. 24

establish goodwill with tenants were extremely reluctant to pressurize people who were financially hard-pressed already. This meant that arrears were sometimes pursued rather gingerly.

Housing Benefit
Housing Benefit introduced another element into the general morass of arrears in authorities that were not coping. It also made the rent control system more remote than ever. No local authority delegated Housing Benefit to the local level at the time of the survey, although this service has since been localized in one or two areas. It proved very difficult to develop a sense of personal involvement or responsibility either among staff or tenants on a poor estate, with the records entirely organized and locked up in main frame computers. The major advantage of Housing Benefit on all the estates was that 'fully passported' tenants were freed almost totally from the arrears debt syndrome. This applied to over half the tenants on most estates.

Conclusion

The local offices brought about savings and benefits on estates whose condition had appeared desperate, if not beyond recall. But they were still a long way from the integrated local management service that they aimed to provide. They could only be replicated if they became more autonomous. Their major asset was that they were in direct contact with the tenants and that the character of the housing service changed as a result.

Notes to Chapter 10

1 The Cloverhall Tenant Management Co-operative, Rochdale, was under way but only took over full management of the estate in 1985.
2 We eliminated from our estimates in all estate areas properties that were empty for major improvements, but included vandalized empty property

that would otherwise have been fit for letting. On one estate, there had always been very few empty dwellings.

3　To arrive at this figure, we averaged rent and rates for two-bedroom properties in all the projects £20 per week, multiplied by fifty (rent paying weeks).

Chapter Eleven

Social Change

When there is a conflict in society, it is always the powerful institutions which find it easy to put out a version of the events which . . . is reported by the mass media as if there were no other truth.

Those without power have no such voice. Our task is to listen to the powerless as well as the powerful. To listen to the ordinary people of this community and the organizations which represent them.

(Gifford, 1986)

The most significant and most difficult turning point on the estates was the restoration of confidence among residents and the establishment of peaceful living conditions. A sense of control or even purpose having been lost, social change was a most sensitive and explosive touchstone for the future of the estates. On estates where abuse had become rampant, only internal patterns of control would re-establish more guarded behaviour. The control of social abuse and the reversal of social disarray were daunting tasks. It was a daily struggle and only implacable determination brought an end to loss of control. Residents played a central role in the process.

Residents and the Local Office

Without a clear sharing of responsibility between tenants and local authority, a local management office was unlikely to reverse the serious decline of an estate. It was a question of the 'buildings *and* the people' (Hill, 1883, p. 41). There was a need for a straightforward trade-off between what the council would do as landlord and what the residents would protect and back in their own communal interest. The centrally based council landlord had not been able to achieve this balance.

In sixteen of the twenty estate-based management projects, there were strong and active tenants' groups (Table 11.1). Fifteen of the sixteen had the support of a paid community worker or organizer and had regular formal meetings with the council in order to discuss the running of the estate. Six had joint organizations between tenants' bodies and local staff. Both the existence of the local office and the support of paid workers facilitated the direct involvement of tenants in the management of their estate.

The involvement of tenants in management tasks was limited on most estates. On only four estates did residents have direct jurisdiction over any areas of management responsibility such as monitoring repairs, helping with lettings, or establishing priorities for improvements. These four projects had elected bodies which were recognized by the council as having a formal say in the management of the estate. Three were pilot Priority Estate Projects. Hackney and Bolton Tenant Boards both registered as Friendly Societies. Other local authorities have since 1982 developed formal structures such as the Broadwater Farm Panel, Haringey (Gifford, 1986, p. 30). However, these organizations depended very much on the goodwill of the council officers and the local leadership that emerged to make them effective vehicles for a cross-section of residents.

Some estates had very varied communities and tenants' representation was not always straightforward. Several of the estate projects went to great lengths to ensure that representatives from racial minorities were directly involved in decision-making. On two estates, co-options from minority organizations to the Neighbourhood Management Committee were agreed to ensure the representation of the sizeable ethnic minorities who might not be elected under a majority ballot system. Secret written ballots were important too in the election of minority representatives.

Table 11.1 Tenant Involvement on Project Estates

Degree of tenant involvement	No. of projects	No. of projects with community work support	No. of projects with regular consultation and liaison between tenants and local authority staff
Strong, active tenant groups	16	15	15
Less active/no permanent tenant groups	4	2	0
Total	20	17	15

Source: Power, 1984, p. 30.

Limited Role for Tenants

Tenants' priorities in improvements were accepted in principle on most estates through the established liaison channels. In practice, constraints of finance, confusion of responsibility between departments and a desire to 'treat everyone alike' throughout the council sometimes led to disappointment and bitterness when tenants' often common-sense opinions were overridden. Ironically, this often arose out of over-ambitious spending plans by councils which could not be realized, which distorted residents' choices and generated consultation exercises that could not be followed through.

On only one estate in the country, Cloverhall, Rochdale (which was not in the survey), did the tenants take over full management and maintenance responsibility from the council. This was a highly complex and drawn-out process, taking over three years to negotiate (PEP working paper on Cloverhall Agreement, 1985). The management record of the Cloverhall Tenant Management Co-operative is impressive, with six estate-based jobs paid for out of a management allowance of £10 a week per dwelling, all empty property now let and a doubling in the level of repairs. But the tenants of the 240-dwelling 'dump' estate are unusual in their determination to run things for themselves.

No systematic survey of residents' opinions was conducted on most of the estates, and it remains to be seen what a broad cross-section of tenants would say about local management. However, on two of the project estates, detailed surveys revealed residents' views of the changes brought about through the local office over four years (Surveys on Hackney & Bolton estates, 1979 and 1983 DOE, unpublished). More residents thought positively about the estates; more expressed confidence in the chance of improvements; more were satisfied with their homes; fewer felt isolated; and fewer felt that the estate would get worse. Most significantly, tenants' representatives were considered to have played a major role in bringing about changes. The recent Gifford report on Broadwater Farm Estate highlights the findings of an extensive tenants' survey (conducted by Jock Young of the Middlesex Polytechnic among 500 households) showing that a majority of tenants clearly perceived the estate as having significantly less crime than previously and being a friendly place. The report attributed a major role to the neighbourhood office as well as to the activities of residents' organizations (Gifford, 1986, pp. 157, 171, 237). The residents' positive views were expressed *after* the 1985 disturbances.

Table 11.2 gives a summary of the main findings of two surveys of tenants' attitudes conducted on the Willows Estate, Bolton, and

Table 11.2 Changes Registered over Four Years

Wenlock, 1983	Willows, 1983
Male unemployment rose fivefold to 20%	Threefold increase in unemployment to 40%
Proportion disagreeing it is a good place to live dropped from 35% to 18%	Proportion thinking the estate is not a good place halved
Opinion that the estate is getting worse dropped from 68% to 24%	Over half thought estate was improving
Fewer people felt isolated	Drop in proportion wanting to move away
Increase in numbers of children, double the proportion of one-parent families, yet children no longer considered the main reason for the estate getting worse	Twice as many thought estate would improve in future
	Vast majority now satisfied with accommodation
Repairs service more heavily criticized	Majority now considered repairs service good
	Large majority used local office and considered service good

Source: Social and Community Planning Research and Public Attitudes Survey 1979 and 1983.

Wenlock Barn Estate, Hackney. The first survey on each estate was in 1979, prior to the opening of the estate offices, and the second in 1983, after four years of operation. On both estates, tenants believed that the Tenants' Boards were primarily responsible for bringing about improvements.

The degree of local involvement and contact between staff and residents on all the survey estates was much greater following the opening of local offices than on the average estate, and, without exception, local staff were deeply committed to working with residents. Residents everywhere argued for local offices and claimed that access to housing services locally gave residents 'more chance'. But residents were not uncritical of the quality of management and very often expected a level of service and control that was not supplied by the council. In this sense only locally based and locally controlled management organizations such as co-operatives could work.

Beat Policing

Crime and the prevention of crime were major preoccupations of the residents. All projects except one suffered previously from an atmosphere of tension and fear of crime. The police were asked to play a visible, locally based, preventive role, very much as the council was. Communities invariably wanted 'law and order'.

Beat policing played a role on nineteen of the twenty project estates. Good policing was impossible without community resolve and because tenants everywhere felt vulnerable and dependent on good policing, the success of beat policing was linked with the rebuilding of tenants' confidence and control. It required direct dialogue between police and residents. The establishment of a local management office almost inevitably led to a change in policing from reactive response to a preventive beat approach to crime.

On thirteen estates, beat policing had an impact in improving police/community relations and was considered a success by residents and local staff. Beat policemen called in regularly at the estate office and patrolled the estate on foot. Only five worked exclusively on the estate. The five locally based police projects were undoubtedly the most successful (Newcastle/Gateshead Inner City Partnership, 1983, Appendix J). The policemen had close liaisons with residents and project staff. They spent a lot of time with children and were able to do preventive work, especially with the youth. Where the police covered a wider area than the estate, the results were on the whole less satisfactory because they were more diluted.

Thirteen projects reported that beat policing had helped inspire confidence and a sense of security in the community (Table 11.3). There was one clear failure, based on the police's inability to provide low-key, friendly policing in a hostile environment, and the total rejection by the youth of the estate of the kind of heavy-handed 'search and arrest' swoops that were the common response to repeated emergency calls. The estate was racially mixed and policing was strongly felt to be anti-black (Power, 1984, p. 73). The estate is discussed in greater detail below.

Actual crime records were available for only two projects.[1] Therefore the evidence of other 'successes' in beat policing was based on project staff assessments and on feed-back to them from residents. It

Table 11.3   Beat Policing on Nineteen Estates – Local Assessment of Impact

		Beat covered project area only	Beat covered wider area
Very successful	3	2	1
Satisfactory	10	3	7
Unsatisfactory	5	0	5
Failed	1	0	1

Source: Power, 1984, p. 28.

was also based on the police's own assessments of the value of beat policing. Residents and project staff universally argued in favour of local beat policing as opposed to more remote Panda car patrols and emergency responses, even where local policing had proved unsatisfactory.

We felt that local opinion was a valid way to assess the impact of crime and policing on an estate since the way people felt about security was a fairly clear measure of the actual effect of crime and vandalism and police activity. It was important that tenants *felt* safe in their homes, safe to walk around the estate, and confident enough to challenge vandals and report criminal activities, as this in turn brought policing into a more preventive role with strong community backing. At the end of the day only this worked (Scarman Report, 1984). Beat policing could only succeed in a high crime area where other processes were at work.

Social Control

It was not quite clear what actually brought the project estates into some kind of social order from disorder, but a transition did take place. The reduction in crime and vandalism and the increased feeling of security among tenants reported on fifteen of the estates resulted from a combination of factors, of which beat policing may have been only one element.

Many improvements in security related to the existence of the estate office, the introduction of door security, a reduction in the number of empty dwellings, the role of resident caretakers in patrolling the estate grounds, the employment of guards, wardens and door porters, the closure of walkways, and the demolition or securing of garages. The reduction in vandalism which was reported in thirteen of the project areas was probably a result of several changes, including stronger doors, better protected lighting, break-resistant glass, evening patrols, door guards, more responsive policing, the local office and the involvement of residents.

Tenants themselves had a part to play in increasing security. As estates improved and tenants' feelings about their surroundings became more positive, they were more likely to feel able to protect their homes and environment. Tenants were able to challenge vandalism and report crime if there was sufficient back-up for intervention from the estate office and the police, and if they felt confident that neighbours would support them in resisting reprisals and intimidation. The fact that tenants were calling on police and caretakers for help was a sure sign of a community upturn. The fact that beat policing and other security measures were reducing damage meant that some confidence was flowing back into the estate communities.

The households who were outside normal social controls posed special problems. Many people – residents, managers, councillors – said they were 'the real problem'. On one estate a family with four violent young members was held responsible for tyrannizing the estate and causing grievous bodily harm to an older resident. The atmosphere calmed down when two sons were sentenced and imprisoned. The evidence gathered would suggest that such households formed a small minority, though their impact was often out of all proportion to their numbers (CHAC, 1969, p. 81, para. 90). Estate offices reported a number of disruptive households on each estate – roughly 3 per cent of households per estate. That is a much, much higher proportion than in the population at large which Cullingworth in 1969 suggested was about 0.5 per cent (ibid., p. 33, para. 98; p. 31, para. 90). The concentration shows the effect of 'dumping' policies.

However, if 97 per cent of the population were determined, they could normally cope with 3 per cent of households who broke the norms and made estate-living unacceptable. One problem was that many other families were involved around the edges, but not quite to the same degree, whether out of fear of reprisals, childhood friendships, street or balcony social patterns, or simply being in the same boat. A central problem in curbing abuse was that the majority of tenants who caused no nuisance to neighbours and who simply wanted to live their own lives in peace did not want to stay on the estate, did not like its environment, did not identify with their neighbours and did not know how to curb the aggressive, anti-social behaviour meted out by the few. The rapid turnover of population also made normal controls difficult. There had been a sense of total defeat in the social atmosphere of all the estates that was reflected in the tenants' own verdict that neighbours were more to blame than the council for the estate being bad (Priority Estates Project, 1983). Council officers and caretakers frequently echoed this view. However, 'it is a gross error to equate problem families with the housing poor' (Cullingworth, 1979, p. 40).

Sometimes it needed an outside catalyst, a new initiative, or a determined stand by someone with authority and back-up to reverse this sense of defeat and powerlessness. A strong tenants' leader, invariably a woman, would sometimes emerge through the other initiatives with a clear belief that 'enough was enough, we've got to stop it' (Rock, 1986). We found that management pressure curtailed some of the problems – dogs and noise. Families who should never have lived on crowded communal estates were offered a chance to move off. The estates subsided to relative normality, helped by local lettings which resulted in the rapid occupation of empty flats. Beat policing was an important back-up to this change. On a London estate, a series of overcrowded parties, using stadium-sized amplifiers, was curtailed when an injunction was secured to prevent an all-night 'rent party' on a balcony flat.

In Kirklees, on a very run-down estate (not in the survey), housing officers were putting substantial pressure on tenants with uncontrolled dogs, on households with rubbish causing a health hazard, or on people causing distress to elderly or frail tenants. The Tenants' Association backed the council in this strong stand and was prepared to provide evidence in court if necessary. In one case, police protection was needed. Kirklees was one of the few authorities that had taken successful action in court to make social pressure stick. A tenant was evicted on grounds of statutory nuisance involving gross abuse of elderly neighbours. Tenants went to court as witnesses in the case with police protection. In other cases, the nuisance stopped in advance of court action.

The estates where it was difficult to make headway were those where the level of demand for council-rented accommodation was so low that dwellings could not be let except on a give-away basis; there, social abuse and disarray were often most severe. Greater Manchester, Merseyside and Tyneside all suffered from this overwhelming problem and the projects, to the extent that they were successful, were 'poaching' tenants from other waiting lists. Nor was there any point, as happened in two northern deck-access estates, in the local office presiding over the slow emptying of the estate through lack of demand. In both cases about a quarter of the dwellings were empty, and demolition and sales were being considered. On one of the estates on Tyneside, the increase in empty dwellings related directly to the local project office's success in reducing arrears, thereby helping tenants to gain a transfer to better accommodation, of which there was a ready supply. 'Lopping off' upper storeys to turn blocks of flats into terraced houses was an attractive alternative to full demolition or half-occupied, semi-derelict blocks. This had been done in three areas. Furnished bed-sitter experiments had to be tried in some cases as there was often heavy demand for this type of accommodation from young single people. It was not always a straightforward task to resolve social problems.

Broadwater Farm Estate in Haringey was referred to in the investigation of difficult-to-let housing as the estate that 'should never have been built' (Burbidge *et al*, 1981, Vol. 3). It was possibly the most interesting case in the study. It was included in our survey because Haringey Council opened an estate office there in 1981. In 1983, it became part of the national Priority Estates Project. In 1985, it was the scene of 'the most ferocious riots ever seen on the mainland' (Gifford, 1986, p. 3).

Its brief history is intriguing. It was built in an absurd way and ended up with major policing problems, yet it proved to be more resilient than was forecast. A major slum-clearance programme was initiated in Haringey in 1965, generating the need for large-scale housing development. Allotment land near Lordship Park was seized upon as an obvious location, in spite of serious drainage problems. The housing department drew up its requirements in terms of bedroom size, and the planning department worried about roads, vehicular access and car parking. As speed was of the essence, the government's advice to use industrialized building methods was followed. The scheme was not designed as such. 'An outline sketch and a notional bill of quantities' were the only basis on which the local authority asked the largest and most experienced industrialized building firms to tender. Many vital elements, such as enclosing the massive service ducts and the 'cavernous' underground car parking areas were omitted from the final product because of the way the tendering agreement was reached with Taylor Woodrow Anglian. The essential design feature of Broadwater Farm was that it was to be all concrete and all on stilts, with walkways in the air entering all blocks, because of the frequent flooding of the land on which it was to be built. The estate of 1,063 dwellings took only three years to build and cost £6,000 per dwelling, about the same as it would have cost in 1965 to rescue and modernize a dilapidated terraced house from the slum-clearance programme. There were two eighteen-storey tower blocks, built in the same style as Ronan Point and with the same method of construction. The rest of the estate was in 'scissor' maisonettes, interspersed with some blocks of flats. The scissor maisonettes had awkward internal layouts and noise problems because of the large number of adjacent neighbours. The few attempts at landscaping could not 'blunt [the estate's] overwhelming effect on the environment' (Burbidge *et al.*, 1981, Vol. 3).

Broadwater Farm was nicknamed Windscale by Haringey's lettings officers because of the combination of its awesome style, the fear it generated in residents and would-be residents, and the climatic changes caused by its towers and its stilt structure.

The most extraordinary feature of this saga was that an international building firm was left to draw up its own design and shape the development. Haringey Council had minimal input or practical control. The difficult-to-let investigators were so appalled by the physical problems of the estate that they felt 'at best the local authority can hope to make it tolerable for the next decade or so, but eventually because the estate is so monolithic ... the possibility of demolition is one that will have to be considered' (Burbidge *et al.*, 1981, Vol. 2, p. 31).

However, the government team's devastating long-term death sentence on the six-year-old, £6 million estate was belied by their own analysis of some of the management and social problems of the estate. True enough, it was difficult to let and unrepresentative of the population as a whole, as Table 11.4 shows. But the council's lettings policies generated many of the problems that Table 11.4 illustrates. One-bedroom flats in one of the tower blocks were let primarily to young, black, single mothers. Three-quarters of all empty dwellings were let to homeless families and lettings appeared to be racially biased. The 1981 Census showed the proportion of New Commonwealth-born heads of household on Broadwater Farm to be 36 per cent. Because of the larger numbers of children in minority households, 42 per cent of all residents lived in households where the head of the household was born in the New Commonwealth or Pakistan, four times higher than the area as a whole.

The Department of the Environment described the increasing management problems as 'a catastrophic slide'. The council for its part changed its allocation policies towards Broadwater Farm, restricting lettings to exclude homeless families, one-parent families and unemployed people from all lettings on the Farm for two years.

Table 11.4 Lettings Problems on Broadwater Farm

	Broadwater Farm	Haringey
Rate of refusals of lettings offers	53%	35%
Lettings to homeless families	75%	25%
Rate of transfer applications	20%	10%
Rate of termination of tenancies (eviction)	9%	4%
Proportion of manual (unskilled and semi-skilled) workers	44%	30%
Rate of Social Services referrals	26 per 1,000 households	4 per 1,000 households*
Rent arrears	74% in arrears (£266 owed on average per arrears case)	53% in arrears (£120 owed on average per arrears case)

*Social Services referrals for the rest of the South Tottenham area where estate is based, not including Broadwater Farm estate.
Source: London Borough of Haringey, 1976.

Certain physical improvements were introduced as well. The lettings restrictions also had some effect and morale improved, but as soon as these were abandoned at the end of a two-year period, the estate went into sharp decline again.

Meanwhile, major problems had developed between the large numbers of disaffected, unemployed black youths on the estate and the local police. Because of a high crime rate and the major security problems generated by the design, the police tended to respond in force to emergencies only. Nervous, elderly tenants would call the police at a sign of trouble from congregating youngsters. The police would come in Panda cars and conflict would erupt. By 1981, the estate was considered a virtual 'no go' area.

From the point of view of housing management, many mistakes were made. Not only were lettings made without sufficient care or forethought and with considerable discrimination against vulnerable groups, but there was only one estate officer for the whole estate and there was no local repairs team. However, there was resident care-taking.

The final blow to the community, fractured and racially divided as it was, came when the council landlord offered one of the vacant shops to the police for them to set up a home-beat station on the estate. The inference was taken to be that the place was out of hand and only the police could stand in authority over the community. The tenants, leaderless, divided and demoralized as they had appeared, saw red, and in a series of meetings, petitions and encounters with their landlord forced the council to withdraw their offer to the police and provide accommodation for the fledgling Youth Association instead. The estate officer had meanwhile also been given an office in one of the shops.

From that point, the survey's prediction of demolition within a decade became a challenge to the ingenuity of council and residents alike. The story of the upturn of Broadwater Farm does not belong with the difficult-to-let survey, which concluded that 'The hasty design and construction of Broadwater Farm has been repented at leisure [and] regretted even more by the tenants.' The pessimism was misplaced.

A remarkable tenant with teenage children took the initiative, deciding that the energy of youth could help the estate. Crime was as bad for the youth who were commonly associated with it as it was disastrous for the victims. She organized, with her own teenagers and their friends, the Broadwater Farm Youth Association, with the declared aim of winning over the youth of the estate to constructive activities and away from crime. She was as concerned for the elderly white population as she was for the black youth. As a result of taking

227

over a derelict shop to house a club for the youth, her standing rose sky-high. The youth began to take a pride in leaving money and goods around in their club. It was a challenge to anyone to dare offend the name of the Youth Association by 'nicking'. The Youth Association has organized a food shop, a nursery, a mothers' support centre and a lunch club, and also runs meals on wheels for elderly residents of the estate. The service it provides is regarded by two-thirds of residents as good (Gifford, 1986, p. 157). Meanwhile, Haringey Council established a highly efficient neighbourhood housing office on the estate in 1983 and the police introduced a beat team (Zipfel, 1985).

The serious disturbances in October 1985 in Tottenham were seen by many observers as an indictment of the estate. Calls for its demolition were heard again in several quarters. However, the Gifford report (Gifford, 1986) describes carefully the role of the community organizations, the Youth Association and the Neighbourhood Office in improving conditions on the estate. The emotive trigger on 5 October 1985 of the sudden death of Mrs Jarrett during a police raid on her home led to a major outbreak of disorders, but it came after a long period of tension, recorded during our survey visit in 1982 (Power, 1984, p. 73). The question remains whether the police will be able to rebuild the confidence of the racially conscious, highly motivated and jealously communitarian tenants who want community policing but are seriously mistrustful of the police (Gifford, 1986).

Broadwater Farm was one of the few estates where almost every management initiative was in train – a local repairs team, locally supervised resident caretaking and cleaning, tenants on the management panel, local recruitment for estate jobs, and a multi-racial local staff team, 50 per cent of whom were residents on the estate. The total cost of the management and maintenance effort there was £13.50 a week in 1986. Social and management problems in the late 1970s had provoked almost total despair, which in turn galvanized the tenants into their own remarkable turnaround. The council has been more than anxious to respond. In spite of popular press coverage to the contrary, the crime rate there fell by 50 per cent between 1983 and 1985 and has remained low since the riots; about sixty estate-based jobs have been created, and the estate has an excellent record on caretaking and repairs as well. The role of the youth, the tenants and the estate office in the reversal of decline has been critical. The Gifford inquiry summed it up:

Four factors coincided to save Broadwater Farm from total decline. First there were members of the local community who were prepared to start from nothing and retain their hope against all the odds. Secondly there were a number of trusted local community leaders who at crucial points were catalysts in the organisation of change. Thirdly the local authority was willing to change its structures and to admit great errors in its previous action. Fourthly there was skilled support from outside by the Priority Estates Project and the Department of the Environment. (Gifford, 1986, p. 233)

The Children

There were many children on most of the project estates. Evidence from the difficult-to-let investigation and our own survey suggests that 30 per cent of the population might be under 16 compared with 22 per cent in the population as a whole (Lambeth, 1984). Children and young people were often blamed for the damage, crime and disruption that was so common (Wilson, 1978). Some of the older children and teenagers were certainly capable of substantial damage and were hard to reach. This cycle had to be broken down.

The children and young people were a key to protecting the environment and the general security of the estate. Their direct involvement often diverted their energies away from more destructive activities and made them want to protect improvements they had helped create. Children had to be seen as an asset to community life. Their *joie de vivre*, their ability to survive, their ingenious defiance of their too harsh childhood, made them the most special members of the community. Competitive sport and heavy activity (boxing, football, camping), material rewards (crisps, a coke, a free swim) and access to the outside world were the prizes they coveted and the things that won them over to helping. They never wanted to help for long but it helped them stop destroying. Like the children in *Lord of the Flies* and Graham Greene's *Destructors*, they were often horrified at their bullying power and wanted to find the limit. The feeling of things giving way under their pressure made them feel deeply insecure and even more destructive. The closer the limit could be drawn with the toughest of the youngsters, the more likely the estate was to curb its social disarray. But it was not a discipline that could be imposed easily. Almost everyone wanted lines to be drawn and it was a matter of making the first move very carefully and then the second, with enough of the key actors helping both draw and hold the line. Adults from within the community were needed to back the involvement, the restraint and the encouragement of youngsters (Donnison, *The Observer*, 14 March 1982). Youth leaders' and playleaders' jobs often went to residents once more permanent youth provision developed, though far more training and local job opportunities were called for.

However, wanton destruction, curbed through the initial efforts, did not stay at bay for long and new gangs had a nasty habit of forming immediately in the wake of the reformed gang that had just converted to gardening. So, like rubbish, vandalism was not something that was overcome once and for all. It had to be fought day in, day out. Some estates were more resilient than others. There was something about the environment of some estates that invited damage, no matter what was done, and only a much greater degree of social control and tighter guarding seemed likely to overcome the vandalism. In the end, only extremely tough-minded residents could do it. The local offices were doing a holding operation with the help of the residents, but the future of the estates was far from secure.

Tenants, estate staff, caretakers, police, all needed to know that the other adult groups were prepared to set limits. They needed to advance in concert. Otherwise estate workers held on to outmoded views of tenants' lack of care and destructiveness, while tenants continued to feel that the council was a useless landlord because it could not keep things in order and stop the estate from being 'a bad place'. That was why in the end, tenant consultation and involvement and the local workforce based in a local office were vital. Through that network of contact, the council landlord discovered, often with surprise, that the disarrayed community had a total identity of interest with the housing authority: to make the estate liveable in and able to pay its way for a decent service; to protect the capital and social investment; to enhance the chances of the next generation of 'problem' children; to call the bluff of the bullies; and to call out the courage of the silent mainstream, the ordinary people who had never been asked before and who did not want to speak out of turn, but who in the end wanted to feel satisfied with their home, and exercise some control over it. A retired caretaker put it best:

> I'm seventy this week, and in all my life so far no one's ever asked me for my thoughts about anything ... I've often thought it might be a good idea if the GLC sent people round say once every year or so, asking people on the estate what their feelings were. But of course they never did, which is why it's such a sad place now.
>
> ... When they first built it twenty years ago or more it was going to be paradise, wasn't it? ... They'd all been living in very bad conditions, in slums and places like that, and here was this marvellous modern new housing estate ... in those early days there was a great sense of community among the people who came to live on Providence. They all knew that they had all come here to have a new start in life.
>
> ... it just strikes me as a funny thing that's all, that all the years

230

I was working on the estate no one ever asked me my views about it.

Oh yes, it is a sad place now. (Parker, 1983, p. 255)

Note to Chapter 11

1 The Springwell estate, Gateshead, showed a decrease in reported crime and vandal damage of 30 per cent in the twelve-month period, March 1981–2. Three beat policemen were based full-time on the estate during that period. (Newcastle/Gateshead Inner City Partnership, 1983, Appendix J).

Chapter Twelve

Summary of Main Themes and Conclusion: A Way Forward

All is far from well with large numbers of council estates. But there is growing experience of attempts to rectify the most severe problems, partially adopting the tried and tested methods that set in train the social housing revolution of late Victorian times. Octavia Hill had pioneered an intimate, custodial, and locally based housing management organization that depended on the goodwill and support of the tenants as much as it did on the dedication and care of the landlord. It was a workable scale of organization that the new public landlords failed to reproduce as they steadily emerged to be the largest landlords in the country.

In summarizing the main themes of this book, I hope to show that a way forward can be found for the much needed rented sector through the management initiatives that we have examined.

Victorian Housing Troubles and Reform, 1862–1914

The rapid development of towns and the spread of factory employment led to dense urban housing in tightly packed terraces that quickly became slums under crowded and impoverished conditions. Octavia Hill, inspired by the awful conditions in central London, persuaded rich benefactors to buy up slum houses, and hand them over to her. She developed a system of intensive management among the most destitute slum inhabitants that relied on constant personal contact, careful business management, essential but modest repairs and improvements, and retention of the existing community in old but improved dwellings. Octavia Hill trained many women in this new style of landlordism and inspired a powerful movement among leading philanthropists like Lord Shaftesbury. She bitterly opposed the building of large blocks of flats. She argued that women were naturally

232

better housing managers than men. She did not think elected councils should become direct landlords, and she pleaded for each family to have its own patch of outdoor space, no matter how small.

The Victorian housing trusts began at about the same time as Octavia Hill was working, but developed a new style of model dwellings built in dense blocks of tenement flats, housing only the 'poor of good character' and charging rents beyond the means of the most needy. However, the trusts did establish intensive, local resident management based on close relations with the tenants. They have managed to run seemingly unpopular, densely built blocks effectively to this day.

Local authorities began building model dwellings in the last twenty years of the nineteenth century, copying the new style of flat-building of the housing trusts but incorporating very little of their management technique. The early council blocks in London were sometimes hard to let and were run from the beginning from County Hall where housing functions were acquired by different departments. The land-lord service was remote and fragmented from the outset. Rents generally were high; the most desperate families were pushed into a diminishing supply of private accommodation. Early council housing was expensive and housed a privileged population of artisans and securely employed workers. By 1914, councils and the trusts together provided only a tiny fragment of housing; 90 per cent of households still renting from private landlords, often in poor conditions.

The First Attempts at Mass Slum Clearance and Rehousing, 1918–39

The acute housing shortage and accelerating decay, which were highlighted by the First World War, led to innovative general subsidies for new buildings. Councils produced many new high-quality estates on the edge of cities. But from 1930 onwards a radical shift took place. Subsidies became tied to slum clearance, to the rehousing of slum dwellers and to relief of overcrowding. Higher subsidies were made available for flats on expensive city land, and the modern pattern of welfare housing in dense, inner-city, flatted estates was established. The governments of the day were determined to tackle slums. Over a million council dwellings were built under these subsidies before the Second World War.

Social problems quickly emerged in the uprooted new communities, and while the women housing managers were increasingly influential on the welfare aspects of slum demolition and rehousing, they were largely ignored on matters of overall housing management by the rapidly expanding local authorities. The public landlords carried out their duties to tenants through assorted departments: Finance, Engineers, Surveyors, Sanitary Departments and Town Clerks. They threw up their own municipally oriented housing body, founded in 1932 as the Institute of Housing, which openly opposed the integrated and localized emphasis of the rival, and better qualified, Society of Women Housing Managers, founded in 1916 to carry on Octavia Hill's work and tradition.

Many estates were difficult to run, and tarnished with the same reputation as the slums they were built to replace. A coherent housing management structure had not evolved within local authorities, though some attempts were made by a small minority of housing departments to graft a social and welfare role on to the more 'professional' aspects of housing.

The landlord service was delivered in a fragmented way, attracting less attention and interest than building, and argued over in acrimonious and jealous terms by the various professional protagonists. The government collected evidence of this great confusion for its 1939 CHAC report, which admirably summed up the problem but failed to give any sense of direction to the way forward for public landlords. Local authority housing departments like the LCC were complacent about the management service, blaming failings on the minority of bad tenants who could not adapt to the better conditions now offered.

The Postwar Housing Boom, 1945–80

By the end of the Second World War, with extensive bombing of cities, further rent freezes and disinvestment in old slum areas, the housing situation was chronic. For twenty-five years a massive public housing boom was generated by Labour and Conservative Governments, with generous subsidies for slum clearance, demolition and flat-building. The higher the block, the greater the proportion of subsidies. Councils were the major providers throughout the period and flats became the dominant form of new construction.

Because of the vastly ambitious scale of public building (4 million council homes in thirty-five years), the desire to produce large, dense, flatted estates in a monotonous, almost mindless style was unsurprising. Industrial building and high-rise flats seemed obvious answers to the numbers game. Massive clearance of seemingly obsolete houses, often condemned for lack of amenity and overcrowding rather than structural flaws, was an insensitive response.

But the cities emptied partly as a result of clearance, and new estates housed only a small proportion of existing residents. The exodus to suburban owner-occupation was fuelled by slum demolition and council building. Small job centres were often demolished too.

The result was a largely unpopular style and scale of new housing, reduced demand in many urban areas, and major problems of damp, structural defects and communal layout, that led to vandalism, fear of crime and increased difficulties in letting. By the time councils stopped building unpopular housing monoliths, much demand for public housing had effectively evaporated. The result was a sharp decline for the largest and sometimes most modern estates.

The Development of Housing Management within Local Authorities, 1945 to 1985

The massive building boom of the postwar era, producing large, costly and difficult-to-run estates, generated an unprecedented scale of management problems.

The typical housing department comprised a lettings and welfare section, with repairs, rent collection and building dealt with by separate departments of the local authority. The recruitment of staff for the rapidly expanding housing departments proved difficult, standards were lowered drastically and training was minimal. 'Rationalization and streamlining' were the order of the day, with severe cutbacks in the already poor estate-based services.

At the same time, the bureaucratization of procedures narrowed and tightened functions, limiting room for manoeuvre and enhancing the sectional division of responsibilities. Power was increasingly concentrated in fast expanding town halls, and estate-based staff became more and more divorced from decision-making and control, as well as increasingly ineffectual in relation to tenants. They were expected to cover more and more ground with less and less power to deliver. Contact was reduced to a bare minimum, and often done away with altogether, with the withdrawal of rent collectors, the centralization of repairs, and the reduction in cleaning and caretaking services. Staff numbers increased at the centre but were actually cut at estate level in the period of rapid expansion from 1950 to 1975.

Because slum clearance generated such huge instant demand, and because the imperative to build large and high seemed so overriding, housing departments operated under a siege of applications, waiting lists, 'decanting' and demolition. Little or no thought went into the long-term management implications. Even weighty government reports on living in flats, rehousing 'unneighbourly' families and organizing a 'comprehensive housing service' failed to address the fundamental issues of flat-building, localized services, diseconomies of scale, landlord–tenant relations, repairs, and the more basic welfare or service role of housing. Housing departments grew in importance and sophistication, but also in complexity and size. Rarely did they control all aspects of estate management, and up to twelve entirely separate departments might be involved in any one estate. The housing department itself might consist of half a dozen separate hierarchies of functions. By the 1970s, individual housing departments often employed hundreds of staff, controlling thousands of properties – 38,000 in the average metropolitan area – worth hundrds of millions of pounds.

By the time public housing started to fall seriously from favour in the mid-1970s, the public landlord had almost lost control of estate management. Unpopular dwellings were coupled with a remote service that tenants could not identify with or locate. Meanwhile, housing staff found it increasingly difficult to deliver on anything but the narrowest part of the total service. The attempt to organize a comprehensive housing service in the mid-1970s tackled the problem at the wrong level and on the wrong scale – mid-1970s local government was too complex to respond.

Access to Public Housing: Need or Merit

Since 1945, the allocation of council housing was the most strife-torn and confused area of housing management. Having started out with carefully selected, economically secure tenants, local authorities shifted in the 1930s almost totally to poor, overcrowded slum dwellers, whose conditions were overwhelmingly bad. After the Second World War, public housing was declared 'for all', but the massive shortage made rehousing more like a mad scramble than a priority system. When slum clearance began again, rehousing from demolition areas took overriding precedence, but although access according to need was widely accepted, the major issue of distributing an uneven stock between conflicting groups remained to be resolved. A system of points was developed, which sometimes included the grading of a family's standards, their merit based on behaviour and rent-paying records. This system required lettings officers to sit in judgement over who 'deserved' the most popular or least popular homes. A complicated 'system' of matching quality of applicant with quality of rehousing was developed and applied in most local authorities. Access to council housing was no longer the dominant issue, rather the key question was who gained access to *popular* estates or areas.

236

Vulnerable categories, such as the homeless, racial minorities, welfare recipients and unemployed, tended to receive the lowest grade offers and became disproportionately concentrated in the least popular estates. There was such a large area of discretion within a highly complex and therefore largely invisible central lettings system that sifting inevitably took place.

Large-scale transfers made matters worse by offering more ambitious and 'respectable' existing tenants the chance to upgrade their housing. The instability and substantial vacancies created by transfers off the worst estates reinforced their unpopularity, resulting in widespread lettings on these estates to the most desperate households. Lettings therefore became the tool of segregation and discrimination in the public sector, resulting in a polarization between good and bad estates, forcing residents of the bad estates constantly to seek a way out, and trapping the 'lowest category' applicants in the areas with the worst reputation.

Meanwhile sharpening social polarization between a growing owner-occupied sector and a declining council rented sector – during a period of growing unemployment and increased family break-up – heightened management problems on the least popular estates. The investigation of difficult-to-let council housing was the first published report by the government concerning the specific problem of socially and physically undesirable estates (Burbidge *et al.*, 1981). Its evidence was damning, cautiously worded as it was, and it highlighted beyond doubt both the magnitude of the design failure of modern estates and the total inadequacy of housing management and maintenance organizations. Most importantly, it highlighted the social distress and ghetto-like communities generated through a lettings system that pushed the most desperate households to the worst estates, and it exposed officially for the first time a crude over-supply of council dwellings in some areas of the country.

The difficult-to-let investigation forged a partnership between a worried central government and desperate local authority housing departments that led directly to the advent of local management on many unpopular council estates.

Local Management Survey

In 1979, the Department of the Environment created the Priority Estates Project to develop and monitor, with local authorities, experiments in reversing conditions on unpopular estates through a local management office with the full involvement and backing of tenants. A survey was conducted in 1982 of the first twenty special housing initiatives on run-down estates in nineteen local authorities, giving valuable details about the nature of the problems and possible ways of tackling them.

The twenty estates were spread across the country and ranged from cottage-style, prewar estates, through balcony-style flatted estates, to the modern concrete complex estates of the 1960s onwards. The average size of the estates was 1,000 dwellings. The main design problems related to the scale of the estates, their communal nature, the poorly maintained environment and, on the flatted estates, the oppressive, dense style and the constantly damaged and poorly protected lifts, stairs, rubbish chambers, garages and drying rooms.

Every communal part was abused. All the estates suffered from youthful vandalism. The modern concrete estates suffered from leaks, damp, condensation, and noise in more intense form than the others. Cottage estates could be just as decayed and unpopular as the flatted estates, but it was easier to see how they could be restored. The thirteen flatted estates in the survey were depressingly large, anonymous and even frightening.

The design of the twenty estates led to major social and management problems. Allocation of housing was probably the single most dominant question and the survey showed that there were above average concentrations of many disadvantaged groups on the twenty estates. Thus homeless families, one-parent families, large families, racial minorities and unemployed adults were all over-represented.

At the same time, there was a higher rate of turnover of tenants, causing instability and unrest, with many tenants aiming to upgrade their housing by leaving. A corollary of the lettings and turnover problems was a high proportion of empty dwellings. This applied to almost all the estates too. Some estates had as many as a hundred empty dwellings and one estate was almost a quarter empty. Empty dwellings created a chain reaction. More people refused to come and live there because of the atmosphere of dereliction. Vandalism and theft to empty property increased with the volume of empty dwellings. The cost of all this damage was substantial and, coupled with the loss of rent income, generated serious financial losses. Often squatting developed.

Communal facilities, where they existed, were often ill-used. Where they did not exist, the estate seemed barren and spiritless. Rent arrears were exceptionally high on almost all the estates, but there were wide variations and some management systems seemed unable to cope with them. The disappearance of door-to-door rent collection was a major setback. The alternative of legal sanctions was ineffective, costly and extremely damaging to landlord–tenant relations.

Repairs presented serious problems and were invariably run independently of housing management under a remote system. Homes were generally poorly maintained. Cleansing, parks and social services departments all ran their separate operations, unconnected with each other or with the housing department. Generally, performance was poor and the estate received a service commensurate with its generally low reputation. No estate had a local management office prior to the projects, and no estate caretakers worked in a team with estate officers or repairs or social workers.

Tenants were often isolated, frightened and desperate to escape. Councillors were often at their wits' end. Steps to remedy this situation were taken in nineteen local authorities.

The Impact of Local Management

We examined the local offices which were opened on the twenty estates in an attempt to stem overwhelming decline. When they were set up, their impact on the local community was immediate, opening up extensive and frequent contact between landlord and tenants and providing an on-the-spot service, cutting through red tape and acting as a pressure point and arbiter with the council. The cumulative experience of the first twenty local management projects has provided the basis for many further initiatives. The most important lessons can be summarized as follows:

(1) Local estate offices which were open all day to tenants, with full-time staff, direct management responsibility and all housing records, brought about an impressive improvement in landlord–tenant relations.

(2) Almost all estates were undergoing physical modernization and adaptation, often incurring major expense. On the whole this reinvestment was successful in rebuilding the popularity of the estates, but it relied heavily on local management to ensure long-term maintenance. Responding to tenants' priorities was a pre-requisite of success.

(3) Local management of repairs, rents and lettings was only partially handed over to the local office. Where local repairs teams were introduced they were highly popular, efficient and cost-effective. Local lettings brought about a significant reduction in the number of empty dwellings and also substantial savings in vandal damage and loss of rent income. However, local lettings and local repairs were introduced on only eight of the twenty estates.

(4) Rent arrears were on the whole being contained but continued at a high level, except in four projects where the amount of arrears actually fell.

(5)   Resident caretaking was a vital part of local management and was felt by everyone to be the backbone of the landlord service. Standards rose in most projects and resident caretaking was recognized as essential in *all* blocks of flats.

(6)   The environment of all the estates was upgraded by communal effort, local initiatives involving children and youth, and changes in layout.

(7)   Most local offices were not given enough direct responsibility to execute all management functions but they were able to put pressure on central systems and on the whole brought about an improved service. The more local autonomy, the more effective the local office was.

(8)   Beat policing was needed to reduce crime and help curb social abuse. In all projects major efforts were being made to build up a sense of security and to re-establish some coherent sense of community control. The local housing office, with the backing of residents and police, appeared to be the key to achieving a normal, peaceful living environment.

(9)   The residents were directly involved in myriad ways in the development of the twenty projects. This was inevitable when once the office doors had opened. It appeared to be the most effective and long-lasting way of ensuring an upturn in the fortunes of unpopular estates.

(10) The local management projects had more staff on the ground than previously. But the projects were not, as is commonly imagined, expensive. They were affordable by the nineteen local authorities, and indeed they brought about substantial cash savings. No local authority questioned the value of the invest-ment in local management.

Were these improvements no more than a flash in the pan, the renowned 'Hawthorne effects' whereby change itself improves perfor-mance temporarily? We can look for comment to Miss Janet Upcott, who died in 1986 aged ninety-seven, the last of the original trainees of Octavia Hill herself. She was reported to smile wryly as she watched well-tried, 'old-fashioned' management techniques being rediscovered in the 1980s. She had far too long an experience of housing manage-ment to call it 'the Hawthorne effect'. The local management tech-niques had remained valid for 120 years, but had only rarely been applied to council housing.

The Future

There are many financial questions which impinge directly on unpopular estates and the future of their management. Levels of housing benefit will significantly influence levels of rent arrears and will affect income for management and maintenance. Far more must be spent on repairs if the stock is to be preserved (DOE, 1985).

Rate-capped local authorities, generally the hardest-pressed with the most formidable problems, may be obliged to reduce their rate contribution to housing without being able to reduce their debt liabilities. Again, spending on management and maintenance will suffer. But special help is needed for the large stock of dense flatted estates in the London boroughs and other major cities (Audit Commission, 1986).

As long as the right to buy favours the better-off in the better property, the council sector will be increasingly polarized. It is hard to see how new incentives to buy flats will impinge on the least popular estates without intensive management. Yet proposed restrictions on service charges for sold flats will limit the scope for management and maintenance.

There are other unresolved issues. The number of manual jobs in local authorities is decreasing and white-collar jobs increasing. The white-collar unions often exercise a stranglehold on essential services and resist change or extract a high price for it. Official homelessness is on the increase, yet families are reported to refuse accommodation on the worst estates in many London authorities, and the number of families in temporary bed and breakfast accommodation is rising, sometimes in the very boroughs with the most empty council dwellings. The cost to councils per family is much higher than alternative solutions to the problem. More building in areas of high demand would ease pressure through the process of 'filtering up', but would not itself help the homeless and the very poor unless the least desirable housing was improved and run properly. The experience in the United States of many hundreds of thousands sleeping rough while 'filtering up' has raised general standards illustrates the problems of access and management as well as supply of housing.

Some housing departments are attempting to decentralize services on a borough-wide basis. But there are major barriers to relinquishing central control and establishing viable local entities. Meanwhile, the areas covered by decentralized 'local' offices usually involve several estates which rarely have a common sense of identity or organizational simplicity. Thus local offices may fail to resolve the core problems of the worst estates. Local housing management works where it is estate-based and the optimum size is up to about 1,000 dwellings. The estate itself normally defines the area covered.

Large areas of the country have a crude lack of demand for conventional family council housing, of which there is an over-supply. Waiting lists are often overweighted with single teenagers wanting to leave home, hoping to get access to property that more highly pointed applicants reject. Needs and housing supply are in serious imbalance, by size and type of unit.

Major economic and social issues impinge heavily on council housing. Large institutions – mental hospitals, children's homes and hostels – discharge vulnerable people 'into the community'. As there is a chronic shortage of supported, sheltered accommodation, such households often end up on the largest and most disarrayed estates where there are vacant dwellings but the least resources to help. Poor estates also contain a high concentration of the unemployed and, with the rise in unemployment, this tendency has increased. The poorest housing communities outside the south-east have generally more than 50 per cent of the adult male population out of work. In the north, as few as 10 per cent may have jobs on the worst estates. Even in London on some estates, over half of households may have no wage-earner (Gifford, 1986, p. 155). A very low-income community has fewer inner resources because more people are close to the margin of survival.

Many factors – crime levels, truancy, drug abuse and general poverty which disproportionately affect the weakest sections in society – spell a bleak long-term future for council landlords and tenants, unless more creative use is found for the physical capital and human energy which has in the past been so undervalued.

Housing Management of the Future

Councils, especially city councils, are generally too big and too complex to co-ordinate or execute effectively the meticulous delivery of landlord responsibilities. They thus suffer from distant and some-times acrimonious relations with tenants, although the extreme condi-tions we have described only apply to one-quarter of the total council stock.

A minority of households is often blamed for the problems of estate management, and new building is the most commonly proposed solution. However, neither changing the population of council estates nor embarking on a major new demolition programme is a realistic or humane way forward in the immediate future. The poorest people suffer the greatest hardship as a result of demolition, which destroys existing, if fragile, communities.

There are a number of changes in organization which could make a significant difference to the operation of housing services on the worst estates. The first is a specific management and maintenance allowance for all council dwellings, to encourage management and maintenance budgets separate from all other housing spending and from other central council costs. The amount needed would be in the region of £10–15 per dwelling per week (1985 figures). A proportion should be designated for planned maintenance. A target amount would facilitate the provision of budgets for each estate and encourage local management organizations to flourish. Estate budgets facilitate local decision-making, help protect services and monitor quality.

The second change is to reorganize the traditional council housing management hierarchy into locally based entities along the lines of schools, hospitals, banks and other services. All basic housing management, rents, repairs, lettings and welfare support should be part of the local organization. As there is no known economy of scale in housing services, such a reorganization, while reaching the customer more effectively, should not add significantly to real costs, except where local authorities are seriously underspending on housing management and maintenance. The localization of housing services is the first step on the most run-down estates. Other services, such as health, social services and police, may require similar local bases.

The third change would be to tailor capital investment and major repair and improvement programmes to the priorities of residents, and to scale down all building contracts to locally manageable proportions, putting them under the control of the local office. Work should be done incrementally on a smaller scale than hitherto but as part of a permanent programme of renewal. Crash capital programmes on a yearly basis are often chaotic and counter-productive. Careful reinvestment is urgently needed and should form part of planned maintenance programmes funded through the management and maintenance allowance.

The fourth development would be to enhance the formal role of residents in the running of their estates. Only where the community is at the forefront of changes do improvements succeed in inspiring its support. There are several formulae for the residents' role. A locally constituted management body, comprising elected residents and council nominees, could preside over the running of all day-to-day estate affairs, in conjunction with staff, within the policy guidelines laid down by the council, with a discreet budget to cover running costs and with performance targets to meet. Management co-operatives, community-based housing associations and trusts are other models. The major requirement is a management entity of realistic size – anything from 100 to 1,500 dwellings – with a locally based controlling body and locally based staff. Administrative and policy links can be retained as long as they do not strangle the service. Many other services operate on the basis of a 'franchise', and housing management is ideally suited to delegated structures (Inquiry into British Housing, 1985b).

The fifth point is that manual jobs are vital to the healthy operation of landlord services. Caretaking, local repairs and cleaning make the critical difference between a habitable estate and a veritable slum. These jobs can only be sacrificed at the risk of hastening demolition programmes already under way in some councils, often for social and custodial rather than structural reasons. The Audit Commission's proposals for economizing on caretaking (1986) do not make management sense, although they represent a severe criticism of some caretaking standards. Without a local management organization and close supervision of staff, the least agreeable jobs are unlikely to be well performed. With local supervision, caretakers are worth their weight in gold. There is no case for reducing manual jobs on most estates.

The sixth element would attack the size, scale and anomie of council housing in the least popular areas from as many angles as possible, by physically breaking it down into small, manageable units; by enclosing much of the unused public space and making it into individual gardens; by guarding and maintaining all necessary communal services and access points; by personalizing details such as colour schemes, door designs, gardens and other areas; by encouraging individual initiative, enterprise and vitality; and by enhancing the enforcement of basic social norms through the close working liaison between landlord and tenants' representatives, cleaners, repair and maintenance workers and gardeners.

The most difficult change would be to broaden the socio-economic base of the most unpopular areas by introducing a variety of tenures on the large, socially segregated estates, and by having a much more open lettings system throughout the council sector, without residential qualifications, points assessment or grading for the mass of applicants, using the simple concept of queuing, but with a fall-back priority system for households who cannot find their own way into the local housing market. The corollary of priority rehousing would be intensive management, recognizing that vulnerable households might need other forms of support if they are to survive in the community and make their way without falling back on the large institutions that have previously sheltered so many. By opening up areas of low demand to a more flexible, open-door access system, the extent of housing demand, which may not be reflected at all accurately in housing waiting lists, will be uncovered and difficulties in letting decline. A new look should be taken at the need for furnished lettings too, as new demand may come from young single people requiring an organized housing structure coupled with independence, but not necessarily unrestrained freedom or sole use of and responsibility for a self-contained council flat. At the same time, in unpopular areas, the local waiting list administered by a local manager should encourage people with ties in the area to apply, thereby strengthening the community. Homelessness is to some extent created by restricted access to council accommodation. Access therefore must be made easier.

The right to buy and sales of unwanted blocks of flats should be balanced by allowing local authorities to acquire street properties so that the disequilibrium between council flats and houses in inner areas can be gradually redressed. There is a need for at least 30 per cent of the total housing stock to be rented, according to major building societies. Housing associations, trusts and co-operatives could expand the direct provision of rented dwellings while local authorities could develop special programmes to combat homelessness and other local crises. It is important for the right to buy to be implemented more widely on flatted estates so that monolithic, segregated, one-tenure communities become more varied. Sound local management and greater social stability are keys to this happening.

It is relatively easy to diagnose the problems of estate management under historic local authority regimes. The tenants are a loosely knit group of disparate households required to liaise from time to time with a housing district or housing department – usually both. There is no focal point. A local management office replicates all the central confusion if it is simply a referral point for tenants. Everything hinges on the local manager having delegated authority and being clearly in charge of the total housing service to the estate. Then other departments can work through the local office. Ideally, they will be estate-based too and will form part of the local team. From a management point of view, clearly the horizontal, unitary organization shown in Figure 12.2 is more workable than the centipede structure of Figure 12.1.

The process of change will not be easy, as those authorities pioneering decentralization are finding. The average local authority will require up to thirty highly trained, competent and imaginative co-ordinators to head local teams. Unless people of suitable aptitude and ability are recruited local offices will founder. Meanwhile, housing associations and co-operatives may expand their role, but their careful organization, their local base and their small scale, which are their greatest assets, require steady rather than explosive growth.

Figure 12.1 The housing management service to a large estate within a large authority.

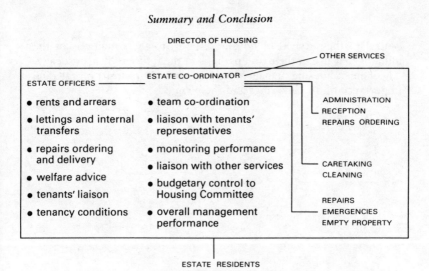

Figure 12.2 An integrated estate-based management structure.

Building societies, developers and other private organizations will not rush to take over the housing that has been so run down and has caused so much dissatisfaction. Indecent haste in the attempt to reduce the vast stock of public housing will not work any better than did Labour's 'siding with municipal landlords, jealously opposing any independent movement of tenants which threatened their political guardianship of the working classes' (Cooper, 1985, p. 144). There is an emergent consensus that small-scale social landlords, preferably tenant-based, can reduce the political controversy of housing owner-ship to the more important and less contentious issue of housing service.

Change will not come overnight, and those impatient with recurrent problems will look again to the bulldozer. But they must remember the wise words of Archbishop Worlock of Liverpool as he contemplated with an old resident the bare site that had been his home: 'The land over which the bulldozer is poised is not the Garden of Eden. And there are already more than two people living there.' (Worlock, 1984). A custodial approach to our built environment, ugly as some of it is, will augur well for the future of our cities and their residents.

The theme of *Property Before People* has not been the politics of construction, ownership or tenure, but the policies of housing management. The political lack of interest in property *after* it has been built and people *after* they have been housed led us to examine a relatively unexplored area of housing policy – an area that proved central to the survival of housing estates, to the conditions of the millions that live in them and perhaps to the future of British society. The women housing managers were surely right to insist on the dual importance of 'the buildings and the people'.

Bibliography

General References

English House Condition Survey (1981), Department of the Environment (London: HMSO).

General Household Survey, Office of Population Censuses and Surveys 1971 onwards (London: HMSO).

Greater London Council, *Annual Abstract of Statistics* 1966 onwards (London: Greater London Council).

Greater London Council, Minutes of the *Housing Committee* 1965 to 1982.

Housing and Construction Statistics, Department of the Environment 1966 onwards (London: HMSO).

Housing Rent Statistics, CIPFA (Chartered Institute of Public Finance and Accountancy) 1968 onwards (London: Chartered Institute of Public Finance and Accountancy).

Housing Returns for England and Wales, Ministry of Housing and Local Government 1949–66 (London: HMSO).

Housing Revenue Account Statistics, CIPFA 1978/79 onwards (London: Chartered Institute of Public Finance and Accountancy).

Institute of Housing, *Housing*, Journal of Institute of Housing from 1942 onwards.

Labour Force Survey 1981, Office of Population Censuses and Surveys (London: HMSO).

London County Council, Minutes of *Housing of the Working Classes Committee* 1889 to 1920.

London County Council, Minutes of *Housing Committee* 1920 to 1965.

Management and Maintenance Statistics, CIPFA 1978 onwards (London: Chartered Institute of Public Finance and Accountancy).

Municipal Year Book, 1897 to 1939; 1954 to date (London: The Municipal Journal Ltd).

National Dwelling and Housing Survey, Department of the Environment (1978) (London: HMSO).

Priority Estates Project, household surveys in Hackney and Bolton 1979 and 1983 carried out by Social and Community Planning Research and Public Attitudes Survey (London: Priority Estates Project).

St Pancras Housing Association in Camden, *Housing Happenings*, Journal of the St Pancras Housing Association 1929 onwards (London: St Pancras Housing Association).

Social Trends, 1970 onwards, Central Statistical Office (London: HMSO).

UK Census 1931, 1941, 1951, 1961, 1971, 1981, Office of Population Censuses and Surveys (London: HMSO).

Specific References

Allaun, Frank (1973), *No Place Like Home – Britain's Housing Tragedy* (London: Andre Deutsch)

AMA (Association of Metropolitan Authorities) (1984), *Defects in Council Housing, Part 2: Industrialised and System Built Dwellings of the Late 1960s and 1970s* (London: Association of Metropolitan Authorities).

Andrews, C. Lesley (1979), *Tenant and Town Hall* (London: HMSO).

Atkinson, A. B., Hills, J., and Le Grand, J. (1986), *The Welfare State in Britain 1970–85 – Extent and Effectiveness*, Welfare State Programme Discussion Paper No. 9, July (London: London School of Economics).

Attenburrow, J. J., Murphy, A. R. and Simms, A. G. (1978) *The Problems of Some Large Local Authority Estates – An Exploratory Study*, CP18/78 (London: Building Research Establishment).

Audit Commission (1984), *Bringing Council Tenants' Arrears Under Control* (London: HMSO).

Audit Commission (1986), *Managing the Crisis in Council Housing* (London: HMSO).

Balchin, Paul N. (1981), *Housing Policy and Housing Needs* (London: Macmillan).

Barclay, Irene (1976), *People Need Roots* (London: Bedford Press).

BBC (1984), *Enquiry: the Great British Housing Disaster* television documentary 4 September.

Berry, Fred (1974), *Housing – The Great British Failure* (London: Charles Knight).

Besley, Mary (1938) *Memorandum upon Housing Management by Local Authorities*, conference paper (Scarborough: National Housing and Town Planning Council).

Bevington, Peter (1986), *Coordinator's monthly report to the Cloverhall Cooperative Management Committee 29 April 1986* (Rochdale: Cloverhall Cooperative).

Blowers, Andrews *et al.* (eds) (1982) *Urban Change and Conflict – An Interdisciplinary Reader* (London: Harper & Row).

Bourne, Larry S. (1981) *The Geography of Housing* (London: Edward Arnold).

Bowley, Marion (1945), *Housing and the State 1919–1944* (London: Allen & Unwin).

Bowmaker, E. (1895), *Housing of the Working Classes* (London: Methuen).

Bright, Jon *et al.* (1986), *After Entryphones: Improving Management and Security in Multi-Storey Blocks* (London: Safe Neighbourhood Units of National Association of the Care and Rehabilitation of Offenders).

Brion, Marion and Tinker, Anthea (1980), *Women in Housing – Access & Influence* (London: Housing Centre Trust).

Brown, Muriel (1982), *Introduction to Social Administration in Britain* (2nd edn) (London: Hutchinson).

Brown, Muriel and Madge, Nicola (1982), *Despite the Welfare State* (London: Heinemann).

Building Societies Association (1983), *Housing Tenure* (London: Building Societies Association)

Burbidge, Michael (ed.) (1981), *Priority Estates Project 1981 Improving Problem Council Estates* (London: DOE).

Burbidge, Michael *et al.* (1981), *An Investigation of Difficult to Let Housing: Vol. 1: General Findings; Vol. 2: Case Studies of Post-War Estates; Vol. 3: Case Studies of Pre-War Estates* (London: HMSO).

Burnett, John (1978), *A Social History of Housing 1815–1970* (Newton Abbott: David & Charles).

Burney, Elizabeth (1976), *Housing on Trial. A study of Immigrants and Local Government*, Institute of Race Relations (London: Oxford University Press).

Burns, W. (1963), *New Towns for Old* (London: Leonard Hill)

Butcher, Ian (1980), 'The estate as a management unit', *Housing Review* (London: Housing Centre Trust).

Butcher, S. R. (1942), Post-War Housing Management', *Housing*, October (London: Institute of Housing).

Centre for Environmental Studies (1984), *Outer Estates in Britain: Interim Report – Comparison of Four Outer Estates*, Paper 23 (London: CES Ltd).

CHAC (Housing Management Sub-Committee of the Central Housing Advisory Committee of the Ministry of Housing and Local Government) (1939), *Management of Municipal Housing Estates: First Report* (London: HMSO).

CHAC (1945), *Management of Municipal Housing Estates: Second Report* (London: HMSO).

CHAC (1949), *Selection of Tenants and Transfers and Exchanges: Third Report* (London: HMSO).

CHAC (1953a), *Living in Flats* (London: HMSO).

CHAC (1953b), *Transfers, Exchange & Rents: Fourth Report* (London: HMSO).

CHAC (1955a), *Residential Qualifications: Fifth Report* (London: HMSO).

CHAC (1955b), *Unsatisfactory Tenants: Sixth Report* (London: HMSO).

CHAC (1956), *Moving from the Slums: Seventh Report* (London: HMSO).

CHAC (1959), *Councils and their Houses: Eighth Report* (London: HMSO).

CHAC (1961), *Homes for Today & Tomorrow (Parker Morris Report)* (London: HMSO).

CHAC (1969), *Council Housing, Purposes, Procedures and Priorities: Ninth Report (Cullingworth Report)* (London: HMSO).

Cleveland Research and Intelligence (1980), *The Ragworth Estate – A Survey of Social Conditions and Residents' Views* (Middlesbrough: Cleveland County Council).

Cochlaine, Alan *et al.* (eds) (1981), *City, Economy and Society – A Comparative Reader* (London: Harper & Row).

Coleman, Alice (1984), 'Design Influences in Blocks of Flats', *Geographical Journal* vol. 150, part 3 (London: The Royal Geographical Society).

Coleman, Alice (1985), *Utopia on Trial* (London: Hilary Shipman).

Collyer, E. (1957), 'Development of Housing Practice', *Housing*, March (London: Institute of Housing).

Commission for Racial Equality (1981), *Racial Harassment on Local Authority Housing Estates* (London: Commission for Racial Equality).

CRE (Commission for Racial Equality) (1984), *Race and Council Housing in Hackney – Report of a Formal Investigation* (London: Commission for Racial Equality).

Community Development Project (1976), *Whatever Happened to Council Housing?* (London: Community Development Project Information and Intelligence Unit).

Cooper, Stephanie (1985), Public Housing and Private Property (London: Gower).

Corina, Lewis (1974), *A Study of Housing Allocation Policy and Its Effects*, Unpublished study by Oldham Community Development Project.

Cox, Jean (1977), 'Housing Management and Design', *Housing Review*, November/December (London: Housing Centre Trust).

Crammond, R. D. (1964), *Allocation of Council Houses* (Edinburgh: Oliver and Boyd).

Criminology Dept, Middlesex Polytechnic (1986), *Summary of Broadwater Farm Survey* (London: Middlesex Polytechnic).

Crossman, Richard (1975), *The Diaries of a Cabinet Minister*, Vol. I (London: Hamish Hamilton and Jonathan Cape).

Cullingworth, Barry (1966), *Housing and Local Government* (London: Allen & Unwin).

Cullingworth, Barry (1979), *Essays on Housing Policy* (London: Allen & Unwin).

Dahrendorf, Ralph (1982), *On Britain* (London: BBC Publications).

Damer, F. and Madigan, R. (1974), 'The Housing Investigator', *New Society*, 25 July.

Dant, J. D. (1970), 'The Housing Department of the Future', *Housing*, July (London: Institute of Housing).

Daunton, M. (ed.) (1984), *Councillors and Tenants – Local Authority Housing 1919–1939* (Leicester: University of Leicester Press).

Davey, Michael (1986), 'Housing Disaster – well, up to a point, Minister', *The Observer* 5 May.

Deakin, N. and Ungerson, C. (1977), *Leaving London – Planned Mobility and the Inner City* (London: Centre for Environmental Studies).

Department of the Environment (1974), *Difficult to Let*, unpublished report of postal survey.

Department of the Environment (1975), *Census Indicators of Urban Deprivation*, working note no. 6 (London: DOE).

Department of the Environment (1977a), *Housing Management – Access and Allocation*, consultative paper (London: DOE).

Department of the Environment (1977b), *Housing Policy – A Consultative Document*, Part I, Cmnd 6851, Green Paper (London: HMSO).

Department of the Environment (1982), *Management Cooperatives – Tenant Responsibility in Practice* (London: HMSO).

Department of the Environment (1983), *Urban Deprivation*, information note 2 based on 1981 Census information produced by Inner Cities Directorate of DOE.

Department of the Environment (1985), *An Inquiry into the Condition of the Local Authority Housing Stock in England 1985* (London: DOE).

Donnison, David (1979), 'The empty council houses', *New Society*, 14 June, p. 635.

Donnison, David (1982), *The Politics of Poverty* (Oxford: Martin Robertson).

Donnison, David and Ungerson, Clare (1982), *Housing Policy* (Harmondsworth: Penguin).

Duncan, S. and Kirby, K. (1984), *Preventing Rent Arrears* (London:HMSO).

Dunleavy, Patrick (1981), *The Politics of Mass Housing in Britain 1945–75* (Oxford: Clarendon Press).

Edmund, Maurice C. (ed.) (1914), *Life of Octavia Hill – As Told in Her Letters* (London: Macmillan)

Englander, David (1983), *Landlord and Tenant in Urban Britain 1838–1918* (Oxford: Clarendon Press).

English, John (ed.) (1982), *The Future of Council Housing* (London: Croom Helm).

English, J., Madigan, R. and Norman, P. (1976), *Slum Clearance* (London: Croom Helm).

Federation of Hackney Tenants' Associations (1982), *Hackney Building Workers and Tenants Repairs Report 1982* (London: Federation of Hackney Tenants' Associations).

Ferris, John (1972), *Participation in Urban Planning – the Barnsbury case*, Occasional Papers on Social Administration No. 46 (London: G. Bell & Sons).

Field, Frank (1981), *Inequality in Britain: Freedom, Welfare and the State* (London: Fontana).

Fleming, John (1965), 'The housing department – city and county of Bristol', *Housing*, July (London: Institute of Housing).

Forrest, Ray and Murie, Alan (1984), *Right to Buy? Issues of Need, Equity and Polarisation in the Sale of Council Houses* (University of Bristol: School for Advanced Urban Studies).

Fox, Derek (1972), *The Organisation of the Local Authority Housing Service* (London: DOE).

Fuerst, J. S. (ed.) (1974), *Public Housing in Europe and America* (London: Croom Helm).

Galbraith, J. K. (1962), *The Affluent Society* (London: Pelican).

Gauldie, Enid (1974), *Cruel Habitations* (London: Allen & Unwin).

Gibbon, Sir Ioan Gwilym and Bell, Reginald W. (1939), *History of the London County Council 1889–1939* (London: Macmillan).

Gifford, Lord (Chair) (1986), *The Broadwater Farm Inquiry Report*: Report of the independent inquiry into disturbances of October 1985 at the Broadwater Farm Estate, Tottenham, chaired by Lord Gifford QC (London: London Borough of Haringey).

Glasgow, City of, Housing Department (1983), *Annual Housing Review* (Glasgow City Housing Department).

Gray, Fred (1976), 'Selection and allocation in council housing', *Institute of British Geographers Transactions*, vol. 1 (London: Institute of British Geographers).

Greater London Council (1967), *Hooliganism on Housing Estates*, Report by Director of Housing (London: GLC).

Gregory, P. (1975), 'Waiting lists and the demand for public housing', *Policy and Politics*, vol. 3 no. 4, June (London: Sage Publications).

Greve, J. and S. and Page, D. (1971), *Homelessness in London* (Edinburgh: Scottish Academic Press).

Greve, John (1985), *Investigations into Homelessness in London*, interim report (Leeds: University of Leeds).

Hambleton, Robin and Hoggett, Paul (eds) (1984), *The Politics of Decentralisation: Theory and Practice of a Radical Local Government Initiative*, working paper 46 (Bristol University: School for Advanced Urban Studies).

Haringey, London Borough of (1976), *Report to Haringey Housing Committee on Broadwater Farm Estate*, September (London: London Borough of Haringey).

Harloe, Michael (1974), *Organisation of Housing* (London: Heinemann).

Harris, H. W. (1957), 'Changing trends in housing', *Housing*, March (London: Institute of Housing).

Harrison, Paul (1983), *Inside the Inner City* (Harmondsworth: Pelican).

Hastie, William A. (1944), 'Rent collection and office management', *Housing*, October (London: Institute of Housing).

Heffernan, David (1977), *Difficult to Let – What are the Difficulties? Study of Milton Court and Evelyn Estates in Lewisham* (Edinburgh: Architecture Research Unit, Edinburgh University).

Henderson, Paul *et al.* (ed.) (1982), *Successes and Struggles on Council Estates* (London: Association of Community Workers).

Henney, Alex (1985), *Trust the Tenant – Developing Municipal Housing* (London: Centre for Policy Studies).

Hill, Octavia (1866), *Cottage Property in London* (published privately).

Hill, Octavia (1871), *Blank Court* (published privately; republished in 1921).

Hill, Octavia (1872 to 1907), *Letters to my Fellow Workers* (London: published privately between 1872 and 1907).

Hill, Octavia (1883), *Homes of the London Poor* (London: Macmillan).

Hill, Octavia (1901), *House Property and its Management* (London: Allen & Unwin).

Holder, Dave and Wardle, Mike (1981), *Teamwork and the Development of a Unitary Approach* (London: Routledge & Kegan Paul).

Holland, Sir Milner (Chairman) (1965), *Report of the Committee on Housing in Greater London*, Cmnd 2605 (London: HMSO).

Holmans, Alan E. (1987), *Housing Policy in Britain* (London: Croom Helm).

Holme, Anthea (1985), *Housing and Young Families in East London* (London: Routledge & Kegan Paul).

Home Office Research Study (1978), *Tackling Vandalism*, Study No. 47 (London: HMSO).

Horn, Chris J. (1977), 'Area management – an irritant at the fringe', *Housing Review*, September/October (London: Housing Centre Trust).

Hough, Mike and Mayhew, Patrick (1983), *The British Crime Survey*, Home Office Research Study: 76 (London: HMSO).

Housing (1948), 'Housing management in Scotland – a summary of the proceedings of the conference held at the City Chambers, Glasgow on 14 April, 1948', April–June, unsigned article, pp. 5–9.

Housing Development Directorate (1981), *Reducing Vandalism on Public Housing Estates*, Occasional Paper 1/81 (London: HMSO).

Housing Services Advisory Group (1978), *Organising a Comprehensive Housing Service* (London: DOE).

Housing Services Advisory Group (1981), *Reducing the Number of Empty Dwellings* (London: DOE).

Howard, Ebenezer (1902), *Garden Cities of Tomorrow* (London: Swan Sonnenschein).

Inquiry into British Housing (1985a), *The Evidence* (London: National Federation of Housing Associations).

Inquiry into British Housing (1985b), *Report* (London: National Federation of Housing Associations).

Institute of Housing (1968), *Yearbook* (London: Institute of Housing).

Institute of Housing (1978), *Yearbook* (London: Institute of Housing).

Jacobs, Jane (1970), *The Death and Life of Great American Cities* (London: Jonathan Cape).

Jacobs, Jane (1970), *Economy of Cities* (London: Jonathan Cape).

Jeffrey, M. M. (1931), 'Women as house property managers', in K. England (ed.), *Housing – a Citizen's Guide* (London: Chatto & Windus).

Kerner, Otto (Kerner Commission) (1968), *Report of the National Advisory Commission on Civil Disorders* (New York: Bantam Books).

Kettle, Martin and Hodges, Lucy (1982), *Uprising! The Police, the People and the Riots in Britain's Cities* (London: Pan).

Kleinman, M., Pearace, B. and Whitehead, C. (1985), *Housing: 25 Popular Fallacies*, Paper 14, Department of Land Economy (Cambridge: University of Cambridge).

Konttinen, Sirkka-Liisa (1983), *Byker* (London: Jonathan Cape).

Knight, Barry and Hayes, Ruth (1981), *Self Help in the Inner City* (London: London Voluntary Service Council).

Labour Housing Group (1985), *Manifesto for Housing* (London: Labour Housing Group).

Lambert, J., Paris, C. and Blackaby, B. (1978), *Housing Policy and the State* (London: Macmillan).

Lambeth Inner Area Study (1977), *Inner London: Policies for Dispersal and Balance Final Report* (London: HMSO).

Lansley, Stewart (1979), *Housing and Public Policy* (London: Croom Helm).

Lawless, Paul (1981), *Britain's Inner Cities – Problems and Policies* (London: Harper & Row).

Le Corbusier, C. E. Jeanneret (1946), *Towards a New Architecture* (London: Architectural Press).

Legg, Charles (1981), *Could Local Authorities be Better Landlords?* (London: City University).

Littlewood, Judith and Tinker, Anthea (1981), *Families in Flats* (London: HMSO).

Liverpool Inner Area Study (1977), *Change or Decay – Final Report* (London: HMSO).

Local Government Operational Research Unit (1976), *Rent Arrears Procedure – A Case Study 1976* (London: Local Government Operational Research Unit).

London Borough of Islington (1976), *Ethnic Minorities and the Allocation of Council Housing* (London: London Borough of Islington).

London Borough of Lambeth (1984), *Lambeth Estate Profiles – 1981*, Housing Policy and Information Unit (London: London Borough of Lambeth).

London County Council (1918), *Housing After the War* (London: London County Council).

London County Council (1937), *London Housing* (London: London County Council).

Macey, John (1961), 'Housing management – control of maintenance and repairs', *Housing*, March (London: Institute of Housing).

Macey, J. and Baker, C. V. (1965, 1978 and 1982), *Housing Management* (London: The Estates Gazette).

MacLennan, Duncan (1982), *Housing Economics* (London: Longman).

Malpass, Peter and Murie, Alan (1982), *Housing Policy and Practice* (London: Macmillan).

Manchester and Salford Family Service Unit (1982), *Ordsall Flats – Survey Report* (Manchester: Manchester and Salford Family Service Unit).

Melling, J. (ed.) (1980), *Housing, Social Policy and the State* (London: Croom Helm).

Merrett, Stephen (1979), *State Housing in Britain* (London: Routledge & Kegan Paul).

Metropolitan Boroughs' Committee (1963), *General Review of Housing Management* (London: Metropolitan Boroughs' (Organisation and Methods) Committee).

Ministry of Housing and Local Government (1920), *Housing*, journal of Ministry of Housing and Local Government (London: HMSO).

Ministry of Housing and Local Government (1955), *Green Belts*, Circular 42/55.

Ministry of Housing and Local Government (1965), *Industrialised Housebuilding*, Circular 17.

Mitton, Roger and Morrison, Elizabeth (1972), *A Community Project in Notting Dale* (London: Allen Lane).

Moberly Bell, E. (1942), *Octavia Hill* (London: Constable).

Morgan, Patricia (1978), *Delinquent Fantasies* (London: Temple Smith).

Murie, A., Niner, P. and Watson, C. (1976), *Housing Policy and the Housing System* (London: Allen & Unwin).

Murray, Bill (1978), 'New housing approaches in Islington', *Housing Review*, September/October (London: Housing Centre Trust).

NACRO Crime Prevention Unit (1982), *Neighbourhood Consultations – a Practical Guide* (London: National Association for the Care and Rehabilitation of Offenders).

Newcastle/Gateshead Inner City Partnership (1983), *Local Authority Priority Housing Estates* (Newcastle: The Newcastle/Gateshead Inner City Partnership).

Newman, Oscar (1972), *Defensible Space* (London: Architectural Press).

Niner, Pat (1975), *Local Authority Housing Policy and Practice* (Birmingham: Centre for Urban and Regional Studies).

North Islington Housing Rights Project (1976), *Street by Street – Improvement and Tenant Control in Islington* (London: Shelter).

Parker, Tony (1983), *The People of Providence* (London: Hutchinson).

Parker, John and Dugmore, Keith (1976), *Colour and the Allocation of GLC Housing. The Report of the GLC Lettings Survey 1974–75*, Research Report 21 (London: Greater London Council).

Parliamentary Commission for Administration (Ombudsman), *Annual Report for 1983* (London: HMSO).

Peters, T. J. and Waterman, R. W. (1982), *In Search of Excellence* (London: Harper & Row).

Piachaud, David (1979), *The Cost of a Child* (London: Child Poverty Action Group).

Power, Anne (1977), *Racial Minorities and Council Housing in Islington* (London: North Islington Housing Rights Project).

Power, Anne (1979), *Tenant Cooperatives or Tenant Management Corporations in the USA* (London: North Islington Housing Rights Project).

Power, Anne (1982), *Priority Estates Project 1982: Improving Problem Council Estates: a Summary of Aims and Progress* (London: DOE).

Power, Anne (1984), *Local Housing Management* (London: DOE).

Priority Estates Project (1985), *Working Paper on Cloverhall Cooperative Agreement* (London: Priority Estates Project).

Randell, Bill (ed.) (1983), *Trends in High Places – How 6 Local Authorities are Making the Most of Tower Blocks* (London: Institute of Housing).

Ravetz, Alison (1974), *Model Estates – Planned Housing at Quarry Hill, Leeds* (London: Croom Helm).

Reade, E. J. (1982), 'Residential decay, household movement and class structure', *Policy and Politics*, vol. 10, no. 1, January (London: Sage Publications).

Rex, John A. and Moore, Robert (1967), *Race, Community and Conflict* (London: Oxford University Press).

Reynolds, Frances (1986), *The Problem Housing Estate: an Account of Omega and its People* (Aldershot: Gower).

Rock, Paul (1986), *Home Office Seminar Paper*, Cambridge (unpublished).

Rose, J. *et al.* (1969), *Colour and Citizenship* (London: Oxford University Press).

Rowles, Rosemary J. (ed.) (1959), *Housing Management* (London: Pitman).

Royal Commission on the Housing of the Working Classes (1885), *First Report* BPP 1884–5, Vol. XXX (London: Stationery Office).

Runnymede Trust (1975), *Race and Council Housing in London* (London: Runnymede Trust).

Samuel Lewis Housing Trust (1985), *Estate Management Manual* (London: Samuel Lewis Housing Trust).

Scottish Housing Advisory Committee (1967), *Housing Management in Scotland* (London: HMSO).

Scottish Housing Advisory Committee (1970), *Council House Communities – A Policy for Progress* (London: HMSO).

Property Before People

Scottish Housing Advisory Committee (1980), *The Allocation and Transfer of Council Houses* (Scottish Development Department, Edinburgh: HMSO).
Seabrook, Jeremy (1984), *The Making of a Neighbourhood – Walsall* (London: Photo Press).
Seebohm Report (1968), *Report of the Committee on Local Authority and Allied Personal Social Services*, Cmnd 3703 (London: HMSO).
Seebohm Rowntree, B. (1901), *Poverty: a Study of Town Life* (London: Macmillan).
Shankland Cox Partnership (1977), *Housing Management and Design: Lambeth Inner Area Study 18* (London: DOE).
Shenton, Neil (1980), *Deneside – a Council Estate*, Papers in Community Studies No. 8, University of York, 1976, reprinted 1980.
Short, J. R. (1982), *Housing in Britain – the Post-War Experience* (London: Methuen).
Smith, Mary (1977), *Guide to Housing* (London: Housing Centre Trust).
Smith, D. and Whalley, A. (1975) *Racial Minorities and Public Housing*, Political and Economic Planning Report No. 556 (London: Political and Economic Planning).
Smith, Mary (1986), Obituary for Janet Upcott, *Housing*, May (London: Institute of Housing).
Smith, Wallace (1938), *Memorandum upon Estate Management*, Conference Paper (Scarborough: National Housing and Town Planning Council).
Society of Housing Managers (1955), *Housing Management* (London: Society of Housing Managers).
Stanforth, John et al. (1986), *The Delivery of Repairs Services in Public Sector Housing in Scotland* (Edinburgh: Scottish Office).
Sutcliffe, Anthony (ed.) (1974), *Multi-Storey Living – The British Working Class Experience* (London: Croom Helm).
Sutton Housing Trust (undated), *History of Sutton Housing Trust – Its Foundation and History* (Tring: Sutton Housing Trust).
Swenarton, Martin (1981), *Homes Fit for Heroes* (London: Heinemann).
Thompson, Quentin and Plant, John (1978), 'Ready access and difficult to let property', *Housing Review*, January/February (London: Housing Centre Trust).
Tinker, Anthea (1984), *Families in Flats* (London: HMSO).
Titmuss, Richard (1963), *Essays on the Welfare State* (2nd edn) (London: Allen & Unwin).
Titmuss, Richard (1976), *Commitment to Welfare* (2nd edn) (London: Allen & Unwin).
Townsend, Peter (1979), *Poverty in the United Kingdom* (London: Allen Lane).
Trevelyan, G. M. (1944), *English Social History* (London: Longmans Green and Co).
Tucker, James (1966), *Honourable Estates* (London: Victor Gollancz).
Walker, J. H. (1959), 'Housing administration in Pontypool', *Housing*, September (London: Institute of Housing).
Ward, Colin (1973), *Tenants Take Over* (London: Architectural Press).
Ward, Colin (1974), *Vandalism* (London: Architectural Press).

258

Watts, Alan S. (1976), 'Southwark Cottages: An Account of Octavia Hill's Work South of the Thames', *The Lady*, 29 January.

Welsh Office (1985), *Guidelines for Establishing Priority Estates Projects* prepared by C. Lesley Andrews (Cardiff: Welsh Office).

White, Jerry (1986), *The Worst Street in North London* (London: Routledge & Kegan Paul).

White, Len (1946), *Tenement Town* (London: Jason Press).

Wilson, Sheena (1978), *Tackling Vandalism*, Home Office Research Study No. 47 (London: HMSO).

Wohl, A. S. (1977), *The Eternal Slum: Housing and Social Policy in Victorian London* (London: Edward Arnold).

Wolfe, Tom (1981), *From Bauhaus to our House* (New York: Farrar, Straus & Giroux).

Wolmar, C. (1983), 'Building up repairs', *The Camden Magazine* (London: London Borough of Camden).

Women's Group on Public Welfare, *Our Towns: A Close-Up. A Study Made During 1939–1942* (London: Oxford University Press).

Worlock, Archbishop Derek (1984), *Housing and the Inner City Crisis*, address to Institute of Housing Annual Conference, Harrogate, June.

Young, M. and Wilmott, P. (1962), *Family and Kinship in East London* (Harmondsworth: Penguin).

Zipfel, Tricia (1985), Unpublished report to the Department of the Environment on Broadwater Farm Estate, Haringey, October.

Index

Addison Act (1919) 22
allocation policies xiv, xvi, 27, 73, 75,
    91–8, 101–2, 104–5, 107–8, 110–13,
    115, 119, 151–3, 156–7, 159–60, 164,
    185, 208–9, 212, 226–7, 236, 238
  future changes in 244
  publicly declared 100–1, 112–13
  racial discrimination in 105–7, 151,
    156–8, 226, 237
  social consequences of 97–100
architects 55–6
Association of Women House Property
    Managers 39
Association of Women Housing
    Workers 28–31, 39

Baker, Charles V. 21–2, 27, 44, 70, 81,
    88, 92, 94–9, 101, 180
balcony/walk-up estates 130–3, 147, 159,
    169, 191–3, 210, 214, 238
Barclay, Irene 19–20, 28
Becontree estate, LCC 36
bed and breakfast accommodation 109,
    241
bed-sitter experiments 224
Besley, Mary 31
Birkenhead 104
Birmingham 18, 25, 30–1, 45, 48, 52, 94,
    97, 103, 105, 137
Blackburn 53
Blythe Mansions, Islington 110
Bolton 51, 124, 218–19
Boundary Street estate, GLC 20
Brent 205
Bristol Housing Department 78–9
Broadwater Farm Estate,
    Haringey 218–19, 224–9
Bromley 36
building programmes xiv, 23, 26, 37
  Conservative 42, 44, 46–8, 234
  Labour 41–2, 47, 92, 234
  postwar 40, 64–5, 70, 74
Byker district, Newcastle-upon-Tyne 50,
    52, 63

car parks
  on flatted estates 142, 144–5, 225
  over-provision of 76, 130, 145, 225
caretaking
  mobile 179
  resident 72, 81, 143–4, 147–8, 160–1,
    178–9, 181, 199–200, 223, 227–8,
    239–40, 244
Central Housing Advisory Committee
    Reports
  (1939) 32–5, 66, 97, 234
  (1945) 68
  (1953) 71–2
  (1955) 73
  (1959) 74–5
  (1969) 77–8, 98, 100–2
central housing directorate 85, 87
Chesterfield 29
children, involvement in social
    change 229–30, 240
Church Commissioners 15, 29
Clover Hall Tenant Management
    Co-operative 219
Clydeside, rent strike (1915) 22
Coleman, Alice xv, 56, 89, 140, 142, 150
community facilities 34, 138–9, 148–50,
    238
community workers 218
compensatory allocation measures 112
compensatory management 122
Comprehensive Housing Service 84–5,
    87–8, 236
compulsory purchase powers 51
concealed households 60–1
Conference of Women Municipal
    Managers (1928) 29, 39
contract sizes 47, 55
cottage estates xiii, 23, 27, 34, 37, 62, 80,
    127, 131–3, 137–40, 145, 159, 169,
    188, 191–3, 205, 210, 214, 238
  car parking 138–9
  community facilities 138–9, 148
  management costs 72
  modernization of 138, 195

council housing
  abandonment of 119
  building programmes 26, 37, 41–8, 64,
    92, 234
  demand for xiv, 58–60, 224, 235, 242
  empty 107–9, 158–63, 187–8, 191, 198,
    207–11, 224, 226, 237–9
  local organization of 243
  outer boroughs 48, 233
  over-supply of 59–63, 115, 124, 130,
    237, 242
  programmes of renewal 243
  stock 88
  vacancy rate 63
  see also estates, local authority, social
    problems
Cox, Jean 89
Crown Estate Commissioners 29
Cullingworth, Barry 21, 31, 77–9, 100–2,
    107, 112, 115, 223
cuts in spending 65, 206, 235

date-order access 100, 112
decentralization of estate
    management 68, 190, 198, 241, 245
  see also estate-based management
demolition 4, 24, 49–50, 53, 92, 235–6
  of abandoned garages 145
  of car parks 145
  of stigmatized estates 105, 110, 122–3,
    130, 181, 225
  of system-built flats 56–7, 104–5
  public opposition to 51, 64
design problems, *see* unpopular estates
Direct Labour Organization 203
displacement 4, 23, 27–8, 50, 52–3, 63,
    68, 73, 80, 89, 98, 102, 233
Donnison, David xvi, 40, 58, 114–15,
    119, 229
Dunleavy, Patrick xvi, 40, 42, 45–7, 52,
    55, 135–6, 139

Elthorne Estate, GLC 63
estate
  agents 21
  environment 76, 89, 122–3, 134, 155,
    176–7, 191, 203–4, 229–30, 238, 240
  management 29, 35, 69–71, 187–9,
    194, 236, 245
  officers 130, 152, 156, 161, 164–8, 170,
    173, 175, 179, 181, 187, 193, 227, 239
  offices 69, 124–5, 135, 139, 151–2,
    185–90, 194–6, 200, 219–23, 235,
    239–40

local lettings 206–12, 224, 239, 245
  local waiting lists 208–9
estate-based
  management 16, 36, 67, 71, 73–4,
    77–8, 84, 87–8, 104, 107, 124–5,
    128–9, 131, 152, 166–8, 176, 179,
    181, 185–6, 189–92, 194–5, 198–203,
    205, 212–15, 217–19, 221–3, 228,
    237, 239–41, 245–7
  benefits 198
  cost of 195–8, 240
  improvements arising from 191–3
  project leaders 194, 245
  repairs services 200–3, 227–8, 239, 244
estates 20, 23, 27, 33, 54
  difficult-to let xiv–xv, 40, 56, 63, 107,
    112, 119–21, 123–5, 127, 129, 131,
    135, 137, 151–2, 154, 173, 191, 210,
    224–7, 229, 235, 237
  guarding 161, 198, 222
  size of 46–7, 244
  see also cottage, balcony/walk-up,
    flatted, modern concrete complex,
    unpopular
ethnic minorities, housing of 107,
    129–31, 153, 156–8, 226, 237–8
eviction 9, 11–12, 94, 96, 109, 173,
    175–6, 182, 224, 226, 238

Federation of Hackney Tenants'
    Associations 90, 166
flats xiv, 15–16, 23–4, 26, 37, 42, 44–5,
    54, 56, 63, 65, 104, 129, 198, 205,
    233, 235
  difficult-to-rent xiv, 17–18, 21, 56, 59,
    62, 92, 95, 103–4, 119, 127, 129, 137
  high-rise 44–5, 47, 52, 54–6, 63, 73,
    120, 131, 225, 234
  lifts in 143–4
  maintenance of 72
    see also caretaking
  management 24, 34, 37, 71–2, 76, 147,
    178–9, 236
  numbers 45–6, 54
  Octavia Hill's view of 11–12, 18, 232
  owner-occupation 44, 113
  problems of 35, 56, 71–2, 76, 80, 101
  refuse disposal in 178
  removal of top storeys 205, 224
  subsidies for 24–6, 42, 44, 54, 72, 233–4
  system-built 54, 145–6, 234
flatted estates xiii, xiv, 42, 47, 54, 56, 76,
    92, 127, 130–3, 140, 155, 171, 181,
    233–4, 241

abandoned areas 147
car parks on 142, 144–5, 225
children on 141, 145, 155, 207, 229–30
communal space 140–3, 151, 178, 238
compensatory management 122
decks and bridges 144–5
dogs on 141
garages on 145
hooliganism 80
management of 147, 178–9
owner-occupation 113
shopping precincts 142
unguarded lifts 143–4
see also balcony/walk-up estates,
    modern concrete complex estates,
    social problems, unpopular estates

Garden Cities 23
gardens, neglect of 70, 139–40
Gateshead 209, 231
General Household Survey 59
ghettoization 28, 101–2, 106, 109–10,
    123, 136, 153, 157, 208, 237
Glasgow 12, 18, 56, 104–5
GLC 20, 63
    cottage estates 80
    discrimination in 102–4, 106–7,
        109–10, 157
    estate-based management 125
    flatted estates 45, 80–1, 204–5, 241
    home visits 97
    house condition survey (1967) 51
    Housing Department 36, 78, 80–1
    lettings policies 91, 94, 96, 102–4, 112
government involvement 27, 41, 88
grants, amenity installation 50, 60
Great Depression (1929–35) 24
green belt 44, 48
Greenwood Act (1930) 24
group management 71
guarding estates 161, 198, 222
Guinness Trust 15
gypsies 163

Hackney 107, 119, 124, 166, 190, 219
    Tenant Board 218
Haringey 205, 218–19, 224–9
Hawthorne effect 240
heating, costs of 213–14
high-rise flats 42, 44–6, 48, 52, 54–6, 63,
    73, 120, 131, 225, 234
Hill, Octavia xiv, 3, 5–16, 18, 22, 28–9,
    32, 38, 50, 58, 78, 89, 151, 196, 217,
    232–4, 240

Holloway 51
homeless
    allocation of council housing to 96–7,
        107–11, 115, 129, 147, 151, 153,
        155–8, 168, 191, 206–8, 211–12, 226,
        237–8, 241, 245
    Persons Act 63, 108, 110–11
    stigma 109–11, 156–7, 208
    temporary accommodation for 108–9
    see also bed and breakfast
        accommodation
hooliganism 70, 80
houses
    costs 25, 45
    numbers 45, 54
housing
    Acts
        (1935) 27
        (1938) 25
        (1949) 92
        (1957) 92
        (1974) 64
        (1977) 63, 108, 110–11
        (1980) 88, 113–14
        (1985) xvi
    Action Areas 64
    Advisory Sub-Committee on Housing
        Management 28
    associations 65, 90–1, 194, 243, 245
    Benefit xiv, 95, 196, 215, 241
    departments 19–21, 31–2, 66–78,
        80–90, 165, 234–6
    developments, postwar 40–65, 70, 74,
        234
    estate managers 34–5, 235
    Investment Programme returns 120–1,
        125
    maintenance xv, 72, 165–6, 195–6,
        202–3, 206, 237
        costs 197
        see also unpopular estates
    management xiii–xvi, 16, 19–21, 24–5,
        28–38, 65–7, 69–78, 80–3, 85, 87, 89,
        100–1, 120, 122, 124, 151–2, 165–6,
        168, 171–2, 178–9, 195–6, 208, 227,
        232–9, 246
        costs 72, 195–8, 240
        future 242–5, 247
        nineteenth century 7–15, 232–3
        problems 66, 82–5, 89, 94–5, 138,
            235, 237–8, 245
        see also estate-based, flatted estates,
            LCC, local authority, unpopular
            estates, women's role

management—*contd*
    managers 5–6, 8, 13–14, 33–5, 66,
        68–71, 75, 84–5, 88, 90, 94–5, 162,
        167, 170, 180, 233, 235
        see also women housing managers
    Policy Green Paper (1977) 17
    Policy Review 111–12
    Revenue Accounts 195–6, 198
    Services Advisory Group 85–8
    shortages 40–1, 52, 61–2, 233–4
    standards 37, 60
    Subsidies Act (1967) 44
    surpluses 59–63, 107, 115, 124, 130,
        237, 242
        see also unpopular estates
    trusts 4, 65, 90, 233, 243
    welfare 30–3, 38, 67, 69, 71, 75, 77,
        233–5
Hull 103

immigrants 4, 93
improvement grants 50, 60
industrialized building methods, *see*
    system-building methods
Inner Area Study, Lambeth 89
inner-city areas 18, 36, 49
    decline of 47–8, 53
    flats 37, 42, 54, 56
    housing problems 25, 41, 48
    population of 47–8, 52–3, 58
    social problems 48
Inner City Partnership 195
Inner London 48, 61, 119, 121, 130, 196
Inquiry into British Housing (1985) 95
Institute of Housing 29, 32–3, 35, 39, 68,
    70–1, 80–1, 83–4, 89, 234
Institute of Housing Managers 39, 83
Intensive Management Projects 195
Islington 52, 64, 91, 105–6, 109–10, 125,
    181

Jeffrey, Miss M. 29, 39

Kingston-upon-Hull 48
Kirklees 224
Knowsley 104

Labour's Housing for All 41–2, 47–8,
    92, 234
Lambert, John 93–4, 103, 105–6
Lambeth 111, 119, 124–5, 190, 198
    Inner Area Study 89
landlord–tenant co-operation 75, 77, 83
    see also tenant involvement

landlord tradition 3–17, 20–1
landlords
    absentee 69
    local authority xiii–xvi, 3, 13, 16,
        23–4, 26, 35, 41, 46–7, 65–6, 68,
        88–90, 139, 142, 150, 156, 160–1,
        173, 217, 232–4, 236
    private 3, 8, 11, 13, 17, 19, 22, 26, 40,
        64–5, 233
    public 14, 17, 21, 72, 232, 234, 236
    slum 50
    social 247
    tenant-based 247
LCC 16, 18–21, 23–4, 26, 36, 47, 50
    Housing Committee 20, 39, 66
    housing department 36, 67, 70
    housing management 19–21, 30, 36–8,
        67, 69–70, 78, 234
    Housing of the Working Classes
        Committee 19
    Public Health Committee 19
    women housing managers 37–8
Le Corbusier 55–6
Leeds 48, 78
lettings
    discrimination in 96–7, 105–7, 115,
        147, 151, 155–8, 211–12, 226, 237–8,
        241, 245
    points systems 93, 100, 236
    policies, *see* allocation policies
    priorities 92, 110, 151–2
Lewisham 148
Lincoln 31
Liverpool 25, 30, 45, 48, 51, 53, 95,
    104–5, 137, 181, 198, 203, 207, 209
    Intensive Management Projects 195
Lloyd George 22–3
local authority
    housing 4, 16–19, 22–3, 25–6, 41–2,
        44, 46, 54, 65
    committees 88
    management xiv–xvi, 19–21, 25,
        28–32, 35–8, 65–7, 69, 74, 76, 78, 83,
        85, 87, 101, 233, 235–6, 239
    landlords xiii–xvi, 3, 13, 16, 23–4, 26,
        35, 41, 46–7, 65–6, 68, 88–90, 139,
        142, 150, 156, 160–1, 173, 217,
        232–4, 236
    reorganization 84–5
    staffing in housing departments 78
Local Government Planning and Land
    Act (1980) 87
local management, *see* estate-based
    management, unpopular estates

London 18, 25, 104, 119, 121, 127, 137, 171–3, 196
  reorganization of boroughs 80–1
  see also GLC, Inner London, LLC

Macey, John 21–2, 25, 27, 32, 36, 42, 44, 70, 80–1, 88, 90, 92, 94–9, 101, 180
Macmillan, Harold 42
maisonettes
  management problems 54, 207
  numbers 45, 54
  owner-occupied 44
  removal of top storeys 205
  unpopularity xiv, 54, 103, 225
management
  co-operatives 142, 190, 219, 243
  and maintenance allowance 243
  problems 66, 82–5, 89, 94–5, 138, 235, 237–8, 245
  structure 85–6
  transfer 182, 212
Manchester 25, 45, 48, 53, 105, 127, 129–30, 137, 155, 158, 205, 224
mass housing xiv, 40–2, 46–65, 76, 83, 89, 124, 157
Merseyside 62, 127, 155, 158, 205, 224
metropolitan authorities 86–7, 119–21, 127, 196
Metropolitan Boroughs' Committee 82
Midlands 61, 127
mobile caretaking 179
model dwellings 4, 15–16
modern concrete complex estates 130–4, 144–6, 159, 169, 188, 191–4, 208, 210, 214, 225, 238
modernization 138, 195, 203–5, 239

National Housing Conference (1938) 31
Neighbourhood Management Committees 218
New Towns 41, 44, 52–3
Newcastle-upon-Tyne 48, 50, 52, 63, 105, 125, 154, 209
Newham 52
nineteenth century urban conditions 3–4, 6–7, 10
'no go' areas 227
North Islington Housing Rights Project 94
Northampton, Lord 6
Nottingham, populated trends 48
nuclear city 56

Octavia Hill Club 39

Oldham 53
  Community Development Project 93
one-parent families 153, 156, 168, 170–1, 176, 191, 226, 238
open space 12, 176–7
overcrowding 4–6, 9–10, 12, 17, 20, 22, 25–7, 31, 40, 56, 60–2, 93, 154, 233
Overcrowding Act (1935) 25
owner-occupation 3, 19, 26, 40–2, 44, 54, 58–9, 61, 64–5, 93, 113, 235, 237

Parker Morris Report (1961) 23, 39, 60
Parker Morris, Sir 29, 39
parks department 176–7, 239
Parliamentary Commission for Administration 90
Peabody Trust 12, 15
philanthropic trusts 15–16, 22, 176
  housing management 29, 78, 142, 194
policing of estates 80, 130, 142, 144, 150, 220–5, 227–8, 240
poorest households 4–7, 13–17, 19–20, 22–7, 34, 37, 41, 76, 93–4, 97–9, 101, 115, 130, 153, 236, 242
population trends 44, 47–8, 52–3, 58, 115
postwar baby boom 44, 73
postwar housing developments 40–65, 70, 74, 234
prefabs, numbers 45
Priority Estates Project xvi, 47, 124–6, 190, 195, 218, 223–4, 229, 237
private housing xiv, 40–4, 47–8, 54, 59, 88, 114, 233
private sector, contract size 47
problem estates 27–9, 119, 185, 226
  see also unpopular estates
problem families 28, 73, 81, 101, 110, 223, 242
public sector, contract size 47, 55
public transport 34, 120

racial discrimination in council housing xiv, 102, 105–7, 151, 156–8, 226, 237
racial ghettos 102, 106, 157
rate-capping 196, 241
rate subsidies 196
redevelopment 14–15, 18, 37, 47–8, 52–3, 64, 76
refuse collection 177–8
renovation 24, 50–1, 64, 243
rent
  accounting, costs 170

Acts 88
arrears 89–90, 96–7, 131, 153, 167–76, 180, 182, 188, 191, 193, 198, 213–15, 226, 238–9, 241
collection 34, 37–8, 67, 69, 73–5, 80–2, 90, 160, 167–73, 175–6, 188, 213–15, 235, 238
controls 22, 40
loss of 160–1, 238
rebates 17
strike, Clydeside (1915) 22
subsidies 196
rented housing, private 40–2, 44, 233
rents
anomalies 95
levels of 5, 17, 37, 95–6
repairs to housing xvi, 6, 10, 22, 34, 61, 74–5, 80, 82, 84, 87–8, 90, 123, 160, 165–7, 188, 191, 198, 200–3, 206, 235, 238–9
bonus system 166
trade demarcations 166
residence qualifications for council housing 93, 100, 112–13, 151, 244
resident
caretakers 72, 81, 143–4, 147–8, 160–1, 178–9, 181, 199–200, 223, 227–8, 239–40, 244
managers 16, 20, 67, 233
superintendents 20, 36, 69–70
Rhondda 51, 90, 187
right to buy 98, 113–14
consequences of 113, 207, 241, 245
riots 130, 158, 225, 228
Rochdale 198, 205, 207, 215, 219
Roehampton 36
Ronan Point 225
Royal Commission on the Housing of the Working Classes (1885) 4–7, 9–12, 14, 16, 18
Royal Institute of Chartered Surveyors 29, 83

Salford 51, 53, 181
Samuel Lewis Trust 15, 90
Scarman Report (1984) 22
Scottish Housing Advisory Committee 82–3, 112
sectional management 71
security of tenure 88
Seebohm Report 100
Shaftesbury, Lord 4, 6, 232
shared dwellings 59–62

Sheffield, population trends 48
sheltered dwellings 65, 242
'sink' estates 23–4
see also unpopular estates
slums
clearance xiv, 25, 27–8, 31, 37, 40–2, 49–53, 60, 63, 66, 71, 92, 225, 233–6
cost 50, 52–3
estates 30, 34
social consequences of 50, 52–3, 71, 73
subsidies for 24–7, 233–4
definition of 51, 232
stigma 27, 138
social
abuse 21–2, 217, 224, 240
ghettos xv, 101, 109–10, 123, 208, 237
problems 10–11, 28, 30–1, 35, 48, 70, 80, 233, 238
segregation in rehousing 93–5, 97–102, 104–5, 109–14, 122–3, 135, 138, 152–7, 207, 223, 226, 236
support 28, 101
workers 73, 130, 179–80
Society of Housing Managers 28–33, 39, 83
Society of Women Housing Estate Officers 31, 33, 35, 39, 66–7, 71
Society of Women Housing Managers 234
Southwark 56
Spitalfields 4
squatters 130, 162–3, 238
St Pancras Housing Association 20
Stockton-on-Tees 27, 195, 205
subsidies for
building 22–5, 36, 41, 233
demolition in the cities 49, 234
expensive sites 42, 48, 233
flats 24–6, 44–5, 54, 72, 233–4
high-rise flats 42, 44–5, 48, 54, 234
house building 44
inner-city building 41–2
rates 196
renovation 50
slum clearance 24–6, 233–4
suburbia 18, 36, 138, 235
supplementary benefit 95, 114
Sutton Housing Trust 15–16, 199
system-building methods 45, 56–8, 225
cost 57
flaws 57–8, 146, 238
system-built homes xiv, 54, 145–6, 234
see also high-rise flats, modern concrete complex estates, unpopular estates

Taylor Woodrow Anglian 225
technical administration of
    housing 32–3, 38, 71
technical departments 87, 202
tenancy conditions, enforcement
    of 181–2
tenants
    categorization of xv, 91–4, 96–7,
        102–3, 105–6
    problem 34, 73, 76, 102
        see also problem families
    residential qualifications 93, 100,
        112–13, 151, 244
tenants
    associations 11, 15, 77, 130, 224
    groups 218, 220
    involvement
        in environmental
            improvements 139–40, 191, 206,
            240, 244
        in management 218–20, 228,
            239–40, 243
        in social change 217–23, 230
    leaders 71, 223
    management co-operatives 142, 190,
        219, 243
tenement flats 15–16, 233
terraced housing 24, 53, 64
tower blocks 54, 146–7, 207
Tower Hamlets 56, 90, 119
town planning 41
trade unions, role of 81
transfers 98, 113, 188, 212–13
    social consequences of 98–9, 153–4,
        224, 237–8
travellers 163
Tudor Walters Committee 23
Tulse Hill 158
Tyneside 104, 124, 127, 158, 195, 205, 224

under-letting 207
unemployment 24, 62, 95, 114, 127, 150,
    153, 155, 158, 168, 207, 238
Ungerson, Claire xvi, 40, 58, 114–15
unpopular cottage estates 137–40, 145
unpopular estates xiii, 23–6, 53–4, 58–9,
    76, 84, 89, 96, 101–5, 107, 119–20,
    122, 125, 129, 185, 226, 235–6
    building faults xiv, 123, 129, 133, 146,
        238
    child density 154–5, 229
    crime 129–30, 135, 138, 142–4, 147,
        149, 161, 179, 182, 219–22, 227, 229,
        231, 235, 240

design factors xv, 89, 119–20, 122–4,
    129, 131–4, 137–51, 155, 225, 227,
    235, 237–8
empty property 158–63, 187–8, 191,
    198, 208–11, 224, 226, 237–9
ethnic minorities housed on 107,
    129–31, 153, 156–8, 226, 237–8
gangs 150, 230
homeless housed on 109–11, 129, 147,
    153, 155–8, 168, 191, 206, 208, 226,
    237–8, 241
improvement of 204–6, 213, 239, 244
local lettings 206–12, 224, 239, 245
local offices on 185–96, 198–205, 208–11,
    213–15, 217–23, 228, 237, 239–40
local waiting lists 208–9
maintenance 123, 129, 131, 151, 160,
    167, 191, 193, 198, 202, 204, 206,
    237, 239, 241
management of 122–4, 129, 131,
    133–5, 138, 140–2, 147–8, 151–64,
    180–1, 185, 187–91, 193–6, 198, 208,
    218, 220, 226, 237–8, 241
    long-term 193, 241
mobility of tenants 99, 129–30, 135,
    140, 153–5, 159, 163, 176, 191, 193,
    212–13, 223, 237–8
one-parent families 153, 156, 168,
    170–1, 176, 191, 226, 238
refuse collection 178
rent arrears 168–73, 193, 198, 213–15,
    226, 238–9, 241
rents 95
right to buy 113
riots on 130, 158, 225, 228
security 203–4, 222, 240
shops on 139, 142, 149
size of 134–5
social change 217–18, 221–5, 229–31
social factors 122, 135, 180, 226
social services and 179–81, 185, 239
social stigma 114, 119–20, 122–3,
    129–31, 135–6, 138, 153, 193
surroundings 122–3, 134, 155, 176–7,
    191, 203–4, 238, 240
unemployed housed on 158, 237–8,
    242
vandalism 119–20, 127, 129, 135,
    138–9, 142–3, 145, 147–50, 155,
    161–2, 178, 187, 191, 198, 204, 210,
    222, 229–31, 235, 238–9
young unemployed housed on 207
youth on 149–50, 155, 158, 221,
    227–30, 240

unpopular flatted estates 140–7
unpopular suburban estates 138
Upcott, Janet 29, 240
Urban Aid 195
US public housing projects 157–8

vandalism 21, 58, 70, 119, 127, 135,
    138–9, 143, 155, 161–2, 178, 187,
    210, 230, 235, 238–9

wage levels and rents 5–6, 9, 17, 27
waiting lists for council homes 52, 62,
    73, 93, 100, 211, 235
Wales, Priority Estates Project 124

Walsall 125, 187, 190
Walworth 15
welfare housing 25, 233
Welwyn Garden City 51
Wenlock Barn Estate, Hackney 220
Willows Estate, Bolton 219
women chartered surveyors 28–9
women housing managers xiv, 29–31,
    35, 37–9, 232–3, 248
women's role xiii, 13–14, 22, 29–30, 32,
    35, 83

young single people, housing 207, 224,
    242, 244–5